JANET DENNY grew up in London. She trained as a nurse at Westminster Hospital and went on to become a midwife and health visitor. She began writing stories in her head when her family embarked on restoring a derelict fifteenth-century farmhouse in Sussex. While scraping rot from woodworm-eaten timbers and re-pointing old brickwork she was able to let her imagination fly. More tales followed, recounting village life and the unexpected adventures of a bed and breakfast hostess.

After twenty-five years of running a busy retail business Janet returned to 'fiddling around with words'. In 2014 she graduated with an MA in Creative Writing. Her particular interest is in memoir and biography.

The Man on the Mantelpiece is her first book.

D1316779

Praise for *The Man on the Mantelpiece*

'Meticulously researched and beautifully constructed,
with an imagination expertly deployed to fill in
the gaps between the facts.'
– Blake Morrison, author of *And When Did You Last See Your father?*

'A moving memoir about the author's search for understanding.
Sometimes funny, sometimes sad, it is a powerful story.'
– Helena Drysdale, author of *Looking for George*

'A wonderfully rich brew of travelogue, memoir, quest,
and detective story.'
– Stephen Mollett, screenwriter and author of *A House Halfway to Africa*

'An important contribution to WWII literature – skilfully
written and deeply humane.'
– Dave Swann, author of *The Last Days of Johnny North*

THE MAN
on the
MANTELPIECE
Janet Denny

SilverWood

Published in 2015 by SilverWood Books

SilverWood Books Ltd
14 Small Street, Bristol, BS1 1DE
www.silverwoodbooks.co.uk

ISBN 978-1-78132-357-1 (paperback)
ISBN 978-1-78132-358-8 (ebook)
ISBN 978-1-78132-359-5 (hardback)

British Library Cataloguing in Publication Data
A CIP catalogue record for this book is available from
the British Library

Set in Adobe Garamond Pro by SilverWood Books

War Baby

He has not even seen you, he
Who gave you your mortality;
And you, so small, how can you guess
His courage or his loveliness?

Yet in my quiet mind I pray
He passed you on the darkling way –
His death, your birth, so much the same –
And holding you, breathed once your name.

Pamela Holmes

*This book is dedicated to Jim and Pat, who gave me life,
and to my children and grandchildren, who continue it.*

Author's Note

The Man on the Mantelpiece is about the search to find the man who was my father, to trace the course of his short life.

None of the named characters in these pages is entirely fictional. Many I have known personally, others figure in anecdotes told by my mother or are described in my father's diaries. To the best of my knowledge all his contemporaries are now dead, with two exceptions: my mother and uncle, who have provided me with much support and information.

Almost all of what occurs in these pages actually happened in real life. Some are stories I have been told by my family or are paraphrases of my father's diaries. In order to bring the narrative alive there are sections where I have employed 'faction'. Some conversations, stories, and the whole of chapter sixteen are fiction, based on research and my mother's and uncle's memories.

November 2014

Contents

Prologue

The hammering on the door was so loud it seemed to me the whole neighbourhood would wake. I lay still, eyes wide, ears pricked to hear Mum's reaction, but the sound of her regular breathing still leaked through the thin wall. When I was sure she was asleep, I climbed from my bed, stepped gingerly from the rag-rug onto the cold lino and eased back the bedroom door, always left slightly ajar. Creeping past Mum's room in the dawn light my heart beat like an Indian tom-tom against my ribs. The hairy coconut matting on the stairs prickled my bare feet and I could see a head silhouetted in the frosted pane of the front door as I stood on tiptoe to reach the latch. I twisted the knob, pulled the door open and there he was: the man from the mantelpiece in his Air Force uniform.

The garden hedge behind him glistened under a hoar frost but something like warm sunshine suffused my body so I was happy and unafraid. From inside his greatcoat a wet black nose sniffed the air, then a brown and white head poked forward. It was the puppy I longed for. In the man's hand was a worn leather suitcase stencilled with black initials, S.J.G., its handle expertly repaired with oiled twine. He laid it on the ground and crouched to use both hands to push back the levers so that the catches released and the lid flew open to reveal a chocolate treasure trove. There were long bars of Fry's Chocolate Cream in their blue and white wrappers, sixpenny slabs of Cadbury's Bournville like soldiers in red coats with gold sleeves, and thick tablets of milk chocolate with lumpy bits in them, their silver wrapping surrounded by white paper with TIFFIN written in big red letters. I had seen them in Miss Beeson's sweet shop but we never had enough coupons. I dreamed of tasting them when, one day, sweets would come off ration.

The man's pale face beamed and his startling blue eyes crinkled at the edges. He held me in his gaze as he flung his arms wide for me to leap into them.

My dad had come back. But then he disappeared and the stair-matting hurt my toes as I climbed back to my chilly bed.

He came again when, all dressed in brown, Miss Lee – eight feet tall with thick stockings wrinkling round her fat ankles and big men's shoes – pointed at me, screwing cross eyes behind little round glasses to demand I recite my three times table, and my mouth was silent and dry; when Nina James boasted that she had a new baby brother; when Roger Catchpole bragged about pitching a tent in the back garden with his dad. Those were the times he came – *my dad*, the hero.

He was my secret; from Mum, the tragic princess from my story book who was waiting for her prince to come back to her; from Nanny and Grandad, who loved me specially because I was born just after he flew away. I was the image of him – everyone said it – and that made me feel important, proud. I was five years old and the war had been over for three years. But the *Daily Herald*, just the week before, had shown a picture of a really thin man with chewed hair, a stubbly chin and staring eyes. He didn't know who he was or where he lived. Somehow he had survived and walked across Europe from a POW camp and arrived home only then – in 1948. The grown-ups said my dad had been killed, shot down by the bloody Germans, but they never found his body so perhaps, perhaps...

1

Rediscovery

I have only four items that felt my father's touch: three exercise books and a brown leather writing case.

On New Year's Day 1970, my mother was to remarry after nearly three decades without a husband. With a secretly heavy heart I helped her clear her rented council flat of the household items that had been the fabric of my childhood, my youth.

For twenty-seven years my mum had been all mine. She'd had boyfriends of course; I remember days out with 'uncles' and gifts to impress. When I was studying A-Level History one admirer arrived at the door staggering under the weight of Churchill's *History of the English Speaking Peoples* – all four large hardback volumes. My thanks were formal and perfunctory. I was not to be bought. Neither was Pat, my mum. The books remained unopened on my shelf until they found their way to Oxfam many years later.

After decades of tedious shorthand and typing in government offices, Mum had finally achieved her youthful ambition and qualified as a teacher. And she had found love again. I was pleased for her; I wanted her to be happy. But it felt like the stable ground she had laid down for my life was rocking. I didn't consider the earthquake I had caused when I left home to marry my own love.

Together we disposed of much that had been our home. Her groom had plenty of superior furniture in the house he had shared with his late wife: antique, not 'utility'; fitted carpets rather than lino and rag-rugs; silver instead of tin.

'That can go.' Mum pointed to the coal scuttle with the rusty lip. I frowned, remembering the triumph of my eight-year-old self when I'd staggered in with the coal and lit a fire – a surprise to welcome Mum home from work – and my satisfaction at her delighted response. *I am a grown woman now*, I told myself, *how ridiculous to feel a sentimental attachment to a worthless old coal scuttle!* Nevertheless, I sighed as I placed it beside the increasing stack of redundant items awaiting the dustcart.

It was then that I noticed, among a pile of old paperbacks, rent books, bundles of bills and bank statements tied with string, some old school files and folders. I needed to see if they were mine, reclaim them. How could she throw them away without consulting me? They might be an important part of my childhood. When I stuffed them into the fraying hessian bag which had always hung on the back of the larder door, I saw only a mixture of her college notes and rough-books from the school where she taught. I took the whole lot home anyway.

Later that evening, having fed and bathed the children and settled them into bed, I sat down to look through the pile of papers and books. As expected, most went in the bin – there was nothing of mine. But in the middle of a bundle of sheet music were three rather older books slipped inside a shabby leather writing case. My eyes widened when I realised what I'd found. These were the wartime diaries of the father I never knew. They were precious. Surely my mother would not have knowingly disposed of them? I didn't ask. She was embarking on a new life; it was not the time to confront her with the old. After a cursory read through I stowed them safely away for careful consideration at some later date.

Thirty-seven years later I am once again clearing a home; the home where I have spent three happy decades with Steve and our children – Andrew, Laura and Matthew.

Autumn sun tempts me into the garden, warms my aching bones, feeds my flagging energy. For a time it stops the rivulets coursing down ever-deepening grooves in my cheeks, until the dam bursts and tears flow again, unchecked. The days are shortening now, beginning to draw a curtain over my husband's last hot summer.

'Look forward, not back,' he said. *I am trying, for God's sake.*

I had climbed the mountain of grief before, when Andrew died, but then we climbed together.

I lost another man too. That was a long time ago and causes me no pain. Instead, that loss evokes a curiosity, a need to find out who he was. To find out who I am. Could he help to fill the aching void in my life?

Perhaps a cup, or even a glass, of something will turn my face to the future. My knees creak as I pull myself up from weeding the rockery – Steve's rockery. How the hell do I know which are weeds and which are his prized specimens with names I can never remember? Why doesn't he help me? Why didn't I help him with his beloved garden?

I cross the farmyard that is no longer a farmyard – grassed over now – and fling my mud-laden trowel and fork into the bucket of tools in the horseless stable. At the very edge of my vision, I fancy I see my boys kicking a football on the grass, their sister erupting when it lands in the water trough, showering her book with sunny droplets.

I crumple and wonder how I can leave here. This place, full of memories, is where they are. *No, they're not.* Common sense shakes me by the shoulders. They are gone: Matthew and Laura to pursue their lives, raise their own children; Andrew and his dad to live only in memory.

'You will sell the house?' Steve's slow fingers had tapped it out on his voice machine after the disease had killed enough neurones to rob him of the ability to talk, walk and swallow.

'My love, you know I will. I must.'

Next morning he was gone. In two weeks I will be gone too, from this house – though not, like him, from this world. Now I have to cull many of the possessions that fill our old rambling home. And I have to find my father.

Merlot, smooth and fruity as it touches my taste buds, warms my blood and staunches my tears when I drain a large glass. I sit on the floor in the study next to a small pile of dust and grit, shed by fifteenth-century beams. Thirty years we spent rescuing this house from destruction, restoring it to its former glory (plus modern comforts), but we never conquered the dust. Who bloody cares? What is a layer of dust set against three decades of happy family life?

I feel sure my dad is in this cupboard somewhere. I sort through boxes of newspaper cuttings, articles on every country in the world. If anyone asked, 'Know anything about Lesotho, Steve?' or Bolivia or Finland or Mali, his eyes would sparkle.

'Just a tick,' he'd say, then a rifle through the cupboard and he'd pull the info from the shelf.

There are files on the death of Churchill, Princess Margaret's wedding (he slept in The Mall for that, to ensure a good pitch for the next day), and then I find a folder full of photos of Andrew's young friends partying on a beach somewhere in the Antipodes. Sorry, my loves, it's all for the skip. You knew I couldn't keep everything, but I'll always have my memories. Memories of two of my lost men: a loving husband and a treasured son.

A few mouse droppings, Andrew's old scout belt, and the cupboard is bare. My body is heavy, weary with grief. I wipe my sleeve across my eyes. I haven't found my dad.

Next day I am in the attic: old projectors, tripods and a mouldy cine screen with a tear in the bottom left corner (made by the dog when she made a bid to join the children in the paddling pool), a judo outfit, a guitar with a broken string. Then, amongst my old nursing text books with pictures of operating techniques from half a century ago, I find him. My third lost man who left me no memories; nothing, save for these three slender, self-effacing books in a writing case. My father's legacy to me.

Perched on a box in the patch of light falling from the hole in the roof where a tile has slipped from its worm-eaten peg, I begin to devour his words, his story.

The cover of the small soft-backed notebook has a crazed design in pond-sludge green; a serious, understated attempt to emulate ancient leather. JAMES GAYWOOD is inscribed in neat capitals on the inside of the front cover and on the following pages are the titles of his writings, such as 'The Simple Boy' (short story, 2000 words), and a table meticulously recording the magazines he sent them to and the date they were returned. I am impressed in these days when one waits for weeks and sometimes forever for a reply, at the courteous promptness of the rejections. The 'date accepted' column remains blank for all fourteen entries, be they poems, such as: 'An Air Raid at Night', 'Industrial Revolution', 'Conchies' or 'Ends and Means'; or a one act play – *Beauty is Dead*; or stories entitled 'While of Unsound Mind' (1800 words), 'Kink?' (2000 words), and 'The Common Enemy' (1400 words). 'Walter Archibald', a short story of 4000 words, submitted to Penguin New Writing on the 8th October 1941 and returned two weeks later, has a teasing asterisk beside it with the cryptic note, 'See letter in file A'. But I have no file A and I have none of these texts. I only have the notebooks and the writing case.

On the lined page opposite the entry 'Bloomsbury Bosh' (short story, 2500 words), which was submitted to *Men Only* in 1939 and returned with a speed the Royal Mail can now only dream of, are pencilled alphabet exercises in a small child's hand. Subsequent pages show my attempts at a diary for the first days of 1950 with such riveting entries as:

3 GAN [Jan.]

I WENT TO AIVIE'S PARTY TEA nice SpOIlt after by
SHILAR AND REATER
    I WENT TO BED AND RED A BOOK
    JANET GAYWOOD

Clearly my diary resolve at the age of six was even weaker then than now. There are no further entries after January 15th despite optimistic date headings until March 11th.

Other pages carry shopping lists in my mother's hand: half a crown for 6lb of potatoes, cauliflower at one shilling and fourpence and six large oranges for three and six – the prices pencilled in and totalled, presumably by Mr Mangan the greengrocer, so that Mum could check I brought back the correct change. The butter came from Price's, the grocer's on Well Hall Road, where I would poke my nose over the counter and Mr Pinnegar, resplendent in a white starched coat, would reach down with a cheerful greeting to take my list and the ration books. My shoes crunched on the grains of sugar which escaped from the sack when Mr Pegram (who wore a long grey apron), shovelled it on to brass scales then poured it into a strong blue paper bag, folding over the top several times so it wouldn't spill.

The biscuits were in square metal boxes lined up along the wall and tilted at an angle so that the glass lids tempted with glimpses of Garibaldis, Rich Tea, Malted Milk or, for special treats, Chocolate Bourbons. A bag of mixed brokens was the economy option. Behind the counter on a marble slab resided a cheese as big as a squashed football with a silver wire at the ready to cut a wedge for me and Mum, and a bacon slicer carrying a joint of maroon meat streaked with white fat. *One day*, I resolved, breathing in the amalgam of salty, buttery, biscuity smells, *I will work in a shop like this and cut and turn a quarter-pound of butter with those ridged wooden pats, and wrap it in greaseproof as neatly as Mr Pinnegar.*

On the next page of the green notebook Mum reminds herself to collect an oil stove from Mence Smith, the ironmonger in our South London high street, and a roll of Ruberoid. Whatever was that? Why did she need Ladybird baby pyjamas size three and two pairs of striped plastic panties from Woolworths? Not forgetting four doz. bridge rolls, twelve pints of Worthingtons (must have been for Grandad) and a rubber tube…!

We didn't waste paper in those post-war years, so this little book was put to many uses over many years.

For my dad, though, this was a book of importance, as inside the back cover is a request in large letters that, in the case of loss, it should be returned to:

Samuel James Gaywood
17 Eltham Hill
Eltham, London S.E.9.

Eltham Hill is a wide main road which changed relatively little in the twenty years between my father's childhood and mine. It carried few vehicles – some small black cars belonged to policemen, doctors and the wealthy who occasionally ventured into this corner of south-east London. Blinkered horses with nosebags of hay hanging from their harnesses pulled delivery carts. A galvanised bucket and shovel were always at the ready in number 17 to collect the valuable gifts the beasts left behind. You had to be fast to beat the neighbours.

Most importantly there were the trams. To my young eyes, these seemed to be suspended from overhead cables that sometimes lit up with a crackly blue and white electric flash. They had wheels running in metal grooves set into the road surface of grey blocks. I loved those scarlet trams with their warm smoke-filled interiors and enamel notices forbidding spitting (transgressors to be fined half a crown). There was no front or back; these clever beasts were reversible. The driver just moved to the other end and the tram glided up the hill it had just travelled down.

Upstairs was the only place for an excited four-year-old to travel. No aeroplane or ocean liner trip could surpass the exhilaration I felt as I knelt on the polished wooden slats of the curved seat. It echoed the shape of the front of the vehicle as it hurtled down the hill, taking me and Mum to Nanny and Grandad's house – where my dad used to live.

Trams were important for another reason. Grandad's job was to mend and clean them at the New Cross Depot. He got up in the middle of the night and cycled there to tinker with the engines, then hose and scrub them down so that they were spick and span for the new day. He was very proud of them and I was very proud of the important job he did. In that hard winter of 1947, when Jack Frost wove his lacy web inside my bedroom window and the snow was deep and crisp and even, the icy water split the tips of his fingers into great bloody cavities, which he insisted didn't hurt when I explored them with my small soft hands.

Number 17 was a flat-fronted, cement-rendered, semi-detached house rented from Woolwich Borough Council. The Gaywoods had lived there since 1926. A few years earlier the council had offered them escape from a crowded life in Plumstead with the extended family. Their new house in Prince John Road had three bedrooms – one for Nanny and Grandad, one for Nanny's old dad, and one for eight-year-old Nell, the small daughter Nanny had brought as an added extra to her marriage. Little Jim slept in the bed next to Nell. But then baby brother Len arrived, Nanny's dad died and Uncle Harry came to live with them, so they moved round the corner to 17 Eltham Hill with its four bedrooms.

Nanny and Grandad left that house when I was six but I remember the ground floor and garden perfectly. My only recollection of upstairs is the back bedroom. Dusty and cold, no one had slept there for years and I suspected it was inhabited by ghosts. When I steeled myself to open the big brown cupboard behind the door I was astonished to find a horse inside. A white horse with faded black markings like splodgy stars, it had the wind in its mane and strained against the bit between its teeth, legs in a stationary mid-canter. I stood in awe of the wonderful creature, then ran down the stairs to tell Grandad of my discovery. He laid his hand on my platinum hair and curled the ringlets round his rough fingers.

'Ah, that's Tipperary Tim.'

'Who does he belong to, Grandad?'

'Your dad used to ride him,' he replied. 'That was the bedroom he shared with your Uncle Len,' and I thought his eyes got a bit watery.

Len and Jim riding Tipperary Tim

'Oh, I see,' I said, feigning a lack of interest, and ran into the garden. I could not upset Grandad with my probing curiosity but my four-year-old brain puzzled how my dad, who I knew was a big hero of a man, had ridden a horse small enough to live in a cupboard. Now I know that this was the room where he read books unintelligible to his father and began to form his socialist philosophy.

There was no upstairs toilet so I guess, like me, he always used the dark outside lav. I remember perching on the high wooden seat, leaving the planked wooden door (covered in peeling green paint) slightly open in case the metal latch should stick and render me imprisoned under the cast iron cistern high above my head. I pushed the seat back, climbed up onto the rim of the pan and balanced precariously, trying to reach the chain with the chipped porcelain pull at its end.

The 'front' door of number 17 had a horizontal, oval, stained-glass window. It was round the side of the house down a couple of steps beside the silver birch tree struggling to survive in the tiny front garden. On entering, the familiar 'Grandad' smell of Wills Whiffs or Woodbines assaulted my nostrils. I ran through the brown hallway (most houses were unremittingly brown in the 1940s) and past the best room with its 'only for Christmas and funerals' brown leather armchairs and, over the cold black fireplace, the picture of brown shaggy cows with horns paddling in a stream. Then I burst into the living room, where I found Grandad sitting by the fire busy with his golden tin of tobacco and brightly coloured packets of Rizlas. The resultant roll-ups were so thin they bent in the middle and strands of tobacco poked out of the end and became a momentary flare when he set light to them. He drew the pink ends of the matches along the gluey sand on the edge of a yellowish box with a picture of a swan on the front. About every third one burst into flames and I breathed in that tangy smell which tickled the inside of my nose. Then he put the tube in his mouth and coughed. He coughed a lot. 'It's the gas,' he said. *What gas?* I wondered. Surely not the smelly gas in the grey enamel stove in the kitchen – Nanny's pride and joy – which made a loud pop when she held a flaming spill to the burner and muttered, 'It'll have my eyebrows off one of these days.'

A deep porcelain Belfast sink in its first fashionable incarnation was flanked by scrubbed, ridged, wooden boards, usually covered with draining saucepans or vegetables Grandad had dug from the garden. In the larder with the wire mesh window was a meat safe; a metal box with a marble floor, and a gauze door defending a couple of sausages from hungry bluebottles. On special occasions there might be a piece of belly-pork.

I pulled open the solid back door and ran past the coal-hole on my right, the mangle on my left. If it was wash day I watched Nanny turning the handle and squeezing sheets through wooden rollers, always a little anxious her fingers would be swallowed up with the washing and spat out with the water pouring into the tub below. Then she used wooden pegs she bought from the gypsies who called at the door to pin the washing on the line of rope Grandad had erected along the central path. On windy Mondays I could stand at the top of the garden and see identical lines of sheets, towels, shirts and bloomers fluttering in gardens all the way down the hill.

Grandad was a very tall man but I gazed with amazement at his long woolly combinations. They grew longer still when they dripped the water the mangle had failed to squeeze out into a puddle on the path. What was that opening with the cracked rubber buttons where the legs met? Then one day I saw him getting dressed and was shocked into understanding. My friends who had brothers had told me they had sausages in their trousers but, living just with Mum, a naked Grandad was a revelation. Had my dad looked like that?

On each side of the path were vegetables and sweet peas

and, beyond them, on the left, was a large family of unruly children of whom I sensed disapproval of number 17. They wore pudding basins and saucepans on their heads in lieu of helmets and screamed unintelligible words as they chased each other with brooms and rakes in their garden war-games. I longed to join in. Sometimes the girl of about my age with the dirty face and torn frock beckoned me over and I climbed the shallow fence for a game of 'Kill the Germans'. Her brother, whose only name seemed to be 'boy', was always the hero. When I was four he was my hero too.

The garden on the right belonged to Mrs Blendell and her grown-up son, Alec. Mrs Blendell was a nice lady who limped, and whose button-brown eyes regarded me tragically through thick round lenses when she enquired, 'How is your poor mother, dear?'

'She's very well, thank you, Mrs Blendell,' I replied, but I sensed the reason for her concern. I knew why Mum sometimes seemed sad when she thought I wasn't looking. I wanted him back too.

The living room of my dad's childhood home was, for me, full of warmth and love pricked by sadness. Late on Saturday afternoons, I sat in silence as Grandad listened to the football results on the wireless and checked his coupon, screwing it up and tossing it into the fire when the points were not quite enough. Again. 'One day, Cinders, I'll get twenty-four points and then we'll all be in clover.' I knew what clover was of course. It grew on the bomb site where Smokey Joe, the tramp, lived. So why would we want to be there? I didn't question him. If Grandad thought it was good it was good. I was Cinderella and he was my beloved Buttons.

I'd watch him work his spicy magic with fish, vinegar, herbs and peppercorns as he prepared the soused herrings. Then he'd take me by the hand and we'd walk up to the stall by the Gaumont and buy the winkles for Sunday tea. Nanny and

Mum thought winkles were disgusting so we'd prop the *News of the World* between us. They'd have their bread and jam on one side, while Grandad and I giggled with our pins and winkles on the other.

My dad was always there too, of course; in the silences, in the atmosphere, in the pale eyes of my grandparents that sometimes swam into a distant, unfamiliar world, in my mother's wistful smile. He was there in their truncated comments. 'Oh, look at her blue eyes, just the same colour as...' or, 'I wonder what he would think if...' I knew who they were talking about. He was there in the frame on the mantelpiece. But I never asked them to continue. I longed to know more about him but these people round the table were everything to me. They were the bulwarks against all that was out there in the wide world of ration books and bomb sites, and the ghosts who inhabited them. They were my security fence and I was afraid of breaching it; afraid my questions would pierce their emotional armour to reveal their frail humanity; afraid they would cry. I can count on the fingers of my left hand (they said he was left-handed too) the number of times I have seen my strong mother weep, and to this day the ground rocks beneath my feet when I witness it. So I would catch his eye in the frame on the mantelpiece and make a silent promise: *one day, Dad, I'll find you.* He would have to stay in my daydreams until then. Then I'd pick up the pin, smile conspiratorially at Grandad and hook the next winkle from its shell.

This was the house where my father grew up.

This was where he began his diary.

*

It is a bone-chilling day in February 2012 when I spend a day walking back into my childhood and beyond, looking for my father. I have been doing this for some time but today this is physical, this is real. Or is it?

I plan to spend the morning researching in the Heritage Centre located in the old Woolwich Arsenal complex; the place where Grandad laboured in the Second World War; the town I knew intimately as a child. But this morning it is unreal. When I pop my head above ground, emerging from the new railway station under Beresford Square, I am in an unfamiliar land. An aggressive, pedestrianised piazza, barely relieved by vegetation, is dominated by a giant 'Big Brother' screen exhorting people to get fit. Most of the population, however, seem disinterested and overweight as they smoke their aromatic roll-ups and shiver under their hoodies.

Someone, I don't know who, once told me that Grandad was born behind a barrow in the market. I cross the street expecting the buzzy bartering I remember from childhood. Stallholders still hawk their wares, but as well as cabbages, swedes, spuds and cockney costermongers there are mangoes, lychees and saris. The air is pungent with a spicy aroma. Men in turbans smoke hubble-bubble pipes; women in burqas chat to oriental teenagers in American jeans. The world has changed. So has Woolwich market.

Which way to walk? I have no point of reference until I find the Arsenal Gate. Mighty and impressive in my childhood, it now looks small and bereft; a head severed from its body by a dual carriageway running parallel to the unseen Thames. Obediently, I wait for the little green man to allow me to cross. Impatient engines throb, eager to roar towards the city, like blood surging along its carotid artery. I walk through the new 'heritage' Arsenal gates into a kind of toy town. Freezing in the Siberian wind blowing up the river from the east I pass new penthouses. 'For Sale' boards are attached to marketing kiosks in the midst of historic powder stores guarded by cannons.

In the Heritage Centre, I thaw my hands and body with a takeaway coffee and pore over old newspapers and wartime bomb maps. But this is cold historical research, unwarmed by emotional engagement, until the helpful archivist appears at my shoulder: 'Let me introduce you to John Kennett – a member of The Eltham Society who may be able to help you.'

I look up at the tall man in the green jumper. I see his spectacles and my memory judders, jumps into another gear...

...the sun is shining on me as I pick juicy garden blackberries and wish I had put on my coat to fend off the prickles. I reach through the brambles to capture the best purple fruit. I stuff the berries into my mouth, the flavour tingles on my tongue, and in the street beyond the picket fence I see a boy. He is wearing short grey trousers and a green jumper and he is kicking a football against the wall in front of his house. He is wearing glasses...

'I think I know you,' I say.

The man's brow creases, he bites his top lip and his eyes leave my face to search his past.

'Didn't you live in Prince John Road?' I prompt.

'Yes – number 8, when I was a child.'

'I lived at 19, but you were older so you probably won't remember me.'

'That was up on the corner. The name of the people was...'

'Gaywood,' I offer.

'Of course, of course. They were a young couple. He was in the RAF. She had a baby.'

'That baby was me.'

After a gap of sixty something years, we unpick our memories together.

'Do you remember the Powell family, or the Rowes?'

'Of course. What school did you go to? I went to Haimo Road.'

'Me too – so did both my parents.'

'Do you remember that wall at the bottom of the hill which felt so scratchy when you ran your fingers along it?'

'I can feel it now.'

As a six-year-old John hadn't known any casualties of war and remembers the intoxicating cocktail of emotions he experienced – sadness, adventure, sympathy and excitement – when he heard the news that the man up the road, the one he had seen in his smart blue uniform, was missing, may have been killed in a blazing aeroplane, and that the young woman and the baby she pushed around in that big black pram were all alone.

My memories are morphing from black and white to sepia, and now the reality of colour creeps in as this human connection makes my day vital and real.

We shake hands, smile, and promise to keep in touch.

Later that day I take the bus along ever more familiar streets to Eltham. I turn into Prince John Road and stop to photograph number 47, where my father spent his earliest years. I pass concreted, unfenced front 'gardens' – resting places for refuse bins, broken play equipment and vehicles in varying states of disrepair. Before me is the grassy roundabout where four quiet suburban streets meet. I am there in no time; surely these roads have shrunk since my childhood? As I approach number 19, my own childhood home, its plastic 'Georgian' windows and high fence announce it is now in private ownership and my prying camera lens is unwelcome. All traces of the thorny blackberry bushes and the fruitful back garden have been subsumed under concrete. Siberian snow begins to fall through the dusk and I fancy I see the ghost of Grandad clumping up the hill in his gumboots, collar turned up round his brown knitted scarf, cap on head, fag in mouth, sack in hand. He looks up and smiles, 'Just coming to clear the snow from your path, Cinders.'

My feet are numb with cold as I pass the wall John Kennett used for football practice and I am tempted to turn back to the bus stop, but I'm eager to see my grandparents' house.

Eltham Hill is a dual carriageway now, with a narrow snaky

Sam 1947

island down the middle of a road carrying noisy traffic. Could that really be the same tree beside the entrance to number 17? Do silver birches live for seventy years and remain the same size? If not, a good fairy has replaced it in exactly the same position. The house, though, is sad. Like its neighbours it has lost its front garden to hard standing fringed with weeds. A lonely post cries for its gate and I wonder what precise Mrs Blendell would have to say about the broken wire fence that has replaced her privet hedge, always meticulously clipped, however fierce the bombing. I consider for a moment knocking at the door and requesting a look round the back, but courage fails me as I foresee a suspicious reception for this strange woman in the freezing twilight.

The houses and streets are real but they are not the houses and streets of my family's reality – they belong to others now. Mine are stored in the brilliant technicolour of memory.

2

Diary of a Crazy War

Jim pointed his pen at the blue blotting paper and made to throw it like a dart, but it didn't leave his hand. A gob of black ink shot out of the flexible nib, landed on the blotter and spread into an amorphous blob. It was a good pen. He knew this eighteenth birthday gift had made a hole in the family budget. But the way the ink flowed – now meanly, now like a severed artery – was trying his patience. He had to get this right; not like his random musings on previous pages; not even like the stories further back in the book.

He tried his signature on a scrap of paper. That was better; he'd get used to it. His old pen had been as familiar as the left hand that held it. It was as if there was a direct connection between his mind and what it wrote. This, however, was to be a momentous record and it was right to honour it with his new Platignum pen.

He was writing in the book I now hold in my hand, a large slim volume with a serious air. The hard blue cover is embossed with a panel reading:

UNIVERSITY MANUSCRIPT BOOK
MADE IN ENGLAND

As well as being yellowed with age the pages are rippled – evidence of damp dried out over more than seventy years. There are three short stories, but none are those so carefully recorded in the little notebook I later used as my diary. Several pages of 'reflections' follow. I especially like:

A Thought

Last night I thought on wedlock,
It reminded me of a sweaty sock.

How many teenage boys have had that impression, only to change their minds when they fall in love.

Then it begins: the diary that starts to bring my father, not yet my father, to life. His diary of a crazy war: his passions, his politics, his struggles, his hopes for the future. The views of a serious, intelligent, idealistic eighteen-year-old.

Sunday September 3rd 1939

At 11 o'clock this morning the British government declared war on Germany, and at 5 o'clock in the evening the French made a similar move. I have begun this diary by calling this war a crazy war. So it is.

The Gaywoods had sat together in silence that morning, listening to Chamberlain's words on the wireless. Like every family in the land they had been expecting it. But until they heard the words, 'This country is at war with Germany,' it had been something for the future, something that may not happen after all. Jim likened it to when his school friend, Frankie Barker, was being consumed by cancer. Everyone knew there was no hope of recovery, but it still hit Jim like a cannonball in the chest when he died. This morning's news though, while shocking and unwelcome, had an edge of excitement. Jim knew what his position would be. He was certain of what he would fight for and that could not be achieved by war with Germany.

He grasped his pen again and poured his thoughts on to the page:

To get down to the fundamental cause of this war we must go back to the outbreak of the Great War of 1914-1918 in which practically every nation in the world was involved. At the time Kaiser Wilhelm ruled Germany with a despotic government. England was a democracy in which the Socialist Movement was making great strides. Both countries were imperialist and consequently their proximity caused a great deal of competition in the field of trade. This eventually broke out into open warfare. Germany, attacking France, violated Belgium's neutrality and Britain, bound by treaty, declared war on Germany.

*

As I write a news flash pops up on my screen: 'The Act of Settlement to be repealed. Royal women to have equal rights of succession with men.' Later I learn that, had this been the case in the past, the Kaiser would have been king of Britain in 1914 and neither the Great War, nor its terrible successor, would have happened. Just two more accidents of history.

*

Jim continues:

> These are the facts as I see them, but the peoples of Britain and France were told they were fighting for 'liberty and democracy'; Germany that she was fighting to protect her vital interests. Naturally, both sides fought believing their cause to be right and ten million died on the field of battle and millions of civilians died of starvation and disease. At the armistice Germany was blackmailed into the 'Peace' Treaty of Versailles by the threat of starvation and the blockade which caused untold misery to the German people. The treaty dismembered Germany by the transfer of territory and the creation of new states with German minorities.

> From the revolution and turmoil that shook Germany
> there arose a man destined to be one of history's most famous
> men, the National Socialist Adolf Hitler who, from being
> an Austrian house painter, rose to the position of Germany's
> dictator.

In the garden, Sam coughed as he hoed the vegetable patch. It was a sound so familiar it generally didn't impinge on Jim's consciousness. Now it irritated him, breaking his concentration, so he stood and closed the bedroom window to silence his dad. That cough was a remnant of life in the trenches, Jim reminded himself. The chlorine gas had attacked his father's lungs and temporarily blinded him only twenty-two years before. Chastened, Jim returned to his desk.

*

The neat small script develops the history lesson, describing how Hitler's coming to power in 1933 began the events which culminated in the Second World War. I begin to wonder at this earnest young man's interest in, and detailed knowledge of, causes and events. For me the First World War is history. For my children it is distant history. When my grandchildren study it at school it must feel the way the English Civil War feels to me – like a film or a staged drama. Jim was just eighteen years old as he began his diary and his dad's coughing in the garden must have made it feel very recent.

The handwriting, punctuation and grammar of the entries are faultless; the passion of the content leaps off the page. Jim had won a Junior County Scholarship from Haimo Road Primary School. The entrance exam for Colfe's was more difficult but both he, and later his brother Len, made their parents proud when they donned their black and gold blazers and caps and took the tram to Lewisham for their first days as grammar school boys. Len remembers the masters at Colfe's as being very clever but inspiring him with little enthusiasm. Where did Jim's inspiration come from?

September 3rd (contd.)

The British and French now call this the war for justice and freedom. The war to crush Hitlerism, out of which, if these countries win, a new order will arise in Europe based on trust and mutual confidence. An ideological war, in fact. And the German side? During the last few months Hitler has proclaimed incessantly that Germany was being encircled and her vital space and trade kept from her.

Having come back from Germany only a few weeks ago, I can confirm that the people there very largely accept this point of view. They say, 'Look at your Empire (which includes colonies in Africa which you stole at Versailles), then look at us who must wear paper for leather and an unsatisfactory substitute for cotton and wool. You have plenty. Why should we go without? WE DO NOT WANT WAR BUT GERMANY MUST LIVE!' And the English say: 'WE DO NOT WANT WAR, BUT AGGRESSION MUST STOP!' And so we have the crazy situation of two countries waging a war which neither wants, and both fighting for those very things for which the war of 1914-1918 was fought, and which FAILED!

It has been proven that nothing can be settled by war and this war may be the end of civilization and yet they will go through with it believing that by doing so the world will be better off. I say to the reader that I believe this war will end civilization in Europe, and therefore this war is a crazy war.

He had been in Germany in the summer of 1939. Why? It seems unlikely his family had contacts there and, anyway, did they have the money to fund such a trip? Since the Great War, Jim's dad, my beloved grandad, had been a milkman with the Royal Arsenal Co-operative Society.

Sam and his milk cart

Then he rose to be the foreman-in-charge, forsaking his horse-drawn cart. Jim and Len watched respectfully as their tall, ramrod-backed father set off for the early morning tram to Woolwich, six days a week. He wore a suit and trilby hat. His shoes were polished to a mirror shine. Then, as war loomed, he mysteriously lost his job and the boys were never told the reason. I am shocked to hear that Len suspects it was 'due to the demon drink.' The pub was important to Grandad and he never missed a day without his pint or two but I never recall seeing him drunk. Did Jim's suspicions echo Len's? Did the respect slip a bit?

Perhaps Jim was in Germany with the scouts. The 18th Royal Eltham Troop was an important part of his life, and exchanges with troops in Europe were not uncommon. I have seen a photo of him climbing at Kandersteg, the Boy Scout camp in Switzerland. A slender youth with a bony face and thoughtful expression, he wears his uniform with pride. A lock of fair hair can be seen escaping one of those big bush ranger hats, the pride and joy of Baden Powell's boys.

A letter from my Uncle Len explains the German trip. Jim

studied the language at school and his pen friend, Ernst, had stayed with the Gaywoods in Eltham on a school exchange. In the summer of 1939, Jim had saved enough money to fund a return visit to the banks of the River Ruhr. Europe's belly was rumbling with discontent and Ernst's sister, Maria, foretold the war: 'Just you wait, my friend, once the harvest is in hostilities will begin.'

On September 3rd, the harvest was in and war was declared. Eighteen-year-old Jim was back in South London at his job as an invoice clerk. An invoice clerk! Surely he had more potential than merely adding up and processing accounts? But this was the thirties depression and he was lucky to have a job of any kind. Len tells me that staying on at school after sixteen to achieve a Higher School Certificate would have been unthinkable. There was no hope of progressing to university (that was only for the wealthy), and the family income needed supplementing. Their dad had managed to secure a job manufacturing arms at Woolwich Arsenal but the pay was abysmal.

September 3rd (contd.)

Now for news of the war itself. An air-raid warning was sounded about midday, but it was discovered that it was only a friendly plane approaching the coast.

Monday September 4th 1939

At about 2.30am this morning an air-raid warning was given but, once again it was a false alarm. It was learned today that a few hours after the declaration of war the British passenger liner Athenia was torpedoed 200 miles off the north coast of Ireland. The liner, on its way to Canada, is reported to have about fifteen hundred passengers on board. Last night and early this morning British planes dropped six million leaflets written in German over N and W Germany. Official reports say that all planes returned safely.

Tuesday September 5th 1939

I had an undisturbed night (thank God), but the morning papers revealed that British planes had bombed the German Naval Station at Wilhelmshaven. Three million more leaflets were also dropped on the Ruhr district. It rather looks as though the British government is trying to cut short the war by provoking revolution in Germany. Heavy fighting and air raids continue on the Eastern Front and the Germans are said to be only fifty-six miles from Warsaw, where machine gun fire can be heard. Civilian casualties from air raids in Poland are officially stated to be two hundred and fifty killed and seven hundred injured. These figures include people killed when an evacuation train was alleged to have been bombed and machine-gunned by the Germans. Athenia survivors are arriving safely in Scotland and others have been picked up by boats. Survivors (including neutral Americans) say that a torpedo struck the liner just above the engine room, and soon after the submarine broke the surface and fired on the liner. This disproves the theory of the Germans that the ship struck a mine. This incident has shocked the world.

Wednesday September 6th 1939

I was awakened at about 6.30 by the wailing of air-raid sirens and the sharp blasts of police whistles. I dressed hurriedly and the family put on coats and grabbed gas-masks. Nothing happened, however, so we made a cup of tea. We waited about until 8am then got breakfast. Eventually the all-clear signal was heard at about 9am.

Even to me, who remembers policemen with whistles, there is something of *Dad's Army* about this account – nothing like a nice cup of tea to calm the nerves.

He continues:

Planes were engaged with ours on the East Coast and were turned back. One report says that an English plane was brought down, the pilot commandeered a car to the aerodrome and took off again to engage the enemy.

Oh, what exciting tales of derring-do. They could almost have been lifted from the pages of Arthur Mee's *Book of Heroes* which still resided on Jim's bookshelf. Then the concerned adult clicks in again:

The French government is said to have bombed the German industrial centre around Aachen. My dear German friends live in Hagen, just on the edge of the Ruhr. I pray that they at least may escape injury. So far the war in the West has not assumed a serious aspect, but Polish troops are fighting furiously with the Germans.

*

Wasn't the fact that the French were bombing the Germans serious?

*

At sunset, a strict blackout was enforced with heavy penalties for those who failed to ensure their house was completely light-tight. Not a chink was allowed to escape and guide Jerry's bomb-loaded planes towards London.

Cis – Jim's mum, my nanny, was big; big and soft and warm when I snuggled into her as she told her stories. Stories that remain like films forever refreshed by frequent re-runs through my mind – such as her tale of preparing for the blackout.

Nanny joined the queue which snaked all the way from Hind's to Burton's corner, opposite the public toilets by the old stone lychgate of the parish church. It was a good-natured social occasion as they waited for their share of the newly-delivered blackout material. Crowds of housewives from the estate, wicker baskets over their arms, were discussing their varying skills with a needle or offering the use of treadle or hand-operated sewing machines.

'Two yards'll do your front window easy, Dulcie.'

'Don't know what poor Frank'll do...'

'Oh, send 'is girl round to me, luv. I'll give her an 'and. 'Er mum never could be bothered with sewing and now she's gone, God rest 'er soul, that poor lass'll have the whole house to do.'

A rumour transmitted down the line like electricity. 'Hinds have run out, Lil, but someone says George's have got a bit left.' A swarm of women sprinted or puffed their way down the High Street – then, George's ran out too.

'There'll be some on Woolwich market tomorrow. Don't turn the lights on tonight, Ena. Joe and you can 'ave a bit of a cuddle in the dark.' Nanny linked arms with her neighbour and hoots of laughter were heard as they retraced their steps down the hill. This phoney war felt like some sort of black game but their jollity was tinged with a fear they refused to acknowledge.

Everyone now carried a gas mask with them when they went out; strange black rubber affairs with inbuilt goggles (painted to resemble Mickey Mouse on the models for children), and a reservoir of charcoal in the snout to absorb the gas (which never came).

Arthur Jones at number 45, an ARP warden, barked his imperious command to 'put out that light' as he patrolled the neighbourhood searching out light-lawbreakers. A long corrugated 'elephant's trunk' connected his mask to a hessian-covered voice box attached to his belt. If we encountered him today we would think we had been invaded by antique aliens. The tops of pillar boxes were painted with gas-detecting paint and I can almost hear Captain Mainwaring's voice directing a posse of old men with paintbrushes.

The Gaywoods, in common with most of the phlegmatic population of London, were calm, but their ears were always alert for air-raid warnings. The starter of a car, a rarity in a working class area in 1939, was enough to engender alarm.

Jim and his dad queued with their neighbours at the depot in Archery Road for an Anderson air-raid shelter. They carried the corrugated beast, snail-like, over their heads down the road and round to the back garden. A couple of hours' work and they had dug into the sloping ground, flattened a floor in the earth and erected the semi-circular steel structure, like a giant baked bean tin sliced down the middle, with reinforced steel ends. Then they shovelled the displaced soil on top.

'Tell your Ma to put the kettle on, son. No, better idea – we'll go down the Yorkshire Grey. I reckon we deserve a pint, and we haven't had to pay a penny for this contraption.'

'Thanks, Dad, I'd like that, but just one pint. I'm going to a meeting tonight.'

'You and your meetings. Don't know what you find to talk about. I s'pose it's all that pacifist stuff. You'll learn, boy.'

It was a tight squeeze in the shelter when the long wolf-like wail sounded at twilight to warn of an air attack. Designed to accommodate a family of six, it measured less than seven feet by five, and while Grandad was thin he was also tall. Nanny, to put it kindly, resembled a large cuddly cushion. Good job young Len had been evacuated and Uncle Harry did a lot of night duty at The Express Dairy depot. At least the family could huddle together for warmth. They took in a paraffin lamp to lighten the darkness rather than rely on the life of a torch battery. It was damp too. The Corbens' shelter at the bottom of the hill was flooded out every time it rained. My future dad seems to have taken all this in his stride, although every time he mentions the shelter he adds, 'I hope I get some sleep tonight'.

He tells of plenty of jokes doing the rounds, of doughty

Londoners keeping the spirits up, and of newspapers branding Hitler as a 'baby killer' after the Athenia attack. Frustrated, Jim writes in his diary:

> But doesn't it occur to them that our bombs will also be baby killers?

On September 8th, five days into the war, the papers reported the Poles were bombing Berlin and the Germans were rushing troops from the Eastern Front to the west. The war in Europe was hotting up. The text of the leaflets dropped on Germany was also released and Jim quotes the salient parts:

> WARNING. A MESSAGE FROM GREAT BRITAIN.
>
> The government of the Reich has, with cold deliberation, forced a war on Great Britain... The assurance of peaceful intentions given by the Fuhrer to you and the world in April have proved as worthless as his words at The Sports Palace last September when he said 'We have no more territorial claims to make in Europe...' Never has a government ordered its subjects to death with less excuse... Your rulers have condemned you to the massacre, miseries and privations of a war they cannot ever hope to win... We are too strong to break by blows and we could wear you down inexorably... You, the German people, can, if you will, insist on peace at any time...

Where was Jim going every day with his gas mask in its cardboard box? His brother tells me his first job on leaving school in 1937 was in the office of the Gutta Percha factory in Silvertown, north of the river. Gutta Percha, I discover, was a type of rubber used for insulating cables. He took the tram to the Woolwich Free Ferry. Still free today, as it has been since Londoner Joseph Bazalgette (the man whose crowning achievement was designing

42

the London sewer system) launched the project in 1889. Free as it was when, as a teenager, I spent many summer days crossing and re-crossing the Thames with my friend Avril, laughing and flirting with the men in blue overalls who maintained the huge engines as we stood at the open viewing windows. The gigantic solid brass pistons moved smoothly, almost soundlessly, glinting with the lubricating oil I can still smell when my memory transports me back.

Since he was sixteen, my dad had alighted from the tram in Beresford Square every working morning and joined a stream of humanity making for the south shore of London's river. The crowd divided as hundreds of men and women entered the gates of the Arsenal to manufacture weapons in anticipation of the coming conflict, and the remainder turned left to board the ferry to the industrial area on the north bank. Fog horns boomed on the water, smoke rose from dozens of chimneys and Jim's nostrils breathed in the smell of burning rubber as he approached the factory gates. Two years into his employment, with the country at war, he had a difficult day.

The hooter sounded and Jim's colleagues put down their pens and filed the papers they had been working on in the communal office overlooking the Thames. He waited until their relaxed end-of-day chatter receded down the echoing corridor before approaching the door of the inner sanctum. Summoning up his courage he knocked on the obscured glass panel, aiming firmly for the middle A of the gold lettering announcing this to be the domain of the MANAGER. He waited. And waited. He was just about to turn away confused by feelings of disappointment and relief when a deep 'Come' issued from within. Jim's moist hand slipped on the brass handle as he turned it and entered.

A few wisps of late sunlight squeezed through small smoke-encrusted panes overlooking the river and fell onto the rug in front of the iron grate, coals set ready to be lit at the first sign of autumn chill. The desk lamp cast a green glow on the man sitting behind it. He downed the remains of his tea from a bone china cup and his finger delicately removed a wandering tea leaf from his tongue. His Harris Tweed suit and wing-collar were further embellished by a gold chain snaking across the mound of his waistcoat. He studied the watch which hung on it, replaced it in its pocket and then looked up, eyebrows lifting into horizontal question marks above his gold-rimmed spectacles.

'Sir, I have to tender my resignation.' Jim's words hung in the air while his boss considered his reply.

At last the manager's expression softened. 'Ah, you've enlisted have you, young fellow?'

Jim's pulse thumped in his ears and he unstuck a rough tongue from a dry palate. 'No, sir. I am a deeply convinced pacifist and can no longer work for a company which supplies cable for submarines – which are part of the war effort.' There. It was out.

What was the reply? 'You are a fine worker and I'll be sorry to lose you. But I applaud your bravery in acting according to your principles.'

I doubt that, and prefer not to imagine the actual scene and allow Jim to make a rapid escape.

Saturday September 9th 1939

Today I gave up my job. This was inevitable for the firm I work for has been executing an ever increasing number of government orders. Being an *absolute pacifist* who will have as little to do with this silly war as is possible, I could not help with the armament programme. I shall finish at the end of next week.

I have always known he was a pacifist, but it still sets off a little adrenaline surge to see it proudly stated in his own handwriting.

Now, he had to tell his family he had voluntarily given up his income.

Jim stepped off the tram right outside his home. It had always been convenient to have the stop almost on the doorstep, but now he wished he had more time to rehearse his speech. The tram clanked on down the hill, a flash of warning sparking in the cables. Jim's heart was unbalanced – one side euphoric at his decision to obey his conscience, the other heavy, anticipating a hostile family reaction to his news. His resolution faltered a little as he crunched on the golden leaves tumbling from the silver birch and went round to the back, past the mangle standing damp and bereft in the dusk. He kicked the galvanized tub beneath, disturbing the occupants of the henhouse at the end of the garden into a cacophony of cackles. A familiar smell of slightly burnt stew and over-cooked apple greeted him when he pushed his shoulder against the blotchy back door – it always stuck in the damp.

'Hello, Jim dear. Good day?' Cis's gaze was full of love and respect as she beheld her elder boy, but she was frightened of the dreams behind his piercing blue eyes. He passed an arm round her ample, soft shoulder, clad as ever in a faded overall, and planted a kiss on her cheek.

'Not too bad, Mum. Dad home yet?'

'Just home, dear – he's in there.' She jerked her head backwards.

In the living room his father's yellowed fingers thumbed through the pages of the *News Chronicle*. 'We'll get the bastards,' he wheezed. 'We got 'em last time and we'll do it again, eh, Jim, my boy? And with bright 'uns like you, we'll do it quicker this time, once you've stopped playing your silly pacifist games. No Somme, no Verdun, no trenches, no gas...' His list tailed off into a prolonged fit of coughing.

Cis waddled in with steaming plates. 'Oh, Sam, put that

45

paper down. And you, son, wash that ink off your fingers and come and tuck in. You need a bit more flesh on those bones.'

Jim wished Len was there. Len would support him.

It was not until they were scraping the last of the stewed apple and lumpy custard from the bowls with the faded roses round the rims, and Sam was smiling, that Jim broached the subject.

'Mum, Dad, I've something to tell you.'

'Tell your mother, I'm off to the Rising Sun.'

'But, Dad…'

'She can tell me later, but I don't want to hear any more about that Russian stuff. Don't know where you get your crazy ideas from – was that all they taught you at the grammar school?' He jammed his cap firmly onto his receding hairline and was gone.

'Mum.'

'Mmm?' Her mind was miles away with her younger son in the country. Len was safe from the bombs but his absence had left a hole in his family, a wound too tender to touch, but which his mum fingered constantly. The tingle of pain felt like a constant connection, an ephemeral umbilical cord. Cis stacked the bowls and made for the kitchen.

'I've given up my job.' A spoon clattered to the floor and she froze.

'You know how I feel about the war, Mum. The firm's contributing to it, so I have to leave.'

'But, Jim, you're only in the office, you're not making the stuff…'

'You don't understand, Mum, that's not the point. I have to go. I've given a week's notice. Then I'll find something else, don't worry.'

Cis's eyes glittered and she shook her head. 'Your dad won't be pleased, you know.' She hesitated, unsure of how disapproving she should be; how much pressure to exert, knowing the perilous state of the family finances. She gave up the struggle.

'Oh, never mind, Jim. I'll tell him later.'

She broke the news to Father in my absence. It seems he stormed a bit but it passed over.

I suspect the storm was violent but Nanny downplayed it.

Saturday September 9th 1939

I learned at a meeting last night that other pacifists are unemployed for the same reason. This afternoon about six of us sold Peace News in Eltham High Street and, strange to relate, we had no insults or scuffles, and our sales were actually the highest ever. I fully expected trouble of some sort; indeed I was surprised that the paper was published at all.

He had been to a meeting of the Peace Pledge Union in the Scout hut in Southend Crescent. Jim admired Harry Phippen, who was there, as always, arguing with an explosive passion, for internationalism and an end to violence. Crimson rose from his collar to his prematurely balding head as he worked himself into a sweat in the chilly hall. Bob Tilling, a schoolteacher from Orpington, was a regular and had brought his brother who was all for fighting and said so in no uncertain terms. Charles Lockyer and Gilbert Rose, men in their twenties from Bexleyheath, made few contributions to discussions but there was a steely determination in their silence.

Jim chewed his lip as he applauded his friends, trying to subdue a slight feeling of unease.

Peace News was the official paper of the PPU and carried contributions from well-known subversives such as Gandhi and George Lansbury. Indeed, some contributors were so sympathetic to the grievances of Nazi Germany that one sceptical member found it difficult to distinguish between letters to *Peace News* and those to the newspaper of the British Union of Fascists. *Peace News*, though, also urged the British government to give sanctuary to Jewish refugees from Nazism.

I begin to see where some of Jim's strongly held opinions came from.

Sunday September 10th 1939

The war cabinet is reckoning on a three-year war and is making plans accordingly. I think they are optimistic. As regards the war in Poland, Germans claim they are just outside the city of Warsaw.

Fighting continues on the Western Front but nothing spectacular has taken place.

Monday September 11th 1939

The Germans claim to have entered Warsaw, but stories of a heroic stand by the Poles keep coming through.

I heard from my brother today. He seems quite happy. I shall cycle down to Tunbridge Wells to see him next Sunday.

'Hey, lad, where are you going with a face like a wet weekend?' Jim's two Scoutmasters were having a chinwag by the post office after Geoff had finished his rounds.

'Evening, Leslie, evening, Geoff.' He told them he would be unemployed by the end of the week, and the reason why.

'Well, all power to you, boy, even though I don't agree.' Geoff tapped his fingers against his chin and considered. 'Can't promise, but I think there may be a place in the sorting office. I'll let you know.'

'Thanks, Geoff, I would be grateful. See you Wednesday.' His step was a little lighter as he walked home.

Tuesday September 12th 1939

British troops are now officially stated to be in France and are reported to be getting a great welcome. I wonder what percentage of them will return sound, physically and spiritually?

How the army must change our minds. How warped and narrow their outlook on life must become. God grant that I never lose my internationalism! They have started bayonet fighting on the Western Front. How is it possible to bayonet a fellow being? How is it possible for a 'Christian' Church to condone such things? Isn't it time we turned away from Christianity and went back to the religion which Christ taught? Or which Buddha taught? Or is the world lunatic enough to think that those two men would do the same in the circumstances? A remarkable fact about the war is that the British and French governments repeatedly state that they are fighting Hitlerism and not the German people. Yet it is the German people we are killing. It is the German people we are trying to starve. It is the German people who must suffer... Hell! What fools are men!

Wednesday September 13th 1939

The German government has announced its intention to bomb and shell open towns and villages – in direct opposition to Hitler's statement that he wouldn't do this. The British government now reserves the right to take appropriate action. Does this mean we are seeing the beginning of a war method which seeks to destroy as many people as it possibly can? That will indeed mean an end of European civilization. My mother is talking about going out to work now that I am leaving mine. I must find a job.

Friday September 15th 1939

Today was the great day I severed my connection with my employer and joined the ranks of the workless.

Two days later he rode Len's bike to Tunbridge Wells where his brother was staying with a young couple in their new house on the outskirts of the town, while completing his education at Skinners Grammar School. The brothers walked over the common and climbed on Wellington Rocks. Len announced that he liked the area so much he would like to live there forever. *Yes*, Jim thought, *he really is a country boy*. Where did that come from? Their grandfather, perhaps. He had been part of the Victorian migration from the farmlands of Essex to the economic promise of London. Maybe that agricultural heritage was locked into his brother's bones.

Len wanted to keep his bike, so Jim returned on the train which was packed to its absolute capacity, and considered himself lucky to get home at all.

Sunday September 17th 1939
As one wit said, 'ole Hitler wouldn't stand for this!

The humour died when he arrived home to hear that 'ole Hitler had occupied Poland.

There was no work in the Post Office, so the next day Jim went to the Labour Exchange and was sent after a job, but the post was already filled. With the optimism of youth he decided on a change of tack.

Tuesday September 19th 1939
Today I wrote a short story which I intend to submit for publication. It is just possible that I may be able to make a living that way.

I wonder if this story was 'The Simple Boy', the first one recorded in the little green notebook.

Wednesday September 20th 1939

Poland seems to be virtually finished. The government has fled to Rumania. Poor Poland!

Yesterday, HMS *Courageous* was sunk by a German U boat. About 1200 people were on board. The U boat is said to have been destroyed.

He went back to the Labour Exchange but it was looking doubtful that he'd get benefit, having left his job of his own free will. Or at least as his conscience dictated. In the High Street he bought a paper when he saw the headline about the Courageous. Six hundred and eighty-one had been safely landed but over five hundred were dead.

Oh the vile stupidity of war!

Yesterday Hitler made a speech in Danzig. It does not alter the situation, but he threatened to use a weapon 'which, so far, Germany has not used and against which there is no defence.' Or words to that effect! The morning newspapers consider that he means the bombing plane.

And that's it. No more diary entries. This is when I have to play detective, tail Jim, and piece together the next two years of his life.

3

The Attraction of Books

It was love that caused the end of the diary. The same love that caused the beginning of me. But not yet. He'd known her forever. She was not the girl next door but the girl round corner – at 19 Prince John Road.

They'd shared a double wooden desk in Miss Brentnall's infants' class at Haimo Road School. They had giggled, swapped marbles, shared wax crayons and smuggled a frog into school which hopped around the classroom during scripture, causing hilarity and terror in equal measure. Pat cried when, at seven, they were promoted to the juniors and separated. After that Jim had to barge through the entrance with BOYS engraved in the stone lintel whilst she jostled through the GIRLS door on the other side of the building. Even the playgrounds were divided, but I like to think they waved or talked through a hole in the fence. I put this to my mother but she destroys my romantic view by telling me it was impossible as the division was a high brick wall.

When Jim passed the scholarship to the boys' grammar school, Pat left half the questions on her paper blank to sabotage her chance of promotion to the one for girls because she knew all the snooty ones went there and she wasn't like that. So she went to the Central School in Plum Lane and occasionally bumped into Jim on the way home. My mother nods and laughs as I weave a picture of what may have ensued.

Pubescent hormones raged, acne flourished and desire

began to inflame their meetings. But he assumed she was Freddie Freak's girl. Jim's school chum lived opposite her and regaled the class with tall stories about his girlfriend, Pat Sheridan. She, however, remained silent on the matter. There was only one boy she ever fancied but her mum had told her she was far too young to be interested in the opposite sex.

Jim's school library provided a diversion in the form of a book on cinematography. It inspired a new hobby. He valued his Kodak Brownie but bemoaned the lack of funds for a movie camera. Mr Jackson, the art teacher, seeing potential in this quiet, artistic pupil, offered Jim his own on an extended loan basis. Filming then became a passion, even an ambition for a future career, and he used his family as guinea pigs for his early efforts, both as subjects and an audience.

On the night of the premiere of *The Tiny Terrier with the Tremendous Heart*, Jim switched off the wireless. The main news was the war in Spain, a problem that had been nagging at his conscience for a while. But for now he pushed from his mind the dilemma of staying in school or running away to join the International Brigades. Running away seemed romantic, but killing? No. He was born to be an artist, not a soldier, and tonight was his filmmaker's debut.

He pulled the heavy chenille curtains across the window and secured the gap with a clothes-peg, making the living room dark enough to satisfy any future ARP warden. Then he attached a white bed sheet to them with large safety pins. An unsteady tower of chair, stool, Bible and bits of cardboard supported the projector at just the right height. Jim's tongue escaped his mouth and curved around his lips as he concentrated on feeding the holes along the edge of the reel of celluloid onto the sprocket-wheel. When it was in place a flush of anticipation crept from his shoulders to his brow.

'C'mon, Mum, c'mon, Dad. Hurry up – the show's about

to start. Where's Len? And Nell? Uncle Harry's here and so is Bob.' He pushed back the lock of hair which insisted on falling over his eyes. 'Come on!'

'Len's helping with the washing up, Nell's gone out with her young man and if you gave a hand we'd get done a lot quicker.' Sam was impatient, anxious this amateur film show would delay his departure to the pub. He muttered to Cis under the cover of the whistling kettle, 'And it wouldn't hurt your brother to do a bit too, instead of just sitting there with that silly grin on his face.'

Cis pushed the knitted crinoline-lady cosy over the big brown teapot with the chipped spout. 'Oh go on, Sam, he'd only smash the plates, clumsy oaf – best left where he is. I'll pour the tea and then we'll go to the pictures.'

A timorous voice from the other room tried a weak joke: 'What, no ices?'

'Get away with you, Harry. Be grateful for what you're given. And yes, I have given you two sugars.' Cis handed him his cup and settled into the big old leatherette armchair, resting her head on the crocheted antimacassar.

The HMV gramophone in its coffin-like black box was fully wound, the needle screwed into place. Jim lifted the heavy chrome head, placed it carefully on the outer groove of the shellac record and the opening bars of Hoffmann's 'Barcarolle' filled the room, drowning out the sound of Uncle Harry's teaspoon chinking repeatedly against his cup. Then it was on with the projector lamp, off with the ceiling light, and a small black and white dog ran up a rippled garden path on the sheet screen before them. Bob barked in recognition of the star of the show. Jim scowled as all attention turned from his film to the dog running round their feet wagging his tail in appreciation of their laughter.

'That record's scratched, son.' Sam stated the obvious; there was no mistaking the regular 'tch' interrupting the music every couple of seconds.

'Well, Bob has got sharp claws!' Len piped up, grinning, delighted with his witticism.

Thwack! A folded newspaper landed on his head. 'Shut up, little brother – this is art.'

Three years later the war had swept all thoughts of the silver screen away. Jim was thankful, after his resignation from the rubber factory, to have landed a job in the office of the Albion Sugar Company. No connection there with the war effort. Of course troops had to be fed but he guessed they didn't get treacle on their porridge. Anyway he had no wish for soldiers to starve.

After a day of paper-pushing and form-filling at the factory to a background of noisy machinery, hooters signalled the end of the working day. Tributaries of men flowed from every factory gate and joined a human river flowing parallel to the Thames until it reached the dock. Jim was among the press of humanity that crowded onto the ferry. He leaned over the rail on the starboard side and watched a lighterman escort an official-looking craft upriver. A grey heron fishing at the water's edge was disturbed by the wake and Jim envied its unhurried flight up and away from danger. Standing in the tram on the next leg of his journey he was pressed up against a stevedore whose body odour forced Jim to take as few breaths as life would allow. He was looking forward to the peace and quiet of the library on his way home.

Eltham Lending Library held a world of exciting possibilities for Jim; a sweet shop for his hungry mind. He revelled in the dusty silence, pervaded with the scent of old leather and paper, where even a cough elicited a grimace from the spinster at the desk. Those thin, rectangular cardboard tickets – green for fiction, blue for poetry, red for works of reference – were like gold in his hand; a passport to the rich country of the rest of his life. H.G. Wells, J.B. Priestley, Shakespeare and Blake were all here for the reading. And oh, how he could relate to those satanic mills.

On a December evening when weak, shaded torches

struggled to penetrate the swirling fog, he was sitting at the library reading table thumbing through *The New Internationalist*. An unsavoury old character next to him dozed over a newspaper. Only here for the warmth, every now and then he woke himself with a snort, causing the librarian to look up and frown, before he drifted back into his private dream. Jim ignored him but even *The New Internationalist* couldn't keep his mind off what was currently preoccupying him. She was scanning the 'C' section of the fiction shelves; the familiar slender figure with high cheekbones and eyes the colour of water he'd be happy to drown in. She wore a blue felt beret on tawny hair which was carefully folded into a roll at the nape of her neck. Her face glowed against her tan raincoat – *like the first almond blossom lighting up a leafless tree,* romanced Jim. Folding his paper and making to replace it with its companions, he 'accidentally' knocked her elbow. 'Sorry,' he whispered, casting a wary eye at the desk. 'Oh, oh, it's you, Pat. I didn't realise… What have you got there?' Getting close enough to peer over her shoulder he could feel her warmth, smell the sweetness of her breath.

'Jim! You made me jump.'

'A.J. Cronin. What sort of stuff does he write?'

'Lovely stuff, Jim, about doctors and romance. It says on the back he's a doctor himself.'

'Well, he should know about romance then,' he said with a wry smile.

I don't know if he asked her if she came to the library often but it would certainly have fitted the picture. He walked her home – what gallant young man wouldn't on a cold foggy night? – courteously holding her elbow and switching to her other side when they crossed the road. The time-honoured custom of protecting a lady from slops thrown out of overhanging windows was hardly necessary in twentieth-century Eltham High Street where there was just the odd puddle in the gutter, but the chivalry still impressed.

If she didn't previously 'go there often' she did from then on. Pat generally stuck to the romantic novels, deciding that the heavy political treatises and avant-garde volumes Jim eagerly tucked under his arm were the natural mental nourishment for a man who was to be admired in every way. It never entered her mind to enquire as to the content, let alone consider reading them herself. Every Tuesday and Thursday throughout that winter of 1939/40 they contrived to meet among the shelves, then took the long route on the walk home. Conversation ranged over families, friends, the war, politics, pacifism and, like the young of every generation, how they could put it all right if they were only given the chance. A tumult of excitement engulfed their minds and hearts. (And other regions, but let's not go there – they are my future parents after all.)

When the sap was rising in the silver birch, swelling its buds until they could no longer resist a green burst of energy, there was a spring in both their steps as they left the library. A gypsy on the pavement proffered a sprig of heather: 'Be lucky, my darling.'

'I'm lucky already,' Pat laughed, 'so I'd rather have those.' She handed over a sixpence in exchange for two bunches of primroses from the woman's basket. She grinned as Jim raised his eyebrows. 'One for your mother and one for mine.'

Silvery twilight stole across the suburban sky as they sauntered through the crocuses in the Well Hall Pleasaunce.

'Can you feel her ghost?' There was mischief in his voice.

'Whose ghost?' There was alarm in hers.

'Margaret Roper's. She lived here, you know; one of the first women to write a book. She was the beloved daughter of Sir Thomas More, Henry the Eighth's chancellor, and after her father was executed she rowed up the Thames, took his boiled head off a pike and kept it with her until the day she died.'

'Uurghh! That's horrible.' She shivered. He reached for her

hand and felt her fingers curl around his own.

'I was wondering if you're interested in amateur dramatics,' he ventured. 'You see, I've joined this new group – we meet on Friday nights in the room over the Co-op by New Eltham station. You'd be welcome to come with me; they're a very friendly crowd. That is, if you…' His words tumbled from his mouth, tangling with each other as his enthusiasm was snagged with the fear of rejection.

'I'd love to.'

He basked in the warmth of her smile, pleased at her interest in the dramatic arts. But didn't he realise that if he had asked her to cross the Atacama Desert or accompany him to Hindustan her answer would have been the same?

'Um, I ought to tell you it's no ordinary drama group – but I'm sure you'll love it.'

'I know I will.' If she wondered what extraordinary band of thespians she would be joining, she didn't ask. She didn't care.

Flushed with success he put his arm around her shoulder and when they turned to smile at one another their lips were very close.

Better see her home now, Jim. You know the curfew is a quarter-to-ten for this eighteen-year-old suburban working girl.

4

Rebels

'Every time it rains it rains pennies from heaven...' Jim grasped his mum in his arms and waltzed her round the kitchen.

'Phew, you're cheerful tonight, son,' she puffed when he released her.

'What d'you expect, Mum? It's Friday; half day tomorrow and dramatics tonight.'

This boy she had worried over for being too quiet, too serious, wrapped up in a chrysalis of books and pacifism had, over the last few weeks, emerged as a dancing butterfly, full of colour and life. She recognized the signs but puzzled over who could be responsible for the metamorphosis. No name had passed his lips but, whoever she was, she clearly made Jim happy and, with this tension about when the 'real war' would begin, any happiness was welcome.

'Can't stop, Mum. Got to go.' A quick peck on her cheek and he was out of the door, on his bike, whistling about pennies and feeling he was in heaven. He lifted his face to the weeping sky and pedalled up the hill and round the corner to 19 Prince John Road. No sooner had he lifted the knocker than the door flew open; she must have been waiting in the hall. Mr Sheridan appeared behind her, pinstriped and business-suited – an outfit befitting his senior position as an inspector of factories. He pulled himself up to his full height but still had to raise his eyes to glare at the lofty young man on his doorstep, while attempting a look of superior disdain.

'Jim Gaywood, is it?' he sniffed, tapping his watch pocket. 'Well, you both know the rules I hope?'

'Of course, sir, we won't be late.'

'You certainly will not.' He turned on his heel. Pat made a face at the back of her father's bald head, pulled the door shut behind her, grasped the handlebars of her sit-up-and-beg bicycle and they were off to sample the joys the Co-op hall had in store.

'So then, Jim, tell me about this mysterious group you are taking me to. Are they all witches or...'

'Oh yes, quite terrifying. Black hats, talons, lots of hubbling and bubbling, and a few wizened wizards too. But never fear, my dear, Jim is here to protect you.' His front wheel wobbled when he reached out to put an arm round her shoulder. 'Whoops! No, seriously, it's a sort of offshoot of the Unity Theatre. Do you know what that is?'

'Well, I think I've heard of it.' But she hadn't.

'Have you heard of The Rebel Players?'

'Um, well...' She recognised his serious, campaigning expression.

'Theatre by the people, of the people, for the people.' Only the slightest hint of irony tinged his words. 'They used to perform working-class political dramas on street corners until they were offered a Methodist Church Hall in Britannia Street near King's Cross. When they got too big for it they got a lease on a big disused chapel in Goldington Street and...'

'Where's that?'

'Oh, somewhere near St Pancras Station, I think. Anyway, they turned it into their own theatre. All the unions helped out – free of charge – and they've put on all sorts of shows, by the working classes, for the working classes. I've heard their *Babes in the Wood* panto was a scream, lampooning Chamberlain's appeasement policy. Even Paul Robeson performed there and wanted to go on the cleaning rota – can you believe it? – and sweep the floors, just like the rest of the cast.'

'Paul Robeson!' In common with countless others, Pat admired the black American singer. Listening to his deep velvety voice issuing from the wireless was like being transported to the slow warmth of a romanticised American south, a world away from England and the war. 'Did he then? Sweep the floors?'

'No, they wouldn't let him – thought the dust would damage his vocal cords. Probably put him on lav duty instead.' Jim hurried on with his explanation. 'Alec was one of the originals but what with work and the war and moving out to Dartford, he can't get there any more, so he started our group along the same lines. Most of us are members of the ILP.'

'What's that?'

'The Independent Labour Party. I thought you'd know about it, with your dad being Labour, and on the council. I can see I've a lot to teach you.' He relished the prospect.

'I'm a fast learner.' She giggled, hit the kerb, splashed through a puddle and her wheel sent a shower of tiny mud spots up enticingly bare legs. A stack of bikes adorned the drainpipe outside the Co-op. The side door stood open to release the chatter and laughter falling down the concrete stairs. Jim and Pat added their bikes to the pile and ran up to join the crowd, hanging their wet macs with all the others on the first landing.

Defying orders they should be left ajar to minimize bomb damage, all the metal-framed windows in the hall were shut tight against the rain streaming down the outside. Tears of condensation ran down the inside too, as if foreseeing the shattering of so many windows, so many lives, soon to come. The perimeter of the green-painted room was lined with chairs and six pendant lights encased in opaque glass shades illuminated a sea of youthful faces.

Pat saw a familiar figure and ran across the room. 'Ellen! Whatever are you doing here?'

Her diminutive next-door-neighbour grinned. 'I might ask

you the same thing, dear, but looking at that young man's face, I don't see the need.'

Pat tilted her head, putting on a questioning frown which soon dissolved into laughter as Ellen's familial humpbacked shoulders shook with mirth. Her brother Fergie's frame was even more deformed than Ellen's and my mum now wonders if it was a genetic inheritance or the result of the malnutrition their mother had suffered in the Glasgow slums, where she had grown up in the neighbouring tenement to Pat's father.

'C'mon everyone, let's get started.' Alec, script in slightly trembling hand, peered through his horn-rims. 'Ah, Jim, do I spy a new recruit?'

'This is Pat, Alec. She's very keen on drama and she, well... she has definite socialist leanings.'

Alec's left eyebrow jumped up half an inch and his mouth formed an ironic grin. 'Mmm, and she's pretty too, isn't she?'

My mum tells me choral speaking was frequently on the agenda. Franco had triumphed in the Spanish Civil War but socialist feelings still ran high. Jack Lindsay's 'On Guard for Spain', a rallying call for the International Brigade of Volunteers who had fought on the republican side, was a Rebel Players' favourite. Tonight, though, they were trying a new piece about the rise of the unions. Pat was placed next to Sebastian (real name Albert Reynolds), whose laconic manner did not match his fiery colouring.

'Are you here for the drama, the politics or the chaps?' He squeezed the words out of the side of his mouth like toothpaste from a tube. 'I'm here for the girls, but don't worry, I can see you're taken.'

Pat allowed herself a flushed smile and showed a great interest in her shoes. 'Oh no, it's not like that. I am really interested in drama and politics. Well, drama anyway – don't know much about politics.'

'Are you with us, Albert, or with the young lady on your right?' The leader's classroom voice silenced Pat's neighbour. A pile of thin booklets, some portions of their torn red covers still in place, were passed along the lines of would-be dramatists but ran out before they reached the new girl.

'Now, three groups, please. The first on the left, second on the right, and three is the middle section.' Alec pointed his hands at each group, palms facing each other as if he were sandwiching slices of ice-cream between wafers. 'Albert, you'll have to share your script with, er – yes, Pat isn't it? And remember to speak in perfect unison for the full effect. Okay, let us begin at the beginning.' He lifted his arms, for all the world as if he were about to conduct the London Philharmonic.

Lawks, thought Pat, as they launched into the chanting, *whatever's all this about?* She was in the mass of downtrodden workers agitating for union action, whilst Jim was one of the threatening bosses. Little Ellen, in the third group, was doing her

Rebel players

best to be a politician but subduing her giggles was a challenge too far. After several run-throughs and a break for those who had come straight from work to eat sandwiches and drain their Thermos flasks, Alec was getting twitchy, impatient with the chatter.

'C'mon, boys and girls, my train goes in ten minutes so we'll go through it once more and this time without the jokes. Heck, my class of thirteen-year-olds is more serious than you. A bit more gravitas needed from the bosses – pretend you are Churchill!'

'Not blooming likely, I'm no warmonger,' whispered Jim.

When Alec had grabbed his tweed jacket, jammed his trilby onto his unruly hair and run for his train, Stan Adams, the expansive Welshman who had been amusing the crowd with jokes at every opportunity during the evening, cuffed Jim's shoulder. 'Weather's cheering up, Jim boy, how about a ramble on Sunday?'

5

The Socialist Sunday Hikers

It was the end of August 1940 and there remained a few late summer weekends to resume the hikes the Rebel Players had enjoyed before the Luftwaffe and the RAF had put a stop to them in June. Britain had felt a marginally safer place since the 'few' had triumphed in the skies over the south of England.

Like a litter of excitable puppies the hikers boarded the bus on Sunday mornings en route to Kentish fresh air and exercise and a welcome interlude from offices, families, landladies and war. Some of the friends from the Players had joined up to fight, some just didn't do hiking.

Otto, a pleasant Austrian engineer, had been welcomed on their early summer walks. Pat and Jim had detected an unspoken attraction between him and Pat's friend, Ethel. Otto had fled to England rather than use his skills to assist Herr Hitler, and Jim's sense of injustice burned now that he had been interned as an enemy alien. The core of the group remained: those who were too young for service, those in reserved occupations, those who objected to the war and those, of course, who were female – these girls didn't fight.

Among the hikers was red-headed Sebastian (aka Albert Reynolds), Pat's neighbour in the drama group, who declared he was going to educate the working classes as soon as the bluebirds appeared over the white cliffs. There was tall, raven-haired Ethel and little humpbacked Ellen from next door in Prince John Road, whose sunny nature shone in her constant smile.

Ron Stratton of the superior countenance clearly had an eye for Ethel and did not share Jim's regrets about Otto's internment. The others were wary of Ron, stifling their puzzled amusement when he brought along his admired Chinese colleague, Zhing Ho from the Royal Arsenal scientific laboratory. Zingo, as he was soon nicknamed, habitually wore a city suit for rambling and translated everyone's name into Mandarin. Bowing low, he presented each hiker with his or her name translated into Chinese characters, then retreated backwards as if they were royalty.

Stan Adams from the Welsh valleys tapped his nose and pursed his lips when he mentioned his secret work at the Admiralty and challenged himself to put a smile on the face of Spike Mullins, a humourless civil servant who looked and behaved like a miserable bloodhound.

Joyce Amos, the daughter of one of Pat's father's colleagues on the council, brought along her reluctant brother to join what their mother called 'a nice group of young people whose hearts are in the right place.' That was, on the Left.

Pat and Jim squeezed their bodies into the last vacant space in the back row of the Green Line bus, the resulting closeness welcome to them both. Out of his pocket Jim pulled a small white paper bag, unfolded the top and offered it to Pat.

'Blimey, how did you get hold of those? Black market?' Her eyes widened at the sight of the sweets.

'Hope you like 'em.' Jim had paid over the odds to a fellow in the factory for two ounces of boiled sour sugar.

'Mmm, I adore acid drops, Jim. I love that tingle you get on your tongue, don't you?' Her mischievous grin as she licked her lips sent a shower of tingles from the tip of his head down through his body and right into the velvety bus seat.

On the road near Farningham, a chorus of 'Knees up Mother Brown' floated through the open windows. The bus passengers roared their approval and applauded as they overtook the open lorry carrying the singers.

'Hop-pickers,' Jim supposed. 'They look as if they're all set for a good time.'

The Sunday hikers tumbled off the bus at the end of their journey and thanked the driver. Her uniform jacket, probably requisitioned from the stack of surplus left when her predecessors exchanged them for service uniforms, was bursting its seams with unfamiliar female filling. Having enjoyed their merriment for half an hour she wished them a good day, wondering how long their laughter, or even their lives, would continue in such uncertain times.

Jim, too, was preoccupied. The war was going badly. With his old friend Nobby Clark he had gasped with disbelief as the German army overran the Low Countries in the late spring with little opposition. Then it had virtually sauntered into France, cutting off the British Expeditionary Force and causing a humiliating retreat from Dunkirk.

'Can you believe it, Nobby?' an incredulous Jim asked when Marshal Pétain, victor of the Battle of Verdun in the Great War, sued for peace with Hitler. 'The Fuhrer is insisting the armistice is signed in the very railway carriage where Germany signed the surrender in 1918.'

'A cruel irony of history,' rejoined his friend.

'So in less than two short months the German Wehrmacht has accomplished what the army of the Kaiser didn't manage in four bloody years of the Great War.' Jim shook his head in exasperation.

'You know what Churchill is saying, Jim—'

'Oh yes. Now he's wormed his way into Number Ten, he's loving the sound of his own voice even more.'

'He says, "The war for France is over. The war for Britain is about to begin."'

'Are you going to volunteer, Nobby?'

'Certainly am. How about you?'

'You know my feelings, Nob. I will not kill.' Jim shook his head in certainty.

He had cheered with the rest of the country when brave young Spitfire and Hurricane pilots saw off the mighty Luftwaffe with exciting bravado in the Battle of Britain and, since June, apart from a few carefully targeted bombs, the skies had been quiet. Now the whole country was waiting, breath held, in anticipation of the next onslaught. Jim knew they were right. It was coming.

'I will not be a part of it,' he insisted to the disturbing voice that whispered in his head, remembering what he had written in his diary the previous year:

> I will not kill other human beings; young men like me, like my friend Ernst in Germany – he only wants peace and an equal world for all. Surely that's what most men want to fight for, German, French or British. And with words, not weapons. Men who have sweethearts, wives, children…

Now in the Kentish countryside he turned his thoughts to less troubling things. His pacifist fervour softened as his eyes fastened on his own sweetheart, just ahead of him, laughing, arms linked with Ethel and Ellen.

'Where to next, Jim?' asked Stan. 'Left or right? You're the Boy Scout with the map and compass.'

'No flipping signposts round here.' It was Spike Mullins' lugubrious voice.

'Well, there wouldn't be, would there, Spike? There's a war on.' Jim's humour was edged with irritated sarcasm as he unfolded his map. 'Over the stile and down the hill into the valley. We'll follow the river for a couple of miles, then cross the stepping stones – here.' They crowded round like raw recruits waiting for their orders, following Jim's forefinger across the map, the nail newly bitten. 'Then through that field. It'll be sunny on that side so we'll stop there for our lunch.' He patted the strap of the khaki haversack straddling his chest, packed by his mum for him and Pat that morning.

'I've done you two each, dear,' she'd said as she handed him the crackly packet, 'one corned beef and one sandwich spread. Will that be all right? And here's a Thermos of tea.'

'Thanks, Mum.' He smiled at the thought of stale doorstop sandwiches with a minimal filling of Fray Bentos (that tin would have to do Dad's sandwiches all week) and slathers of slimy spread so vinegary it made eyes pop and lips disappear into a grimace.

Fanning out across the meadow they skipped with morning energy down the grassy slope. Contented grazing ewes and fat market-ready lambs, ignorant of what awaited them, scattered in all directions.

A grey wagtail danced among the stones as the river bubbled over them. It lifted its head and flicked its tail to show a bright yellow rump like a can-can dancer revealing her bloomers. When the water slowed to meander down the valley, sticklebacks darted under the clear satin surface when, all at once, it shattered into a million kinetic droplets, each dancing, shining like a tiny ballerina. Sebastian had plunged in his freckled, golden-haired fist and pulled out a lump of weed declaiming, 'A minnow, a minnow, I have him by the tail!'

Sweaty feet were refreshed in the cool water lapping the stepping-stones and when the hikers rested to pull on their knitted socks, Pat scanned the field and asked, 'Where are they off to?' Eyes and knowing laughter followed Ron leading a reluctant Ethel towards the orchard beyond the hedge. Ten minutes later they were back and she untied a woollen bag fashioned from her cardigan to reveal a pile of apples. Ron spread his palms, offering them to the friends who after the first bite tossed them aside to cries of 'Yuck, they're sour!' and 'I suppose you think that's funny, Ron, picking all the unripe ones.' Ron arched his eyebrows sardonically and said nothing while Ethel blushed and moved away from him.

Crossing the lane at the top of the hill, Pat spied a figure down at the crossroads in the valley. Jim focused his field-glasses on him. 'It's only some old fellow dressed up as an air-raid warden. He's holding a placard and I think I can just make out…' He lowered the binoculars, shook back his hair, turned the focusing wheel and lifted them to his eyes again. 'Well, would you believe it? It says, AIR-RAID WARNING – TAKE COVER.'

'Silly old duffer,' snorted Ron, 'he'll be telling us to turn the lights out in a minute. They don't have air-raids in these godforsaken parts – there's nothing to bomb except cows. He probably got shell shock in the last lot and has been haunting these lanes ever since.'

Jim flung a scowl in Ron's direction, licked his top lip as he concentrated on the map, then looked ahead. 'Oh, I see. Through this gate and beyond that group of elms the footpath goes right across the middle of the field.'

They set off but when they rounded the trees they were confronted by a herd of heifers lumbering towards them. You don't find many cattle in Eltham so, while the girls' giggles turned into screams, the boys faked unconvincing bravado. Stan, hero of the hour, pulled from his pocket the piccolo he had brought to entertain and impress.

'Don't you worry now, my friends!' His lilting voice always sounded like a smile. 'Cows love my music. Well, Welsh cows do anyway. Now you walk that way, fast like, and I'll draw them this way and calm them with a little ditty I play back home.' Looking over their shoulders as they retreated the friends saw Stan backing away from the herd playing his pipe more and more tunelessly as his nervous fingers failed to find the notes. The beasts, appreciative of the music, seemed to increase in number and size as they gained on him until he turned, fled, and vaulted the fence like the athlete he never knew he was.

Two girls in dungarees, one dumpy, with an unfortunate nose which somehow transported Stan back to Punch and Judy on Barry Island, and one with blonde curls bursting out of her headscarf, giggled as they leant on their pitch forks in his field of refuge.

'Well, they like my tune too much, that's all.' His grin was sheepish. 'Probably they're homesick for Wales. Maybe Scotland the Brave would be better.' He raised his piccolo to his lips and attempted to emulate bagpipes. The Land Army girls put their hands over their ears and broke into a run.

In the untidy field margin, summer had melted the beauty of the bee orchids' sugar-pink wings and dark velvet bellies into swelling seeds. Scarlet poppies, blue scabious and creamy ox-eye daisies waved their patriotic welcome when the hikers settled to eat their sandwiches.

Pat poured tea from a Thermos into cream enamel mugs with green rims while Jim blew at a dandelion seed head. One

Sunday hikers

o'clock, two o'clock... How long would he be able to resist the pressure to fight?

She offered him his tea and wished there were just the two of them there to lie hidden in the tall grass which, crushed under the weight of bodies, released the ripe fragrance of fading summer; to listen to the optimistic call of the chiffchaff in the hedgerow and to gaze at swallows swooping against the background of unbroken blue, scooping up airborne insects before their long flight south.

Spike was telling an endless dull story when a pair of tall brown ears poked above the stubble in the next field. The hare, motionless, alert to a distant drone, streaked to safety as the sound drew closer. The picnickers looked up to see angry, growling bombers in German livery pursued by the familiar sound and shape of agile little Spitfires.

Jim was jolted from his reverie. 'My God, that lunatic was right, it is a raid! Better find some cover!' Half-eaten sandwiches, mugs, bits of greaseproof wrappings, were stuffed into bags and pockets, possessions were gathered and hands clasped as Jim unfolded the map. 'There's a pub marked just down the lane there. C'mon, folks.'

Breathless, they arrived to be greeted by a corpulent licensee who had abandoned his bar and reverted to playing the sergeant major he had been twenty-odd years before. His missing front teeth and the tin helmet he wore with pride reminded Jim of the childhood war-games he had played with Len, when he was always the Tommy and poor Len had to be the Hun.

'Through there and look smart about it, chaps,' the publican ordered, aiming a sly kick at the black and white sheepdog attempting to round them up.

The blossom on the hawthorn hedge had turned into tight berries which, before winter, would ripen to blood red. In its shadow were lines of slit trenches, dug by the old soldier and his regulars. The gashes in the earth were deep – friable topsoil giving way to clay, striated with green and purple. When they lowered their bodies into the cleft, Pat sniffed the sweet acidic smell of the soil and thought of the half-eaten sandwich in her bag. The picture of small scraps of brightly coloured who knows what encased in sandwich spread was reminiscent of the vomit she was struggling to subdue.

Valiant fighters appeared from all quarters of the sky. Swooping, diving, they spat their fire at the monsters lumbering across the sky. Heavy with explosive payloads, they were intent on destroying Kenley airfield a few miles to the west. The sound of fighter-fire was drowned out by the mighty engines of the German bombers but every trail of smoke raised a cheer in the dugout. This was no dogfight; more like clumsy animals worried by tiny flies puncturing their bodies with poisoned darts which may, or may not, cause the beasts to succumb.

Poking their heads above ground the shelterers saw a single white parachute unfurl and a figure descend slowly, silently, from a flaming Spitfire. He was so close they could see his face encased in a brown leather helmet until he disappeared behind the trees. Then there was a screech, a crump and a thunderous dark cloud as the plane ploughed into the woodland, leaving a wing hanging in the branches, its tail in the brambles, the engine setting fire to the golden bracken. A single thought ran through the watchers' minds: *One of ours.* Ethel gasped and covered her eyes; Ron shrugged his shoulders.

The collie's herding instinct spent, she sat, head tilted skywards and howled.

When the skies cleared the friends emerged to greet a group of women, children and old men climbing from the earth a little way off. They had been celebrating the end of two weeks of hop-picking fun and fresh air. Now, effing and blinding, they returned to the bar with the hikers in a buzz of hysterical relief. Jim stared into the free beer the munificent host served to one and all. Pat knew he was a world away even though her hand was gripping his fingers beneath the table.

At the sound of a slow clip-clop in the lane, one of the hop-picking women, sweltering in a fur coat in its terminal moult, peered out of an open window. Her over-lipsticked mouth formed a silent O and she paused before filling the air with her screech: 'Oh my Gawd!'

Jim, shaken out of his reverie, was one of the first out of the door. Sitting on the back of the farm cart, his fur-lined boots dangling over its open end, was a young man in a flying suit. The breeze ruffled his coppery hair as he jumped down into the jubilant crowd, waving his helmet with one hand and clutching the remains of his parachute in the other. He was cheered into the bar. A pint of Bass, already pulled, awaited him, and those East End girls who were not making eyes at him were claiming the parachute silk as their prize, already imagining the alluring cami-knickers they would fashion from it.

About my age, thought Jim as he returned to the corner by the fireplace. *He's fighting for my country, my people.* Shakespeare's 'Sceptred Isle' had always sounded arrogant and self-satisfied but now an urge to protect and preserve surged through Jim's arteries and flushed his skin. 'And I am a clerk in a sugar company,' he muttered to himself. He didn't finish his beer; there was a bad taste in his mouth.

After a noisy post-mortem on the bus journey home and fond farewells when they were deposited back in the High Street, the hikers dispersed to regale their families with their dramatic adventure. The Gaywoods and the Sheridans were incredulous and dismissed them as youthful tall stories.

6

Blitz

Six days after their hiking adventure, on Saturday 7th September 1940, a low sun backlit the figures seated on the grass by the pond in the Well Hall Pleasaunce. Two smiling cherubs embraced atop the cascading fountain.

Jim had been silent all afternoon, morose. In fact Pat had felt him slipping out of her reach since last weekend. When she'd engineered a paternally unsanctioned meeting on the way home from work on Wednesday, it was the same. Yes, his face brightened at the sight of her and his kiss was eager. He nuzzled her neck like a swimmer settling into safe warm sand after battling a rip tide. But then he'd retreated into the dark. She knew he had been to the Peace Pledge Union meeting on Monday. Had something happened there? He was usually fired up with his pacifism after those evenings, but not this time.

Now, as they sat in silence, the corners of Jim's wide, thin lips turned down and he tapped his watch. Her tawny hair smelled of honey as he stretched across her cane basket of rations to plant closed lips on her cheek.

'No! It can't be that time already,' she pleaded and transferred the basket to her other side so that she could move in closer. He took her smooth hand, the perfect oval nails painted with a sheen of clear varnish, pressed it to his cheek and hunched as if the cares of the whole world were laid upon his back.

'What is it, Jim?' Her words were tentative and she distanced herself, emotionally and physically, anticipating a reaction she wouldn't understand. Every part of her shrank and tightened as he turned his head away and she felt the colour and energy draining out of her. She had been certain he was hers forever. A lifelong commitment was something they had both assumed rather than verbalised; at least that was how she had seen it. Now she began to wonder if dreams and desires had led her down a road with a dead end, and instead of stepping through a gate into a future with Jim, she would have to wearily retrace her steps into the drab reality of life without him. She straightened her back. No. She would not have it. He was just in a bit of a mood – and she knew how to change that.

She stretched out one hand to cup his chin and turn his face towards her; the other stroked his thigh. 'Jim, darling, I love you so much.'

He dropped his gaze to the grass and his voice was jagged. 'Sometimes I think you are the only thing separating me from madness.' When he looked up his blue eyes locked with hers, but they were not smiling. 'Oh heck.' He stood, clenched his lips and frowned. He turned his head away, searching for the words. 'What if I'm just a bloody coward?' He banged a fist into the palm of his other hand.

'Sweetheart, you don't have to fight. You're only nineteen and no one has to register before they're twenty.'

He turned to face her again. 'Think I don't know that?' It was as if he were spitting stones, not words. 'Could volunteer though, couldn't I? Nobby Clark's joining up. You saw *The Chronicle* headline this week, didn't you? Those pictures of smiling chaps in their new uniforms. "Brave lads," it said. "How many more of our young men will join them and fight for our glorious country?" Well, not this one, mate.' Certainty was returning to his voice. 'Why is Britain so much more glorious than Germany? Why are we all so inward looking? Why can't we fight for internationalism? Why can't nations work together for the common good? Just look at Russia, they've got it right – equality for all.' He bowed his head and pummelled his temples with clenched knuckles. When he looked up there was resolution in his eyes, idealism in his words, but anxiety haunted his pale sculpted face.

'Can you understand that?' He chewed his lip, waiting for her reply.

'Mm, I think so.' She was not sure she did, quite. All she knew was that she wanted him here with her. Forever.

Caring nothing for the two figures in black habits and white wimples approaching through the rose garden, she held his cheeks in her hands, parted her lips and pressed them to his. He had his answer and the tension drained from his body as he responded.

'C'mon then, Pat Sheridan – race you to the gate!' He picked up her basket and sprinted across the lawn.

'Hold on, Jim, wait for the starting pistol!' She jumped to her feet, brushed grass cuttings from her skirt and ran after him, scattering a group of short-trousered boys playing 'It'. When she arrived at the gate, laughing and breathless, she hurtled into his waiting arms. Jim retrieved his bike from the railings and they walked home with the shopping basket hooked over the handlebars and his arm firmly round her waist. The sun was dipping out of an apricot sky when they reached her gate and he squeezed her goodbye. No kisses here; Mrs Sheridan might be peeping through the net curtains.

'Nine o'clock at the bus stop tomorrow, sweetheart? I thought we'd go hiking out Wrotham way.'

Pat smiled and nodded, made her lips into a rosebud and kissed the air as she waved him goodbye. He cycled down the hill humming, 'Night and day, you are the one...' Oh yes, no doubt about her. But fighting? He was right about that too, he knew it. Why did these doubts keep clouding his resolution? Socialism, not war, was the way forward. And it wasn't just the working classes either. In the library on Thursday he'd read a report in *The Times* of the young intelligentsia at Cambridge meeting to support the Russian system.

*

On my 2012 winter pilgrimage, I jump off the bus at the Pleasaunce and stop for a hot cup of tea in the Tudor Barn, all that remains of Margaret Roper's sixteenth-century home. I think of my future father scaring my future mother with his gruesome ghostly tales, but I don't believe in the ghost of Thomas More's daughter. Margaret is interesting but she is history.

Today the cherubs on the fountain are clothed in icicles and there is no sun to illuminate the vaporous breath of a group of after-school footballers on the crunchy grass. From the corner of my eye I think I see a young couple kissing and laughing on the summer lawn. They are not history, they are my parents. Perhaps I do believe in ghosts after all.

*

Jim thought of his girl, dismissed his uncertainties, and was still humming when he leant his bike against the shed. Cis tapped on the window and pointed to the basket of washing on the ground. He stuck his thumb in the air, picked up the basket and carried it into the kitchen.

'Where's Dad?'

'Down the dog-track. He'd better be home before dark, though. Mrs Blendell heard from Mr Jones there might be trouble tonight so I've got the shelter ready. The cushions and blankets got a good airing on the line this afternoon. Here's your cuppa, Jim. Had a nice time in the sun with your lady love?' He returned her mischievous grin but made no reply. It was just as she handed him his tea that the sirens started; low and quiet at first, swiftly rising to an ear-splitting crescendo.

Jim tensed. 'My God, that's early. It's not even six, nothing like dark yet. Can't be the real thing, surely?'

It was no false alarm. Before long they heard the roar of Heinkel engines increasing as they gained on the capital. 'Here, Mum, I'll take your tea.' Her cup was rattling in its saucer, spilling its contents onto the lino.

Uncle Harry was in the shelter before them, smiling inanely and sitting on the biggest cushion with a rug over his knees. 'Where's Sam, Cis? Gone to the dogs?' he murmured. She nodded, not meeting his eyes, then squealed as they heard the first crump of a distant explosion. Then another, then another – much, much louder. The barrage continued and Cis drew closer to her son, who stroked her hand. Suddenly, Jim jumped from the bench, pulled open the door and stepped out.

'Where are you going?' Cis cried.

'To check there's no lights on, Mum. Blackouts aren't down and we'll probably be here 'til after dark.'

Outside Jim shouted to Alec, who was shepherding his mother into the shelter next door. 'Any idea what's going on, Alec?'

'It's a big one. Mr Jones says Woolworths, Simpson's and the Castle Inn have all taken a hit.' Jim relayed the news when he returned to the shelter.

'But that's – that's just up the High Street!' Cis's bulk quivered like a vast floral jelly. Unearthing an embroidered hankie from the elasticated leg of her bloomers, she pushed her spectacles up onto her brow and dabbed away the tears. 'I wish Sam was back. And what about Len? They won't be bombing Tunbridge Wells will they?'

Jim's reassuring words were lost in a new explosion.

Instinctively they edged their bodies closer. For warmth? Despite the mild September evening they were shivering. For protection, obeying a basic human instinct? For the comfort of loved ones? For solidarity against the enemy?

'Blasted, damned, bloody buggers! We'll show 'em!' Meek Uncle Harry stood (still holding the rug), banged his furious head on the corrugated roof and shook a fist at the unseen sky beyond. Jim and his mum stared in disbelief. The shelter door squeaked open.

'Sam, there you are…at last.' His wife didn't hide her tears as he stooped his lean frame to step in. A layer of ghostly dust covered his shoulders and cap and he drew deeply on a bent Woodbine. Jim saw terror in his dad's eyes and the slight tremble of his lower lip before he stilled it with nicotine-stained fingers.

'Oh be quiet, Cis, it's all right. Stop blubbing, I'm home safe,' he snapped.

'All right, there's no need to shout,' she yelled.

'I am not shouting!'

Harry's tremulous voice interrupted. 'There's a pot of tea in the kitchen, Sam; I wouldn't mind one myself.'

'Then you can damn well get it yourself, Harry. It's bloody hell on earth out there. It's like the, it's like the… Well, it's bad anyway.' His voice tailed away.

Sam thought he'd put all that behind him. The nightmare had come less and less often over twenty-three years but the incident still sometimes re-ran in his head like one of Jim's cine films. Then he was back in Flanders and Arthur was falling from his horse, spluttering, yellow bubbles foaming from his mouth, like the filth on the stagnant creek by Woolwich docks. Yet again Sam heard Arthur gasp out the words, 'I can't…bloody… breathe…Sam, I can't…bloody…' before his face hit the slime. He was still alive. His best mate was alive. Sam would have climbed from his mount, rescued Arthur – he was just about to, honest he was – but then…

When the horror had filled his mind in recent years Sam had ordered another pint of Watney's to put the picture out of focus, then another, and another to draw a curtain over the whole thing. But now, in the back garden shelter, there was no beer and it was all happening again, right here in front of his eyes. He could see it, he could feel the mud, he could smell

Sam on his warhorse

the blood, hear the scream of his horse as it crumpled beneath him. Arthur was drowning in the gas in his own lungs but the CO pulled at Sam's sleeve, yelling, 'Leave him, Gaywood, he's a goner and so will you be if we don't get the hell out of here.' Then a shell screamed out of nowhere. Sam hit the ground and when he lifted his head Arthur's leg was there. Nothing else.

Hearing the explosions around him Sam lived it once more but he couldn't put words to it. If he did, he, like his horse, might crumple and scream and that would never do. So he sat on the edge of the bench, covered his ears with his hands and stared at his feet, willing the image away. His body shuddered violently when the ground beneath rumbled and vibrated from the blasts that were hurling bodies from the dust and rubble of crumbling homes.

When there was a lull they relaxed a little and listened for the signal to tell them it was over. Instead there came another continuous growl from the east which increased to a thunderous roar as it passed overhead. After a minute or two they heard the explosions. Sam's face twitched and he gritted his teeth to subdue the scream erupting from his damaged lungs.

He's really frightened, thought Jim. *My strong father is as terrified as Mum.* He put his arm round his dad's shoulder and silently acknowledged that he, Jim, was the adult now.

They kept coming – wave after wave, bomb after bomb, explosion after explosion – far into the night. The paraffin lamp was making so much smoke they had to put it out. Instead they relied on a torch which grew steadily dimmer. Just as they got the all-clear the battery gave out altogether.

'I'll never see my way down the garden in the dark, Jim.' Uncle Harry adopted his wheedling voice. 'Be a good boy and slip out to the kitchen for the spare torch, will you?'

'Oh, for goodness' sake, Uncle.' He got up from the bench. 'All right, I'll go. But I'm doing this for Mum, Harry, not for you, right?'

He clanged the low steel door shut behind him, just in case there was another lot to come. As he unfolded his bent body he knew there was no need for a torch. It seemed the very clouds were on fire. It might have been a blood-red sunset but it was not in the west and it was roaring like an army of dragons. Skeletons of buildings were silhouetted against the sky. Jim cast his mind back to the hop-pickers, so full of life last weekend. Those were their homes that were burning, in Poplar, Stepney, Rotherhithe, Silvertown.

Dante's Inferno, thought Jim, just as a little hobgoblin danced out of the fire and whispered in his ear.

'Can't let them do this, Jim. Got to fight, Jim. Got to fight.'

'I can't fight.'

'You must fight, Jim.'

'I won't fight. I will not fight.'

'You will, Jim, you will.' The gremlin laughed and danced away.

'What are you doing, boy? We can't wait all night for that torch.' His family staggered out of their iron cocoon and straightened their backs. They saw him standing still as a statue, bathed in red light, and when they turned to follow his gaze their silent mouths gaped in disbelief. At last Cis uttered the words, syllable by syllable, as if in slow motion. Words she would have admonished her son for using.

'Blood-y-hell.'

She didn't apologise for her language.

At least Pat was safe. He'd gone round to check on his way to survey the damage in the High Street the next morning.

Mrs Sheridan opened the door and looked him up and down. 'Good morning, Jim. Pat's not here. She's out collecting clothes for those poor souls who have lost everything. I've turned out what I can but, with rationing, one can't afford to let too much go.'

'I just wanted to make sure you were all right, Mrs Sheridan. Bad night, wasn't it?'

'Very unpleasant. We need all the young men we can get to fight back.' Jim's ears were not deaf to her implication.

The rumours were true. The High Street lay under a heavy Sunday silence when Jim scrunched his shoes over shards of glinting glass and gazed at the patch of sky which, until last night, had been Woolworths. Where Simpson's the furnishers had proudly displayed solid mahogany wardrobes and armchairs covered in the latest uncut moquette, there was now a smouldering black hole.

At first glance the Castle Inn seemed virtually untouched, until Jim realized the roof behind the parapet was missing and daylight streamed through broken windows from the desolation of the public bar. Only its facade survived, complete with the image of an impregnable castle on the hanging sign now swinging at a drunken angle.

A silver-haired man, patch over one eye, wiped a tear from the other and thanked God the bloody Hun had been too stupid to realize that, at six o' clock, the shops had shut and the pubs hadn't opened. But the publican, his family, the manager of Simpson's and the cleaners mopping the floor in Woollies had all copped it.

This is not how wars are fought, thought Jim as he retraced his steps. Those hard-working people they pulled out of the rubble hadn't joined up to fight the enemy. They were fighting to keep body and soul together, to retain some normality in a crazy world.

His expression was troubled and once more he tussled to make sense of his pacifism. But, he reasoned, he had made his decision, hadn't he? He would not be a party to killing anyone, let alone innocent civilians. He knew that was the right course of action. Didn't he?

'Jim, hang on, wait for me.' It was Nobby Clark, his closest mate.

'Nobby. Oh Lord, isn't it awful?'

'Sooner I get out there with a gun in my hand the better.' Nobby pointed the index finger of his outstretched arm and sprayed imaginary bullets into an invisible army. 'Have you heard what happened in Albert Road?'

Jim shook his head.

'Come on, I'll show you.'

The quiet little street looked as it usually did. Late roses clung to the brick walls of the Edwardian terraces. Michaelmas daisies turned their pink and purple faces to the sun in neat front gardens behind picket fences. The smell of Sunday dinner wafted from open windows. The road took a sharp turn to the left and then Jim saw it.

'It seems they dumped their remaining heavy bombs on the way home. A baby was found dead in its pram, still looking absolutely perfect – in there.' Nobby indicated a house with its front torn away, revealing a bed complete with sheets and blankets which looked about to slide off the sloping first floor. 'But its parents were blown to pieces.' His words tumbled out of trembling lips. No more phoney war – this was the real thing; schoolboy adventure stories brought to life on his own doorstep. 'And over the road there, the force of the blast was so great a woman was sucked out of her bedroom window and deposited on the roof – dead of course. No sign of her old man. Dad knows him from the rest centre. They're at their wits' end down there, snowed under with queues of people wanting help. Jim, you can't still be a pacifist when you see all this, can you?'

'Oh, Nobby, let's go home.' Jim felt the weight of despair on his shoulders. He asked himself, *How can I go to work in an office in a sugar factory when this is happening? Surely I should be defending these innocent people?*

No, no, his conscience replied. *War, fighting and killing solves nothing. There has to be a better way.* But what was it?

'See your dad gets into work all right before you get the ferry, will you, son? He's a bit shaken after the weekend, worried about what he'll find. Woolwich got it bad, they say.'

'Course I will, Mum,' he replied to her whispered request as the two men set off on Monday morning. Sam had been quiet, it was true. They had all been quiet since Saturday night. And the old man certainly had one over the eight in the Rising Sun on Sunday, missing his dinner and not rolling home to his wife's wrath until nearly four. Then he shook silently in the shelter when the bombers came again last night.

Now Jim and his dad were beginning a new week in an altered world. The acrid smell of doused burnt timber seeped into the tram before they reached Beresford Square and when they approached the Arsenal witches' fingers of smoke still rose from blackened buildings.

'I'm all right, son. Thanks for coming with me but you get off to work now.' Jim clapped Sam on the shoulder and watched him join the throng passing through the gate. Then he turned towards the ferry.

When it docked the scene was astonishing. A stream of humanity disembarked; refugees from north of the river. Weighed down by bundles on their backs, most carried battered and bursting suitcases as they poured across the gangway. Young men on bicycles pulled makeshift trolleys, old men pushed barrows overflowing with buckets and boxes, eiderdowns and camp beds. Shoeless children whose traumatised eyes stared out of blackened faces held tightly to adult hands. An old woman, her face lined by anxiety and apprehension, carried a singing canary in a wire cage, her lead-less mongrel trotting obediently at heel. A young woman with a man's coat pulled across her pregnant belly pushed a high Silver Cross pram, decades old but still doing sterling service. Cooking pots clanked against its side and, from behind the hessian sacks piled onto the rain cover, a cheerful toddler waved to his fellow adventurers. Jim had seen this before, on the Pathé News at the pictures. But those refugees were French Jews fleeing before the occupying Germans. This was Woolwich.

'What the Dickens...?' Jim spread his hands in disbelief when he reached the ferryman.

'Getting out of the East End, mate. If they've still got homes they're not risking another night in 'em.'

'Where are they going?'

'Chisl'urst. Gonna live down the caves. Think they'll be safer there. Reckon I might join 'em.'

The picture of the laughing hop-pickers last weekend was in Jim's mind and he wondered if any of them were in the crowd.

The raids continued for fifty-nine nights. Every night. On 12th September, the roof of the great hall of King John's Eltham Palace was destroyed. *That was bad enough*, thought Jim, *part of our history gone*, but then a few days later a bomb dropped on a bunker in the vicarage garden where children were sheltering. Eight were killed and twenty-four injured. And so it continued.

On 17th October, the Luftwaffe took advantage of a 'bomber's moon' and scattered their load indiscriminately on the margins of bomb alley, marked by the Thames. In Mayerne Gardens, a stone's throw from Eltham Hill, the house next door to Nobby Clark's was destroyed.

Then there came a night on 2nd November when the skies were quiet. Was it over? They dared to hope. It was not. Hitler was giving his boys a night off and on the 3rd it started again.

The winter of 1940/41 was one of the coldest and driest on record and the Gaywoods felt fortunate to still have a home. They cooked one of Sam's scrawny hens and vegetables from the back garden for Christmas dinner. The shelter had not been used much for the last couple of weeks and they were breathing easier now the siren sounded less often. But they were back in their iron bunker on the 27th, when the tram depot up the road was flattened with the loss of eighteen lives. Two nights later they thought they were safe under heavy cloud but had reckoned without the radio beams developed by the enemy to pinpoint their targets. At 6pm, Jim and his family watched a hundred and twenty bombers fly over the suburbs and an hour later the sky over London was a lurid crimson and yellow crescent of flame. The level of the Thames was so low that little water was available for firefighting. From the south-east it appeared the capital was finished.

It wasn't.

*

Eltham is notorious for a different kind of violence now. In 1941, black faces were a rarity on its streets; now it is a rainbow of skin colours. I leave the Pleasaunce on my voyage of rediscovery and pass the bus stop where a promising young man was stabbed twenty years ago for no other reason than that he was black. I am confident my father would have raged as much about that murder as about Hitler's bombs.

Under the railway bridge I turn right into Sherard Road and instinctively look for the station on my right. All trace of it was swept away by one of the frantic new brooms of the sixties and seventies which made way for the dominance of the motor car. Gone, too, is the whitewashed timber shack at the bottom of the old station approach where my friends and I, and perhaps my parents twenty years earlier, handed over pocket money on the way home from the swimming baths. We bought liquorice bootlaces which blackened our teeth so that we fell about laughing, pretending to be vampires. And sherbet dabs. The top of the yellow cardboard tube containing the tongue-tingling dust disintegrated into damp, grey papier-mâché when the liquorice stick had been licked and plunged into the sherbet a million times. There were pear drops that smelled like Mum's nail varnish remover, aniseed balls the colour of stale blood – good for using as cannon balls when I played with my cousin's toy soldiers – and halfpenny chews which Mum said rotted your teeth faster than the speed of light.

*

When he could, Jim met Pat from her train and he was there, shivering outside the charred wooden walls of the station one night in January 1941, a few days after it had taken a hit. He lit a cigarette and waited, anticipating the warmth of her hand, the touch of her lips as they walked home. He jogged up and down, stamped on his dog-end and repeatedly thumped his arms around his chest in an effort to keep warm. He checked his watch and frowned. The booking hall was dark and deserted so he ventured onto the moonlit platform and proffered a penny to the stationmaster for a ticket.

'What's happened to the six twenty-three?'

'No idea, son. Probably a fire on the line somewhere.'

Jim paced the length of the platform. Up, down, up, down, until he heard the telephone ringing. He ran along to the office and reached it just as the man lifted the handset from the wall.

'Allo, Eltham Well 'All Station. 'Allo, Bob. Right. Where? I see. Is Cannon Street out? What about Blackfriars? So it's a waiting game then? All right, thanks, Bob.' The man drew in a deep breath as he replaced the receiver and exhaled very slowly, like an engine releasing its steam. 'Bomb at Bank station, lad. It's bad by all accounts, being rush hour.'

Bank! How close was that to Pat's office in Leadenhall Street? Too close, Jim decided. She'd told him she didn't use the Underground in the morning. Couldn't stand the lingering smell left by the mass of humanity who hid down there from the bombs at night, but by the end of the working day the whoosh of trains had cleared the stench and the night-shelterers had not yet arrived. So if she was in a hurry, or if it was raining, she'd sometimes get the Underground from Bank to Cannon Street. Jim shivered and his face faded to white as a sudden shot of adrenaline pushed more blood into his thumping heart.

'So what did he say? How many casualties, fatalities? What about the other stations?'

'Can't say, lad, can't say.'

Before long a small crowd had gathered and the Chinese whispers began.

'What's happened to the train?'

'Bomb at the station.'

'Which station?'

'Dunno. Bank, I think.'

'No, someone said Blackfriars.'

'Wicked bastards.'

'And Cannon Street.'

'I bet they've done Charing Cross as well.'

Soon every London terminus was ablaze in their minds as they waited. A young woman in apron and carpet slippers held a whimpering baby in one arm and grasped a snivelling toddler by the hand. She seemed on the verge of tears herself.

'Cigarette, luv?' an older woman offered.

'Mum says I shouldn't smoke in the street.' Her voice wavered and she reached for a fag.

'This ain't the street, it's the station. Go on, I'll hold 'im.'

'Thanks, but I'll manage.' She sat on the ground, taking short urgent puffs with the baby in her lap and her free arm round the child, until a man sitting on the one crowded bench was shamed into exchanging places.

Jim knew his mum would be anxious, wondering when he'd be home for his spam fritters, or whatever delicacy was on her menu tonight. But his only concern was Pat.

'Shush!' A command passed through the crowd and the muttering ceased as they strained their ears. A faint hum transmitted through the rails, which increased to a rhythmic *te-dum de-dum, te-dum de-dum...* When they leant out over the white painted edge of the platform and peered up the line they could just see a silver glint of moonlight on a dark shape gaining on them; a shaded blue light showing the driver the signals.

The train, when it pulled into the station, appeared to be packed with the whole population of South London squeezed into dimly lit carriages with blacked-out windows, like pencils into a tin. They poured out and the slamming of hundreds of doors behind them sounded like applause for the brave little loco which had got them home safely.

Jim watched a man in a cloth cap and shabby raincoat kiss the young woman and gather the toddler into his arms. Mothers and daughters, sisters and brothers were hugging, clasping hands, laughing with relief. But he was still scanning the tired faces for Pat. At last, he saw her – she must have been in the very last carriage – and he sprinted to the end of the platform to grasp her in his arms and twirl her off her feet.

'Jim, Jim, for goodness' sake, you'll make me dizzy. Put me down.'

She hadn't been at Bank station where, they later learned,

fifty-five commuters lost their lives, but the city had been a melee of fire engines, police cars, stranded workers and rumours of bombs everywhere.

'I couldn't get near Cannon Street – too many police and crowds. So I tried Blackfriars – chaos of course, but then they said there was an Eltham train on platform four. Goodness, it was packed. All the seats were crammed full. I was quite glad to have to stand rather than squeeze my bottom between those pinstriped legs. I don't know what's happened to chivalry, though. No one offered us girls a seat. We stood there for ages, waiting for the train to start and more and more people pushed their way in. Then this man with a bowler hat and rolled umbrella, and a moustache a bit like Hitler's, sort of cleared his throat and suggested that men should occupy all the seats and take a girl on each lap. Oh Lord, I thought, I know what that means. But we did as he suggested and my bloke, at least, didn't try anything on. We sat perched on their bony knees and the girl next to me caught my eye and we couldn't stop giggling. We were still stationary and had no idea if or when the train would move. Then another plucky gent suggested that anyone who had any sandwiches left from lunch should share them around. Well, Jim, it seems quite a lot had found something better for lunch 'cause out came all these greaseproof packets and we ended up having quite a party!'

An unsmiling Jim harrumphed. 'That's all very well, but I was here, worried stiff, while you were having this jolly picnic.' He removed his arm from her waist and plunged his hands into his pockets.

'Oh, Jim darling, don't be like that. You haven't heard the rest.' Her smile dissolved into helpless laughter.

'Go on then, I suppose you'd better tell me, but I really can't see what's so funny.'

'Well, the train stopped just outside Hither Green station.' She took a deep breath and tried to regain some composure. 'And the man with the Adolf moustache said to the girl on his lap, "Excuse me, my dear," and stood up. Then he squeezed through the standing passengers – he could hardly get past without standing on their toes – and he kept saying, "So sorry, so sorry," to everyone.' Mirth overtook Pat and she leant on Jim's shoulder, holding her stomach. 'And then – he opened the door and got out!'

'But you weren't in the station.'

'No. We all sat there looking—' Pat took a deep breath, trying to subdue her laughter, 'looking at each other, but no one said a thing.' She wiped a tear away. 'Oh dear, give me a minute and I'll tell you the rest.'

'There's more?'

'Oh yes, this is the best bit. After a minute or two, when we were wondering if someone should go and rescue him, he opened the door again and clambered in, trousers covered in mud, saying to everyone, "I am so sorry. You must think I am an absolute idiot." And then…and then, oh dear…' she was bent double with laughter, 'and then he – he squeezed past everyone again, opened the door at the other side of the compartment and stepped out!'

'Very funny.' Jim's tone was glumly ironic but he couldn't prevent a smile and took her hand in his.

7

Renouncement

In May 1941, attendance at the Peace Pledge Union meetings was declining by the week, but the remaining stalwarts were fired up with their pacifist beliefs when they left the scout hut in Southend Crescent. Harry Phippen, Charles Lockyer and Gilbert Tilling piled into the Rising Sun with several others to continue the discussion, but Jim decided not to join them. His applause for his friends' impassioned speeches was more in admiration of their courage than enthusiastic agreement. For six months he had tried to ignore the pernicious mythological creature, the little gremlin, hobgoblin of flight, which had flown at him out of the blazing London sky, but it kept returning. Its taunting whispers that he must fight had grown so persistent they became the background to all his thoughts.

Speculation about when Hitler's advance on Russia would begin had been rife for months. The Fuhrer had declared time and again that the Germans needed more living space and he had fantastic plans to develop a German colony in Ukraine. His vision was based on the British occupation of India. He said:

What India is to England the territories of Russia will be for us. The German colonists ought to live on handsome spacious farms. The German services will be lodged in marvellous buildings, the governors in Palaces... The Germans – this is essential – will have to constitute amongst themselves a closed society, like a fortress. The least of our stable lads will be superior to any native.

Jim's socialist beliefs were international. Colonialism by any nation was repugnant to him, and combined with the other abhorrent aims of Nazism it presented the blackest of prospects for his world.

While Stalin dismissed the possibility of a 1941 German invasion of Russia, the British were relieved that the Eastern Front was looming large in the minds of the Third Reich, offering the possibility of a respite for the home forces to regroup and re-arm after the ravages of the Blitz. Jim could not share the relief. Although he was doubtful about Stalin's leadership, he was enthusiastic about the Russian political system. He knew Hitler had Russia in his sights but could not believe he would turn his fire to the east for at least another year. Could there be a miracle before then? He shook his bowed head as he walked home.

*

I am lunching with Mum, quizzing her about her memories of the time. She smiles and says, 'Of course, I've told you the story of the break-in, haven't I?'

'No. What break-in, Mum? Where was that? Tell me about it.'

She settles herself comfortably into her chair, relishing the memory and retelling of her tale.

'Well, I often called in at number 17 on my way home from work to make a cup of tea for Jim when he got in. Your nanny was doing war work by then, filling shell cases in Peek Freans biscuit factory in Bermondsey. You know, by the railway line just before London Bridge – it had been requisitioned. The whole household arrived home later than me, but Jim was usually earlier than his mum and dad so those tea breaks were very precious for us.

'One evening I took the spare key from the hook in the coal-hole and unlocked the back door. When I stepped into the kitchen – oh, my God!' She pauses, watching for my reaction, then continues, 'The larder door was open and there was tomato sauce all over the floor. Honestly, it looked like a river of blood. The meat safe had been tumbled off the shelf and a bluebottle was crawling over the sausages which had been bitten into – I could see the teeth marks. A loaf of bread was on the table, torn into chunks, and the whole week's butter ration was slapped on the lino and trodden in by a muddy foot. All the packets and canisters had been opened and emptied just in front of the stove so there was a great heap of salt, cocoa, tea leaves, sugar, dried egg and flour, all mixed up together.'

'Mum, you must have been terrified.'

'Of course I was – they might still have been in the house. I can remember my mouth going dry and hardly daring to breathe, listening for the slightest creak of movement. Then I noticed the washing-up bowl with the rusty rim was in the sink, full of scummy grey water. The kettle was still warm on the gas stove and Grandad's soapy shaving brush stood on the draining board. Damn them, I thought, the devils have been shaving.

'Well, I was frightened of course, but more than that, I was furious. So I stepped out of my shoes and followed a trail of porridge oats into the living room where Nanny's prized aspidistra lay on the carpet, its roots sticking up in the air, with soil and bits of pottery all over the place. Then I heard the squeak of the back door and footsteps in the kitchen behind me.'

'Oh no!'

'It was okay, dear, it was only Jim. I could hear the shock in his voice as he shouted "Who's there?" and when he reached me I could hardly speak. A mixture of anger and relief, I suppose. The net curtain was fluttering in the draught, so we knew they'd escaped through the window. And on the living room wall a huge letter C had been gouged into the shiny anaglypta wallpaper. Nanny was so proud of that paper but it was stained a nasty yellow colour.'

'Grandad's fags.'

'Yes, must have been. Anyway, your dad put his arm round me but I wasn't in the mood for all that, I was so angry. "Damned vandals," I said. Well, I probably used stronger words than that. "As if there isn't enough senseless destruction already." I was trying jolly hard not to cry. We looked around but they didn't seem to have taken anything. Len's trumpet was still on the sideboard.

'Jim checked he had a couple of coppers in his pocket and cycled up to the phone box by the church to call the police, while I tried to clear up a bit. I thought it would break his mum's heart if she came home to such a mess. By the time she arrived a young bobby had propped his bike by the gate, surveyed the damage, pulled out his pencil and was writing in his notebook. I remember looking over his shoulder and noticing he couldn't spell.

'I made Cis a cup of tea while Jim calmed her down and then she said, "What made them choose us? What have we done?"'

'Didn't she understand about that letter C?' I ask my mum. She looks puzzled and I point out that it probably stood for conchie.

Realisation dawns and she smiles at her naivety. 'Well, of course. D'you know, we never thought of that. But I expect Jim did. Oh, poor Jim.' She pauses and, for a moment, is lost to me. 'Now where was I? Oh yes, the policeman said there'd been a few similar cases in the neighbourhood and they had a couple of suspects in mind. He described the two youths in question; one of average height, loud-mouthed with a limp; the other taller, wearing a trilby hat and sporting a spivvy moustache. Then he said, "Sorry about the mess, missus, but at least there's nothing missing. Keep your eyes open and we'll let you know of any developments." And with that he shut his book, picked up his helmet, gave us a sort of half-hearted salute and left.'

My mother sighs. 'Shall we have a coffee now, dear?' She's back in the present, tired by reliving the past.

After coffee she tells me the rest of the story.

Cis's heart did not break and she vowed to get those boys. She regaled her neighbours, friends and workmates at the factory with plots she was hatching to confront the villains, drawing on the fantasy world of Paul Temple, the gentleman detective, whose exploits she enjoyed on the wireless. Temple's wife, Steve, assisted him in his investigations so 'by Timothy,' as Paul would say, why shouldn't Cis play detective too?

Despite the family's amusement she was serious, and a few days after the incident she was carrying her shopping down Eltham Hill when she noticed two lads pointing to her house. They fitted the police description. One of them raised an imaginary trumpet to his lips and toot-tooted, while the taller youth made a show of taking a crust of bread from his pocket, biting into it and tossing it on the pavement smirking triumphantly. In those days of rationing my nanny found that disgusting.

Women of a certain age carrying shopping bags have always been invisible to the young, so they were unaware that she puffed after them all the way down to the Yorkshire Grey. They ambled and limped on along Rochester Way making an exhibition of themselves, laughing and tearing blossom from the cherry trees. Cis phoned the police from the box by the roundabout. They were there in no time, hustling her into the back of the car and following the suspects. At one point the officers stopped the car and ran into a house – just an ordinary house – and came out in plain clothes.

'So it can't have been just any old house,' I said. Mum nods knowingly.

Then Cis spotted the two youths and the car motored

behind them at a safe distance while the coppers discussed what to do.

'Pull 'em in, of course,' interrupted Cis.

'Can't do that, ma'am. They're not acting unlawfully you see, so we can't pick 'em up.'

'Then ask them for their identity cards!' Cis was triumphant when the police thanked her for such a good idea. They pulled up beside the young men and demanded their cards. Of course, they couldn't produce them so they were arrested.

The policemen asked Cis if she wanted a lift home, but she replied, 'No thank you, officer, I'll walk.' She wasn't going to sit with those vermin. Only when she got out of the car did she see she had been sitting right by two rifles.

Mum laughs as she remembers her mother-in-law's hand flying to her mouth, her eyes widening with mock horror as she wondered what would have happened if she'd sat on the trigger.

'And a damn long walk home she had too,' my mother tells me. 'Jim was about to form a one-man search party and Sam was wondering when, if ever, he'd get his dinner, when Cis finally arrived. Of course, someone brought the boys' cards in and they got off with a warning.'

Sensing that the listeners felt this to be the end of the story, Mum says Cis would puff out her significant bosom and continue with a triumphal 'But...' – she had her audience back again – 'a week later Pat was off work with a cold and glanced out of the window of her parents' house and what should she see but the two little buggers trying to force Mrs Rowe's scullery window. So she ran to the phone at the bottom of Lilburn Avenue and dialled 999.

'They got 'em! Red-handed. It was prison, of course, they'd done so many.' Cis would stop for breath and smile to herself at a job well done, then chuckle. 'The police recognised Pat from the break-in at our house and now Len will insist on calling her the Gangster's Moll.' Her laughter would send ripples down her several chins.

Enjoying the story I can sense it was a moment of glory for my mild, modest nanny; relief from the pressures of war, an opportunity to laugh and feel important. I imagine Jim listened indulgently as the tale was repeated many times over, happy to see his mum basking in a splash of limelight. But his own world was growing darker. His thoughts about the war, his future, the world, buzzed round his head like a swarm of bees which stung whenever he affirmed his pacifism.

*

He took to exploring the damaged streets north of the river on his way to work. The factory was in Silvertown on the fringes of the East End, which was still suffering sporadic bombing raids. Early one morning in June, Jim walked as far as Poplar and was shocked at the devastation. It could have been a film set. Roofless facades stared with unglazed eyes onto a rocky landscape of rubble at each side of the cobbled roadway. Where the front wall of one house had succumbed, it was as if the front of a doll's house had been ripped off. In one room an armchair by the grate was blackened, a mirror smashed on the hearth. In another, a pile of splintered wood tangled with an oilcloth, shards of china and the ash-coated remains of a family supper. A broken glass orb hung from the ceiling.

All was lifeless until Jim detected a movement at the periphery of his vision and turned to see the last character in the movie – a hunched figure wearing a flat cap, his jacket suspended from shoulders as thin as a coat hanger. He stooped to burrow in the remains, found something, examined it, then tossed it aside and exited the scene.

Jim narrowed his lips and shook his head, kicking at a soft bag with clothes spilling out – dropped, no doubt, in the terror of flight. The morning silence was heavy, malevolent. Suddenly, he was ambushed by the strident call of a mechanical cuckoo announcing the hour as it leapt out of brightly painted doors on a fragment of wall at his feet. Beyond, he could see no evidence of habitation, merely ash-strewn piles; whole houses reduced to heaps of crushed masonry not even as high as his shoulder. The valley of the shadow of death.

A swarm of flies drew his attention to something lying on a blackened slab of concrete. Recognisable only as a mauled carcass, Jim worked out that it had once been a dog; a small dog, a puppy perhaps, in the graveyard that had been its home. A month, perhaps a week ago, people had lived their lives in this house. A family had laughed, loved, struggled with homework, played in the yard, listened to the wireless, darned socks, argued about money and thanked God after every raid that they were still safe. Until that last night.

A zigzag of light shone through the jagged glass teeth of a broken window and fell on a patch of fur clinging to the lifeless body. A rat slid from beneath and the pelt settled with an apparent sigh into the bony spaces left by decomposing flesh. Acid rose in Jim's throat and he breathed deeply to still the retching, but he couldn't still his tears for the family who had been blasted from their home. Were they dead now, like their pet? Were they maimed? Grieving for lost ones? Or shocked and sheltering nearby? Maybe they had fled London – or were living the life of nocturnal troglodytes in an Underground station. A whisper of breeze lifted the strands of fur, restoring a ghostly breath to the rotting remains. Jim thought of the emaciated old man he had noticed picking through the ruins, a last vestige of life amid the destruction.

His legs were leaden as he plodded back towards the sugar factory. This war was robbing the world of civilisation and, under Churchill's leadership, he could see no possibility of it being restored.

Gerald, one of the labourers from the milling shed, was

whistling the cheerful melody of 'Alexander's Ragtime Band' as he came up behind, steel-capped boots sparking on the cobbles. As he passed, he touched his cap in mock deference to Jim, the office worker. Then, noticing his tears, he looked into the distance, cleared his throat and walked swiftly on.

The lost family filled my future father's mind and he knew he could not sustain his pacifism for much longer. Civilisation itself was becoming a carcass. Imperfect but always vital, its life was now being extinguished, the flesh beneath its skin left to be consumed by Nazi vermin.

On the 3rd July, Jim walked into the London Combined Recruiting Centre behind Euston Station. He made straight for the RAF section where, after filling in a volunteer's form, he was seen by a dour sergeant. 'So what are you qualified to do?' He looked Jim up and down as if he were fit for nothing.

'I am interested in being a pilot, sir.'

The man sighed. 'Ah, another one. Education?' A glimmer of respect crossed his face when Jim explained his excellent matriculation results. 'I'll put "query pilot" then. But there's no guarantee, you understand. You'll hear in due course, but it'll be about six months before we call you up.' He posted Jim's form into a box. 'Next?'

'So you're done with all that pacifist stuff?' Sam was relieved; his drinking companions had been asking awkward questions about his son.

Cis's face crumpled when she was told but she steadied herself. 'Good for you, son,' she muttered and turned back to the stove. Jim's brother Len, home from the country for a few days, said he wished it were him.

Pat had felt it would come to this. He never spoke about it but she knew his black moods arose from a tussle with his conscience. A part of her was relieved. She knew that if he stuck to his pacifist view the future held either prison or some sort of civilian service. Even those employed in the mines or resettling homeless families didn't get the respect they deserved, and at least he had made his own choice. But she shivered – she had too many friends grieving for missing lovers.

Jim touched her cheek, looked into her eyes. 'It's your birthday next week and I know what your present will be.' She cocked her head and raised her eyebrows.

'Secret.' He tapped his lips and grinned. 'Wait and see.'

She found out on Saturday afternoon when they took the number forty-six tram to Woolwich where they chose a solitaire diamond engagement ring and celebrated with tea and currant buns in the ABC cafe.

8

The Wedding

It was to be a Christmas wedding. So what if there was a war on? This would be Pat's big day. Her cheeks glowed as she planned the details with her friend. Ethel had agreed to marry Ron, the strange, humourless member of the Sunday Hikers. Their wedding was planned for the last week of September, only eight weeks ahead, so as a married woman, Ethel was to be Pat's Matron of Honour.

'Ooh, Christmas – that means holly and ivy and snow and…' Ethel's voice faltered.

'Mistletoe,' said Pat, 'we'll hang it over every doorway.'

'And kiss and kiss…and kiss…' Ethel's eyes clouded over.

Pat squeezed her hand. 'You don't have to marry Ron you know. You still have two months – long enough to change your mind. Do you really want to spend your life with a man who brings you sour apples? I've not forgotten that incident on the hike you know.'

'Mmm, I think that was his idea of a joke. He is a true intellectual, Pat. That's what makes him appear a bit odd sometimes. We'll have bright children.'

'He may be clever, but brains aren't everything. A sense of humour helps – preferably one that isn't warped.'

Ethel took a deep breath, tossed an ebony curl from her eyes and changed the subject. 'You'll look lovely in white, Pat. There's a girl at work who's got reams of parachute silk. It's a bit grey but perhaps we could bleach it, and there's that stall on Woolwich market where they sell netting for a veil.'

As my mum recounts the conversation, it stirs a memory of parachute silk. All these years later, I can still feel the fabric slipping through my small fingers. It seemed to me that everyone had a piece of reclaimed silk in the drawer. I loved to play with Mum's offcuts while she turned the handle on her Singer sewing machine. It was a few years after the war and she was transforming into glamorous 'undies' the fabric that had been squeezed tight into airmen's packs. When the ripcord was pulled by young men jumping from blazing aircraft it billowed into gossamer mushrooms as they dropped through the air.

*

'No, no, I've never seen myself in white,' Pat replied to Ethel, 'and anyway it'll be freezing, and what would I do with it afterwards? No, I rather fancy a tailored two-piece costume in blue Harris Tweed. I won't make it myself, I'll commission a dressmaker!'

'All right, Miss Moneybags, if that's what you want. But I'm having white – and a veil I can hide behind.'

Pat shook her head, frustrated by her friend's decision to marry for brains instead of the passionate love that enveloped her and Jim.

A couple of days later Pat had a difficult journey from the city. The trains were delayed by false air-raid warnings. The siren sounded as she hurried home from the station. When she pushed open the door of the shelter she found only her parents there, looking expectant, serious.

'Where's Enid? And Jimmie?' Pat asked.

'They're spending the evening in Mrs Rowe's shelter,' her mother replied.

'Why?' Pat wrinkled her brow. This was an unusual choice for her younger sister and brother.

Her father shifted on the bench, pulled at his ear lobe and gazed at the shelter roof. Her mother straightened her back, lifted her chin and arranged a serious face.

'Pat, these are difficult times. You are to be married and we have some advice for you.' Her tone was imperious and not to be argued with. She cleared her throat. 'Your father and I would like you to avoid getting in the family way until the war is over.'

What a damned cheek! How dare they? Pat was furious. Her heart drummed noisily against her ribs, her breath quickened. She flushed crimson with embarrassment and anger but her reply was icy. 'Mum, as you have just said, I am to be married.' She paused and slowed her speech. 'When, and if, we start a family is none of your business. It is a decision for me and Jim.'

'Well, that is how we feel. But if you do find yourself expecting, you must promise to do nothing about it.'

'What are you talking about?'

'Just remember what happened to Mrs Elliot's daughter round in Keynsham Road. She nearly died. Now, we will say no more about it. Here's your dinner. We ate earlier.' She handed her daughter a soup plate of lukewarm stew and a spoon. The conversation was clearly at an end. Pat's father, having nodded his agreement, announced he was going for a walk and 'bugger the bombers'. Her mother decided to join her neighbours for the BBC News and Pat was left alone to smoulder.

Much later, she discovered that it was Mrs Sillito down the road who could 'do something about it'. She was handy with a douche and a knitting needle, and the story of Mrs Elliot's daughter fell into place.

It was not a Christmas wedding after all. On the last Wednesday in September, Jim opened the back door to find his mum waiting for him in the kitchen. Silently she handed him the small typewritten envelope with Royal Air Force Volunteer

Reserve printed on the back. Her hand trembled as she grasped the edge of the sink. He had the distinct impression that she had been standing with the letter in her hand since the postman had delivered it that morning.

Carefully, he eased back the flap of the envelope and drew out a flimsy piece of paper. Only a few weeks after being told he would almost certainly not be required for six months, here was a formal order for him to report for service at St John's Wood, London, on Monday 6th October. Jim looked directly at his mother. She was shocked to see not her boy, but a man. A man in uniform, a man flying a plane, a man killing, a man dying...

'This is it, Mum.' He put his arm round her shoulder.

'Yes, dear, I guessed. You'd better go round and tell Pat. Arrangements will have to be made.' She sat heavily on the wooden kitchen chair and forced a smile.

Pat lifted incredulous eyes from the letter. 'But they said six months,' her voice wobbled.

'Not guaranteed, it said in the small print.'

'This is real now, then?'

'Yes, it's real.' When she pressed her cheek against his chest he didn't move. His body was paralysed, his mind blank.

Then everything jangled into life. Adrenaline flooded his bloodstream and his muscles tensed as if to repel all the bullets and bombs Hitler could aim at him. Pat was sobbing now and he tightened his arms around her. His mind leapt from imagining himself in uniform, to giving in his notice, to a hurried wedding, to the excitement of piloting a plane. As the stimulation drained away his heart was leaden with the thought, *Then I will have to kill.*

Jim gave a week's notice to the foreman at the sugar company, who accepted it with better grace than his manager at the Gutta Percha factory the previous year. He took the tram to Woolwich to make the necessary arrangements with the registrar. Two mothers panicked about the food. Where was a wedding cake to be found at short notice? What should they wear? They inspected ration books and pleaded with friends and neighbours for some of their coupons. Sam said he knew a fellow at the Arsenal who could get some ham 'off the back of a lorry'.

On Saturday, Pat went to Cuff's in Powis Street in search of an outfit, all thoughts of Harris Tweed forgotten, and settled on a knee-length number in old rose crêpe de Chine. Then she chose navy shoes, hat and gloves. Grasping her brown paper parcels she whirled out of the revolving doors of the department store straight into Jim's arms and he spun her round until she was dizzy.

'What the...?' she gasped, when he allowed her feet to touch the ground.

'Just came for a quick cuppa with my girl, and to do a little bit more shopping.'

'No money or coupons left for more shopping, darling,' she explained over tea in their favourite café.

'Oh yes there is, for special shopping. Come on, they close in half an hour and we have to buy a wedding ring.'

They went back to the same shop where they had chosen an engagement ring less than three months before.

'Closing in five minutes.' The owner smoothed imaginary hair over his bald head, tapped his wrist and tutted. 'You'd do better to come back on Monday.'

'Can't do that,' Jim laughed, 'got to buy a wedding ring – quick.'

The man's face softened. 'Are you off then, son?'

'Indeed I am. We are to be married next Saturday and I'll be in uniform two days later.'

The jeweller pulled a tray from the glass cabinet, placed it on the counter and drew back the red velvet cover to reveal a shining array of gold bands. 'Take your time, my dears.' His voice was fond now, with an edge of sadness. 'Choose carefully, you'll be wearing it a long time I hope.'

*

My mother, now a ninety-three-year-old mistress of her laptop, emails me with a description of the ring:

> The wedding ring Jim gave me was 22ct gold tooled with
> ears of corn (for plenty) and orange blossom (for happiness).
> I think it cost four pounds, ten shillings.
> Love Mum xx

The man in the shop was right; it has been on her finger for nearly seventy-three years. It is smooth now; life has worn all trace of the engraving away.

*

Ten days after Jim received the letter they were married, by special licence, on 4th October 1941. Although religion had not figured in the life of either family, Pat's mother was mortified that there was to be no church service. The couple stood their ground; they were not churchgoers and were adamant they would not use the church merely for the sake of conventional hymns, prayers and blessings. Instead, the ceremony was in a small back office at Woolwich Town Hall where someone had put a few fading pink dahlias in a glass vase. Pat noticed their heads drooped for lack of water and three petals fell as they made their vows.

Her father's Morris Eight, running on black market petrol, transported the bridal party. Stan Adams (of cattle charming fame) was best man and newlywed Ethel was Matron of Honour. A grainy monochrome photo shows the wedding party standing in a line behind the rockery in the garden at Prince John Road.

Like a Victorian family group, the faces are solemn, save

Pat and Jim's wedding

for the suspicion of a triumphant smile playing around the lips of the bride and groom. Jim wears a civvy suit, perhaps for the last time. Pat clutches a large silver horseshoe and a corsage of flowers is pinned to her shoulder. Ethel stands on the edge looking mournful, a pale flower on her dress, and two sets of parents are positioned at either side of the bride and groom.

On their first anniversary Jim procured a weekend pass. On the night train back to Scotland, he wrote in his diary:

Sunday 4th October 1942

The end of a beautiful year despite such long separations. On Saturday 4th October 1941, about 11.30am, we sat in the waiting room of the registrar's office, all feeling rather nervous. Nobody quite knew what to talk about, and the few words that were spoken only served to heighten the tension. I don't remember the friends and relations who were present; I kept looking at Pat and thinking how beautiful she was. But I do remember Ethel's hat with its large feathers that somehow put me in mind of Cavaliers. The others were just a vague row of people wearing heather on their best clothes. Yet I didn't think much about marriage. We seemed to be so much married already (I shall never forget that April evening). My strongest reaction was 'now Pat and I will be left in peace'.

Vows were made, rings exchanged, a form signed, licence money paid and then the registrar said, 'Congratulations, Mrs Gaywood.' At last Jim realised he meant Pat, not his mum, and someone said, 'Well go on then, Jim, kiss her.' And they kissed the first kiss of their married life. Then they were lost in kisses, handshakes and maternal tears.

Jim's mother kept nudging his dad, who bestowed a beatific smile on everyone and ignored her until she stood directly in front of him, head on one side rubbing her thumb and forefinger together.

'What's the matter, Cis?'

'Give the office boy a tip, Sam,' she hissed.

'Oh yes, of course,' he replied, fumbling in his pockets for a florin.

Then bride and groom were escorted down the town hall steps to the car. On the drive home they kept glancing back through the small rear window to wave to those in the car behind.

The table in the front room of Pat's home in Prince John Road was laid for a wedding breakfast, but what they ate is now an ancient mystery to my mother.

'Surely you can remember, Mum.' I tease her memory. 'Did you have sandwiches?'

'Oh no, not sandwiches.' She looks affronted. 'Perhaps it was salad... Yes, it would have been salad, with some ham Grandad got hold of.'

'Anything sweet?'

'Jelly, I expect, or maybe trifle. We'd have had dried egg

and milk for the custard and some of those autumn raspberries from the garden.'

A cake had been found and together we study a small black-and-white photo of a magnificent tiered construction frosted in white with lucky little silver horseshoes on each layer. Quite a cake for wartime. I wonder if one of the tiers was made of cardboard and put it to Mum.

'Oh no, dear, things weren't that sophisticated.'

'Do you think Granny made it?'

'No, my mother never made cakes. It must have come from the baker's in the High Street. Not Fysons, that one further up on the left-hand side. You know the one.'

I don't.

The one-night honeymoon was spent at the Spa Hotel in Tunbridge Wells. On the journey there, Jim recorded later, they were:

> ...unhappily accompanied by both Pat's parents. Mr Sheridan was driving the car and his wife thought she would 'like a spin in the country.' Her real reason can well be imagined.

They arrived in time for tea at the hotel and sat on straight-backed chairs, surrounded by retired colonels from the Indian Raj with their squawking wives.

An old woman in the corner berated the waiter about the honey and Mrs Sheridan, never the soul of tact and in possession of delusions of grandeur, held forth in a loud 'posh' voice about how well the wedding had gone and asked Pat how it felt to be a married woman. Pat bristled, glaring at her mother and Jim's toes curled with embarrassment as curious eyes turned in their direction. The bride's mother drew herself up to her full five foot height and sailed over to reception.

Pat was puzzled. 'Where's Mum going, Dad?'

'Just to make sure everything is in order,' he replied, 'and to pay the bill.'

Jim recognized his cue and, once again, offered profound thanks for their wedding gift of this one-night honeymoon.

Some minutes later, after disappearing upstairs with the acne-ridden bellboy, Mrs Sheridan returned and delivered her verdict. 'The room looks perfectly satisfactory.' Was this the real reason she had come? At last the parents were waved off and the honeymooners were alone.

They only had one night away but, instead of going straight to bed, they went to see a film and found a cosy restaurant for supper. Then there was the hunt for a taxi; Pat's shoes were rubbing blisters and she couldn't walk across the common to the hotel. At last, they were alone in their 'perfectly satisfactory' twin-bedded room.

There to spend a heavenly night.

Uneasy in such a smart hotel, they found breakfast a rather grim business and the excess offended Jim's socialist principles.

We had a week's ration of butter for that one meal! What a relief it was to leave that atmosphere… But in spite of it we were wonderfully happy…

Jim's brother Len couldn't be at the wedding owing to milking duties on the farm where he was now working. Jim wondered where and when they would see each other again so it seemed a good idea to visit him. They broke their return journey near Sevenoaks, tramped the fields, admired the cows, and viewed the prize pig in borrowed gumboots that didn't fit – theirs, not the pig's. After a cup of tea in the farmhouse, they walked to the end of the lane where they boarded the next Green Line bus for home.

Sam and Cis welcomed their new daughter-in-law to their home with smiles, kisses, tea and a rather solid cake Cis had laboured on all morning. It had taken all the week's margarine and sugar rations, and a good deal of dried egg. Sam always described his wife's baking efforts as 'dry yellow', and he wondered what had happened to the remaining wedding cake.

The newlyweds were shown upstairs to the 'bridal suite'. Jim's generous parents moved into the boys' back room so that the newlyweds could occupy the best bed in the best bedroom for one more night before the war called.

9

London Calling

It was dark when Jim slid silently from that bed. He had planned not to wake her. Tearful farewells might undo his resolve to chance his life to the uncertain path of German anti-aircraft fire or the skill of a night-fighter. He had wondered, as he packed his belongings into his old Scout rucksack the previous evening, whether he could change his mind. *Probably not*, he thought. He laid a brand new university manuscript notebook, his Platignum fountain pen and an unopened bottle of ink amongst his underwear, socks and striped pyjamas.

Sam was rolling his first fag of the day and Cis was stirring the porridge when Jim came into the kitchen.

'Ooh! You made me jump, son.' Her spoon clattered against the side of the enamel saucepan. Jim shut the door carefully, put his forefinger to his closed lips and pointed to the ceiling. His parents nodded their understanding.

Grey watery porridge did not tempt him at the best of times, but today felt like the worst of times. So, after a brave attempt not to cause offence, he put down his spoon and pushed the dish aside.

He drained his mug of tea, drew the back of his hand across his mouth, whispered, 'Best be off now then,' and heaved his rucksack onto his back. His dad unlatched the back door.

'Bloody door,' Sam muttered as he wrenched it open.

Cis saw her clever blue-eyed boy, a married man now, going off to war. She kissed him on the cheek, then on the mouth.

Then, cupping his cheeks in her palms, she held him away from her, gazed into his eyes and swallowed a sob. Sam clapped his son on the back. What he saw were the broken bodies of his comrades in the last war, and he closed his eyes, as if shutting out the light could block the image of an exploding plane from his mind. He squeezed Jim's hand and tightened his lips into a thin stoical line as he closed the door behind his son. Jim gritted his teeth as he walked into the dawn light and told himself not to look back.

An early tram clanked down the hill and Pat, in that cobwebby space between sleeping and waking, believed it was her sister tugging at the drawer of their shared dressing table. But no, she remembered, she was married now, and the surge of happiness rising through her body blew the cobwebs away and she reached out to hold him again.

He was gone.

She sat bolt upright, switched on the bedside lamp and opened her eyes to confirm what she knew to be true. She might have guessed he'd do it this way – to try to spare her the pain of separation. But how could he deny her a last look, a last kiss?

Her eye was caught by a letter on the dressing table. It bore the inscription: *For my wife*. She climbed back on to the bed. Nestling into the still-warm depression made by his body, she told herself it could not be long before they were together again, but she doubted her optimism. From the Basildon Bond envelope she slipped a single sheet of paper and read:

Indivisible

Have no fear, dearest. Our love is not doubtful,
We have endured too much to be divided now.
Remember the past and be not regretful,
Look to the future and remember our vow:

We are one!
Nor time, nor place, nor persons,
Nor persecutions, nor prisons
Shall divide us.
I shall hold your hand through prison walls
And in the god-gilded halls
Of Death.

She buried her face in his pillow, but it was no substitute for a husband who had been with her for only one sunrise.

Despite the gloom of early morning, the 6.51 train was well populated. Jim got the last seat in the compartment, opposite a woman in a moth-eaten fur coat – rabbit, his mother would say. Her bare legs were bound with ropey veins and the sole of her shoe had parted company with its top. When she pulled a half-smoked Craven A from its battered packet, Jim smiled and offered her a light.

Next to her, a man in a raincoat, holding a flat cap in one hand and a bent roll-up in the other, nodded to Jim and glanced up at the luggage rack. 'Mighty big bag you got there, boy. Where're you off to?'

'My first day,' Jim replied, 'haven't got my uniform yet – RAF Reserve.' A young man in the window seat wriggled in his black jacket and wing-collar and buried his nose deeper into *The Times*.

'Bloody good for you,' the older man wheezed. 'Don't go getting yourself killed, though. We'll need you after it's over.'

It came to Jim that these were the people he was going to fight for; the people who would benefit from a new socialist world; the meek who deserved to inherit the earth. The woman got out at London Bridge, but not before she had 'God-blessed' him. On the platform at Charing Cross he hefted his rucksack onto his shoulder. The man in the raincoat waved him on. 'Go get the bastards, boy, and good luck to you.'

Early light fell on Queen Eleanor's cross as Jim stepped onto the station forecourt. Cabbies were touting for fares but he marched past with a purposeful step, all thoughts of heading for Euston to plead rediscovered pacifism forgotten. It was early yet. Nine o'clock was the time to report to St John's Wood Road. A grating in the pavement outside Lyons Corner House released the smell of frying bacon from a subterranean kitchen. Jim's tummy was rumbling and he had a couple of bob in his pocket, so he walked through the door and down the stairs to the basement brasserie.

A 'nippy' wearing a newly starched white apron over her black dress, a matching snowy crown on her head, smiled with an over-lipsticked mouth and took Jim's order for a rasher of bacon, fried bread, a poached egg and a pot of tea.

'London lad, are you?' She hung around when she brought his breakfast. 'Home on leave? Going dancing tonight?'

'No, on my way to join aircrew.'

'Oh well, s'pose I can't win every time.' She laughed as she moved away.

Fortified, he emerged from the depths. London was filling up now; policemen with white gloves blew whistles at the traffic, then beckoned commuters across the road in front of halted vehicles. Jim crossed the Strand, turned left and looked up at Nelson. Proud above Trafalgar Square, his one eye stared down at dry fountains and inanimate lions, their backs coated with ash like ageing fur.

*

Lyons Corner House is long gone now, but I am in London to walk his walk of seventy-two years ago. Today there are traffic lights in the Strand and I wait, not for a policeman, but for a little green man to appear and give me permission to cross the road. The square is full of tourists climbing onto the lions' backs for photos and cooling their hands in the sparkling spray of the fountains.

*

The worst of the Blitz was over in 1941 and the population was trying to believe that life was reverting to some sort of normality. But the shuttered theatres in Haymarket and the latticed tape over the shop windows were a constant reminder. Eros, with his cupid's arrow, was missing from his plinth in the centre of Piccadilly Circus, kept safe and ready to direct his amorous fire after the cessation of hostilities. *Who needs him?* Jim thought, kicking up his heels in delight as he pictured his bride, and continued up Regent Street. In Langham Place, All Souls Church – John Nash's classical memorial to the Duke of Wellington, victor of an earlier war – now lay in ruins, thanks to Hitler. Beyond it, Jim looked up at Broadcasting House. Damaged but undaunted, that art nouveau 'galleon' sailed on with Prospero and Ariel at its prow. *We are such stuff as dreams are made on, and our little life is rounded by a sleep.* He thought of the words Shakespeare had put into Prospero's mouth. Jim's dreams were of a new socialist world when the war was over. He was not ready for that sleep yet. Shame Churchill was given so much airtime though, Jim frowned. At least George Orwell got to have his say as well, and his views were more in tune with his own.

*

Prospero, the old magician, and Ariel, the spirit of the air, now oversee a building nearly three times its original size. The extension echoes the shape of the original, but is a miracle of twenty-first-century glass and steel construction from where television and radio programmes beyond Jim's wildest dreams are broadcast to the world.

When I follow my father to the end of Great Portland Street, I will him to stand and look in horror at the once elegant regency crescents, their facades pockmarked in 1941, their iron balconies missing. I don't know if architecture, or any sort of visual art, was important to him and I feel the distance between us lengthening. Then I remember his interest in film, and his big blue book of art photos I used to thumb through as a child (looking for the nudes). My shoulders relax as I retrieve another little piece of my father.

*

A curious mixture of war and peace pervaded Regent's Park as Jim entered. Norland nannies in long brown coats, matching felt hats and sparkling white gloves pushed shiny black perambulators past mounds of debris dumped on the lawns – the Luftwaffe's calling cards. The railings bounding the perimeter had been torn up to join John Nash's balconies to be manufactured into armaments. The summer green of the trees along the margins of the lake was relaxing into the yellow and gold hues of autumn, reserving strength for the coming winter. A breeze fluttered the fronds of willows and water birds searched for food beneath fading rose bushes.

Beside the drained boating lake Jim turned left into Hanover Gate and nearly collided with an athletic figure striding in the same direction. A long kitbag rested nonchalantly over his shoulder.

'Going my way?' the man smiled.

'Looks like it – if you're bound for the RAF too.' Jim was arrested by the man's eyebrows; bushy and mobile they protected dark, intense eyes. There was an immediate connection between the two men. They knew nothing of each other's background, education, politics, attitude to the war, but Jim knew instantly that they would be friends. It might only be for as long as the walk up St John's Wood Road, but he felt a burst of affinity as they pounded the pavement together.

'Charles Lawrence.' A broad hand, downy with black hairs, nails neatly clipped, grabbed Jim's, shaking it firmly. His cultivated accent had a northern burr, but of which side of the country Jim had no idea.

'Jim Gaywood. Pleased to meet you, Charles.'

'Not much prospect of leather on willow for us, more's the pity.'

Jim unpicked Charles's comment until realisation dawned. 'Of course, St John's Wood – Lords!' Mr Gridley, at Colfe's, had always promised to take the boys to the home of cricket but it had never happened. So here he was approaching the hallowed ground, not to watch Don Bradman thrill the crowd but to train to kill.

*

I've never been to St John's Wood, so it is as new to me in 2013 as it was to Jim in 1941. The pedestrians I meet walk with the confidence only money can give. A chauffeur-driven Daimler, carrying two women passengers veiled in black, glides into the underground garage of one of the apartment blocks which sit smugly behind carefully manicured hedges.

I step through the Grace Gate of the cricket ground and explain my mission to the man in the gatehouse.

'Yes,' he says, 'I know the RAF was here in the war. There's something about it on the wall just up there.' On the red-brick wall of the pavilion arch I read on a brass plaque:

> Many entering the RAF through gate no.1 Aircrew
> Reception Area at Lord's during the Second World
> War gave their lives. Our enjoyment of cricket
> reflects their sacrifices.

There is no cricket today and I can only see the stands and the grass through a locked gate.

*

In 1941, Jim and Charles joined the stream of boys – they were just boys – who poured under the brick arch and were marshalled into the Members' Stand, their civilian clothes holding them in that uncertain terrain between two lives.

They were directed to the row of seats labelled with their initial. Jim sat in G and lost sight of his companion searching for row L. Next to Jim was a lad with a Glaswegian accent. He paused every few words to open a mouth full of rotten teeth in a slow yawn. 'There's nae sleep to be had on the night train. Aye, no' a wink wi' the whisky causing all the singing.' A whiff of his breath confirmed Jim's suspicion that his neighbour had been one of the choristers.

A bespectacled fellow a couple of rows in front tried hard to suppress his cough, covering his mouth with a large checked handkerchief. His pigeon chest rose and fell under a tweed jacket several sizes too big; perhaps borrowed from his dad, to look smart for this important occasion.

When they had been processed – Jim chuckled at the comparison with the cans of processed peas his mother served up for dinner – they were kitted out with blue-grey uniforms, far from new and somewhat ill-fitting. Jim wondered who had worn them before. Had they been left when their owners exchanged them for flying suits and never came back to reclaim them? Their forage caps had a white flash to denote their tenderfoot status.

Then the men were lined up and marched around the green parade ground; their first square bashing. Jim was grateful that as a scout he had learned how to march. 'Shoulders back, head up, eyes front, by the left, quick march.' He could hear Scoutmaster Leslie's commands even now; firm, but more benign than the officer who barked officiously at the bunch of raw recruits. Was he a sergeant or a wing commander? How many stripes denoted what? There was a lot to learn.

The first night they slept on groundsheets in tents at the far end of the ground. The grey blanket was scratchy around Jim's shoulders. He was warm enough, but sleep was distant. Beyond the twenty or so prostrate bodies in the bell tent, Jim listened to the recurrent coughing of the boy in the tweed jacket, relieved he was not sleeping near him. How had he got this far? Why hadn't they noticed when he first went to volunteer? Jim had heard coughing like that before; not just from old men, veterans of the last war like his father, but Hattie Drinkwort in Miss Brentnall's class at Haimo Road had coughed like that.

*

'Do you remember her?' I ask my mother.

'Oh yes. We nicknamed her Fattie to rhyme with Hattie, but she was all skin and bone. One morning, Miss Brentnall told the class she'd gone to a sanatorium to get better. She never came back to school. It must have been TB.'

*

In the dark, amongst the twitching, snoring and deep rhythmic breathing of the sleepers, Jim could hear stifled sobs. He reflected on the whirlwind of his recent life. Only a few months ago he had been selling *Peace News* and attending regular pacifist meetings, protesting at the incarceration of friends who objected to the war on grounds of conscience. Daily he had crossed the Thames to a peaceable job in a sugar factory and had spent his leisure time in the library, indulging in amateur dramatics and rambling in the Kent countryside with the girl he adored. Now he was in the RAF – he'd *volunteered* for the RAF – the girl was his wife and he was sleeping on the sacred ground of Thomas Lord and W.G. Grace. He stared up at the brown canvas, just thin enough in parts to admit the faint glow of a full moon. How long, he wondered, before he too was up there among the stars? His heartbeat pounded in his ears so loudly that he felt sure it would wake the man sleeping beside him.

Early next morning, the new recruits were marched to

the restaurant at London Zoo for breakfast. Men carried old-fashioned hurricane lamps at each end of the column to prevent traffic accidents in the dark. After an eternity in the queue, they were given five minutes to down their food before the return march.

'Gaywood, S.J. – Bentinck Close.'

Jim clicked his heels in response to the order, saluted and joined the column of recruits to be billeted in one of several new apartment blocks surrounding Regent's Park.

'Blimey,' one of Jim's companions exclaimed when they arrived, 'they ain't even plastered the walls yet.' Construction had been halted when war broke out, but the lavatories were working and white sheets on their bunks were an unexpected perk for prospective aircrew.

*

When I type Bentinck Close into Google a list of apartments for sale appears on my screen – at nearly two million pounds! Times have changed, Dad.

*

Their second day was filled with intensive examinations of eyesight, hearing, heart, etc. Those with suspect-sounding chests were X-rayed. Men passed fit lined up for inoculations against diphtheria, typhoid and smallpox and were sent for compulsory haircuts. Some tried to bribe the barber with a sixpence to leave a decent thatch, but he was incorruptible and a demon with his clippers – one airman every ninety seconds.

Any man deemed unfit, or who reacted badly to the jabs, was moved to Abbey Lodge, the Aircrew Receiving Centre's Sick Quarters. Those found to have TB (Jim assumed this included tweed jacket man) were held there until a hospital bed could be found near their homes, their service experience over. For the remainder, life would become an unending round of Physical

Training (PT) in the park, kit inspections, aptitude tests, irksome discipline and queuing for near inedible food at the zoo.

A week after his arrival, Jim felt a hearty clap on his back. 'Are we supposed to eat this, old boy? Perhaps it was meant for the animals.'

'Charles! I wondered where you had got to. Thought you might be banged up in sick bay. Where's your billet?'

'Avenue Close.'

Jim told him he was in Bentinck and Charles guffawed. 'So you'll be out on the tiles every night then? Rumour has it the officer-in-charge goes home at night to sleep with his wife and then the mice go out to play.'

What the officer could do, Jim could do too.

Queuing for porridge and toast a few days later, Charles looked quizzically at his friend. 'You look done in, old boy.'

None of the men he had met there knew about Jim's marriage. It was the treasured centre of his life and he wanted to share it with no one but Pat. But now he decided to tell Charles. The previous night, the first time they had permission to go out, he had joined his colleagues in the local pub where they found their uniforms were a passport to free beer. Following the Battle of Britain, Londoners were falling over themselves to buy a pint for the boys in blue, and they made the most of it. Back at Bentinck Close he signed in with the crowd and then retreated out of the door while they caroused up the stairs.

Breathless, he fell onto the last train at Charing Cross and thirty minutes later alighted at a deserted Eltham Well Hall station. He would not wake his sleeping parents; time was short and it was all for Pat. Removing his shoes at the back door he turned the spare key in the lock, clenching his teeth when the click sounded like a shotgun in the silence of the night. He crept through the kitchen with its stale aroma of dinner, past the faint glow of the dying coke in the living room grate, into the hall and up the stairs – avoiding the creaky fourth step. The front bedroom door stood ajar, but he closed it silently behind him and bent to kiss her.

'Jim! What the…? What's happened to your hair?' He put a warning finger to his lips. She smothered her giggles and sat up to watch him tear off his uniform and his underwear and waited to be gathered into his arms.

After much joy and very little sleep, he was gone again into the darkness to catch the milk train.

Jim discovered that whoever had the responsibility of securing Bentinck Close for the night was sometimes neglectful of his duty. He suspected it was the officer in a hurry to get to his conjugal bed. On non-drinking nights, if he judged the other three occupants of his room asleep early enough, Jim collected his clothes, changed in the lavatory and tried the front door. If it opened, he hot-footed to Charing Cross; if not, he returned to his changing room and then back to bed.

He came in the night and he left in the night.

Each evening Pat waited, hoping, straining her ears for the slightest sound heralding his arrival. But on nights when the hands of the Smith's alarm clock passed midnight, she knew he would not come. 'Goodnight, Jim,' she whispered and settled to disappointed sleep.

The times when Jim was lucky, he'd sometimes surprise his room-mates.

'You're a fucking early bird sometimes, Gaywood.' Someone sat up in his top bunk and rubbed the sleep from his eyes when he saw Jim dressed and ready for the day.

Jim just smiled.

*

'But it had to stop when there was a murder up by the swimming baths,' Mum tells me.

The neighbourhood was taut with the fear of dark deeds. Women whispered together on street corners, men cast suspicious glances at strangers, doors were double locked, wives and children kept under curfew.

'A young girl, not local, raped and strangled. Your grandad met me every night at the station. No woman wanted to walk home alone in the dark. The police were everywhere and there were rumours a serviceman was seen running from the scene. "You mustn't come again, sweetheart," I told your dad. "If they find you walking around in the early hours they'll jump to conclusions."'

Jim was not going to let anything stop his precious nocturnal visits. 'I'll wear my civvies, then. Pretend I'm working nights.'

'No, Jim, it's too risky.'

'But I don't know when I'll see you again. I might be posted to John o' Groats after London. Don't worry, I'll work out a plan.'

Before any plan took shape, however, his stay in the superior surroundings of Regent's Park came to an abrupt end. He had passed all medical examinations and aptitude tests and was bound for the No.6 Initial Training Wing at Aberystwyth, with no opportunity to say goodbye.

10

Aberystwyth

After a gap of two and a half years, my father began his diary again. I have pieced together the missing time from family memories, research and informed imagination. The third notebook I possess is covered in red leatherette, surprisingly undamaged by the years. I hold this diary in my hand and touch the pages he touched, reading his own words in his own handwriting. We're getting closer now. I am feeling his joy, I am feeling his pain; I am itching to know what happened next.

I open the notebook and read:

Aberystwyth Thursday 16th April 1942

It is many years since I kept a diary. When I was at school I made various attempts in the little pocket diaries that are the inevitable Christmas presents. Lack of space prevented long entries so I never got further than 'lots of homework today' or 'went to the pictures – rotten' or 'out cycling this afternoon. Weather gorgeous. Enjoyed myself…'

What are you talking about, Dad? Surely you remember those entries you wrote in the university manuscript book in September 1939, when nothing would persuade you to fight? You said then that the only war you would be involved in was the one for international socialism. Those pages of impassioned outpourings are here beside me.

So much has happened in the intervening years. Hitler has

committed atrocities all over Europe. He has scared your mother half to death in the Blitz and invaded Russia, violating that icon of your ideal society. You have renounced your pacifism, you have married the girl you love and been separated from her for months while you trained to kill. You have forgotten all about those pages you wrote at the outbreak of war and have begun again. A new diary of a new life.

...now events are moving so rapidly, so many things may happen to me in the next few years that I feel I must keep a record of events and my reactions. It will be interesting in twenty years' time to read this diary. May the fates spare me to do so! I am optimistic. How many times have I spoken to my darling Pat of when I shall be grey and carry a balloon belly? Yes – I must come through this alive and well. And if I don't? Well maybe those dearest to me will like to keep it and perhaps find me still living in these pages...

You are talking to your daughter, Jim, and you are coming alive to me.

Here goes...

Back from embarkation leave yesterday. A perfect five days with my darling. Through all the bitterness of my pacifism I was never really unhappy. That is impossible with her. Tuesday was particularly joyful as it was our anniversary. On 14th April 1941, she and I were married.

No, no, you've got that wrong, Dad. You were married on 4th October.

No prosaic form filling marriage that, quite unofficial. But on that night we knew beyond all possible doubt that we must spend all our lives together.

Oh I see. *That* anniversary.

> Darling girl, she wrote of it on the train, not an hour after
> our goodbye kiss. If there be a God I thank him for giving
> me such a woman...
>
> And now I am back at no.6 ITW Aberystwyth. John
> Brown was on the platform with the news, 'It's Canada,
> boys!'

Canada. How he had hoped for a posting in England. He was
appalled at the prospect of being so long away from Pat. Weeks
apart were bad enough, but months... With luck, though, he
might be home again in time for Christmas.

Brown had arrived on the earlier train and was bursting
with information. 'We're going to Ansty first for a three-week
grading course – just to see if we have any aptitude for flying,
and if we don't – out of aircrew.'

A voice came from the back of the crowd. 'It's pretty bloody
at Ansty. Jock Jackson went with C flight about three weeks
ago. He wrote to me. The flying school's miles from anywhere,
apparently, and conditions are right shitty.'

'Well, well, we shall soon find out.' Jim was just pleased to
be leaving Aber.

He had disliked Aberystwyth on sight. Everything was grey.
The streets were grey, the buildings were grey, the beach was
grey, the sea was grey. His mood was grey. When they first
arrived, the officer who met them had screamed unintelligible
orders from under a handlebar moustache. He marched them in
convoy down Terrace Road, then along the promenade (where
the wind nearly took away their forage caps) to their billet at the
Queen's Hotel.

*

My summer Sunday journey from London to Aberystwyth is magical, far from being the worst railway journey in this island, as Jim described it. I sit in a comfortable, quiet, air-conditioned train for a mere five hours, listening to 'The Pastoral Symphony' on my iPod. No more London Midland or Great Western railways; platforms now boast they are sponsored by opticians or universities and the trains are Virgin. Soon after leaving Birmingham we pause at Cosford, where the RAF museum is beside the line. A crowd is enjoying an air display and we passengers follow their eyes skyward to watch the Red Arrows race across the blue like a supersonic flight of geese in V formation. Silently they weave and turn, dive and climb, only a hair's breadth between them. Then we hear the scream of engines and red, white and blue tail feathers unfurl against the sky. I always feel a sense of awe when I watch this display by today's RAF and I wonder whether Jim would believe his eyes if he were with me.

My views of the smooth Cambrian Mountains could be pictures from a 'Beautiful Britain' coffee-table book. Fat lambs with woolly mothers seek shade under freshly leaved trees, and, on the crests of hills, the white propellers of giant wind turbines turn with a stately motion.

The valleys grow deep and narrow. Sunbeams fall through branches onto buttercups, dog-roses and a patch of unseasonal bluebells, delayed by the cold spring weather. The River Dovey skitters and rolls over its stony bed, then slows into wide meanders as the land flattens and the margins of the river are lined with bog iris and rushes. The bog becomes salt marsh as we approach the sea and the low buildings of Aberdovey come into view on the opposite bank. Then the line turns south following the coast. Beside the station at Borth, a rainbow terrace of houses – lime green, shocking pink, scarlet, blue and yellow – makes me smile. Laughing families of tattooed holidaymakers board the train clad in swimwear and beach towels. Those pink shoulders will be sore tomorrow.

The next stop is Aberystwyth. It has been a spectacular journey and I wish I could have done it with my dad.

When I arrive, the sea is not grey but glittering under a yellow sun in a clear azure sky. I check in to the Richmond Hotel, where, I later discover, the owners found diagrams of aircraft under the wallpaper when they redecorated. Airmen had slept there too.

Next morning my first task is to find the Queen's Hotel. There is a sketch of it on the Internet and it is described as having been built by a Victorian entrepreneur in 1866. A four-square lump of granite with panels of geological specimens of fossils and quartz in the facade, it was a grand venue for wealthy travellers arriving on the new railway. I can find no address or information on whether it is still standing.

The man in the Tourist Information Centre can't help me. 'No, there's no Queen's Hotel in Aberystwyth.'

I am frustrated. 'But it was here in the war and I need to find out what happened to it.'

He scratches his head and sends me to the new library up the road. The librarian directs me upstairs to the Ceredigion Archives, where I explain my mission to Gwynedd and her colleague Ania, who are enthusiastic about my quest.

Ania is tall. Her perfume is musky, mysterious, and untidy black hair frames her pale face from which dark eyes sparkle. 'Of course I know the Queen's,' she says, 'it was the council offices and we only moved out a few weeks ago.' She speaks with a faint accent which is not Welsh.

'Would you like to see it?' She is bursting with barely suppressed excitement. 'I think I can still get hold of the keys – pretend I've left a file in the basement or something.' She almost trips over her feet as she whirls me down the stairs while chattering into her phone, arranging to meet the key holder.

The sun is warm but Ania chooses to walk on the shady side of the road. 'I was once a Goth, you see. Not now – too old – but Goths don't like the sun and it's sort of stayed with me. That's why I love the Queen's – it's old and spooky and I used to have such fun running along the corridors howling like a banshee. My colleagues thought me mad, of course, but they got used to it.' She does a little skip and a jump and screws her face into a grin. A current of enthusiasm jumps through the air, lands on me and I giggle like a child embarking on an unsanctioned adventure.

The Queen's Hotel is only a few yards along the bay from where I am staying. It looks as if it will endure forever, but Ania tells me it is to be sold and its future is uncertain. As we approach she runs to meet a man who hands her a bunch of jangling keys. She selects the largest and turns it in the lock of the imposing door. When we enter the cavernous Cambrian ballroom sunshine is streaming through the high windows and lighting up the dust, which gives the place that lifeless smell redolent of antique shops. I have a vision of potted palms and Victorian ladies in feather boas peering over their fans at bearded gentlemen in evening suits. Then I remember why I am here and imagine a crowd of uneasy young men in blue-grey uniforms receiving their instructions.

I remember Jim wrote in his diary that when he first arrived he was directed, with three others – Boon, Sanders and McGeorge – to their quarters in room 97. The lift was for officers only so they humped their kit up the wide stone staircase to the third floor.

After admiring the decorative floor tiles, enjoying a renewed lease of life now the cheap municipal carpet had gone, Ania and I travel to the top floor in the forbidden lift. 'We'll start at the top and work all the way down to the basement.' She squeezes her eyes shut and shivers. 'Ooh it's so good to be back again.'

Through the lattice metalwork of the lift-shaft, I admire the coloured windows of the stairway and wonder if they were made by that master of Victorian stained glass, Burne-Jones. Jim would have been relieved to see them still in place, indicating that bombs were not expected in the far west of Wales.

We step out onto the third floor. The rooms are no longer numbered, but an original brass plaque on the wall points to rooms 83 to 116. We count the doors, assuming the odd-numbered larger rooms are on the side facing the sea, and find what must have been number 97 – a large, blue painted room with a corner window. A poster on the wall about welfare benefits, a fiercely coloured carpet and a 1970s light fitting force me to close my eyes to imagine Jim and his colleagues arriving in a very different room.

Ania's enthusiasm for the building increases with every floor she shows me. 'Oh, I must get this' – out comes her phone to photograph a door handle, 'and this' – a window catch, 'so it will not be lost to memory forever. And look, look there! That is where your dad must have peed.' She points me to the Victorian urinals and I wonder what Jim would have thought of his seventy-year-old daughter laughing as she imagines a line of young men relieving themselves. I turn to speak to Ania, but she is gone. I am unsure which of the maze of corridors to follow when the soundtrack of a horror film rises behind me, an unearthly scream echoing through the ghostly building. I am momentarily frozen with fear. Then I understand. Chasing the sound, I find Ania running and howling through the empty rooms and we collapse in a hysterical heap. When we descend below ground, however, and she produces a wolf-like howl which reverberates through the basement full of ancient electrical equipment and heavy metal doors, I am glad to regain the daylight as we mount the stairs.

Walking back to her office, I ask Ania where she grew up.

'In Warsaw,' she replies, 'but I left a long time ago.'

I tell her my granddaughter is half-Polish and also called Ania. Knowing my father had Polish comrades, I reflect on how strands of humanity connect in the most unexpected ways.

Jim was frustrated at the delay in moving from Aber to Ansty. He had spent months studying aircraft recognition, navigation, theory of flight, air force law, meteorology and maths. Any time not spent in lectures at the Old College was taken up with PT and drill. On Wednesday afternoons they played rugby – not his favourite sport.

Thursday 16th April 1942

This morning we were told we would be going tomorrow but now it seems fairly certain that the posting is postponed until Monday. We are annoyed. Now that we must go let us get on with it!

There has been the usual fuss and bustle. A good deal of waiting about – as usual in the RAF; a farcical kit inspection this morning, clothing parade, inoculations and a full 'medical' this afternoon. My arm is stiffening from the needle. Extra tunics issued on clothing parade. We expected new ones that we could keep for 'best'. Instead we received NCO's cast offs. Mine was so dirty and torn I had to go back and change it for one just a bit more wearable.

Of all the absurd things – I have been here since November 8th and done drill nearly every day, and on the very day we are packing for moving off we are given an hour's drill! 's amazing!

In the evening, he records, he escaped to the picture house on the pier with Boon and Sanders. They saw Deanna Durbin and Charles Laughton in *It Started with Eve*. Jim, with his interest in film-making, considered it pleasant but not outstanding.

On the same bill was a Ministry of Information film, *Land Girl*, made by Paul Rotha Productions. Usually he found M of I films good, occasionally excellent, but this was one of the worst he had seen and he expected better of Rotha.

Friday 17th April 1942

Damn inoculation! All day I have felt limp, unenergetic and fed up with everything. I have cursed the RAF, Canada, the war and everything that keeps Pat and I apart more times than I can count.

Hope to God peace may come soon, but I feel sure it is a long way off yet.

An ARP exercise this morning, and like all those exercises it was pretty absurd. Everyone was bored stiff and binding like hell, especially those of us who spent an hour standing in the basement. How laughable these rehearsals are to one who has been right through the London Blitz.

Jim's mood was low – he'd had a rough night. His arm was swollen and painful and he shivered under his blanket while Boon talked in his sleep. But an incident the next afternoon cheered him up. They were sent to Tan-y-Bwlch for clay pigeon shooting.

Friday 17th April 1942

Quite a little mutiny this afternoon. When we got to Tan-y-Bwlch, those of us who had been inoculated refused point blank to hold a gun. We won the day and basked in glorious sunshine instead. A small pointer of what non co-operation can achieve.

*

'Where is Tan-y-Bwlch?' I ask Ania as we explore the archives looking for more information about the RAF in Aberystwyth.

'It's a big house. Is that what you are looking for?'

'I shouldn't think so. They went there for shooting practice.'

'Ah, it must have been on the recreation land.' She shows me on the town map. 'Follow the coast path around the southern bay, here, and across the bridge.' Her black-varnished fingernail finds an area of flat land. 'It must have been there.'

When I reach the place, I see a small mansion hidden in the trees and some boys kicking a ball around on the spit of land between the sea and the river. My dinner table is booked for 8pm but I loiter in the late sunshine as long as I dare, conjuring a picture of happy rebellious airmen.

*

Jim was even more cheerful when he returned to the Queen's to find two letters. The one with Pat's writing on the envelope he tucked into his pocket to savour when he was alone. The other was addressed in a hand which looked as though it belonged to a demented spider. It was kind of Len Allbury to write to him, but Jim was not charitable:

> I do wish that fellow would cultivate a legible hand writing. Some of the words are indecipherable and what one is able to read proves dull and uninteresting. I do so hate letters describing uninteresting details of work and play. I like a letter to be full of opinions and discussion of events and trends of the time.

*

'Do you remember someone called Len Allbury?' I ask my mum.

'Oh yes, he was Ellen Stewart's boyfriend; lived at the New Eltham end of Green Lane.'

'Ellen with the hump back?'

'That's right. Funny bloke, Len – Ellen gave him the boot.'

Poor old Len Allbury. I hope Jim climbed down off his high horse to write a friendly reply.

*

Lying on his bunk later, Jim eagerly slipped Pat's letter from its envelope, but his smile faltered as he read her news. A close friend of his brother's, Bill Mills, had been missing for three weeks. A fighter pilot, he had been taking part in sweeps on France.

> One of the finest fellows I ever knew – straight, honest, clean, adventurous, likeable. I pray he is not dead. Maybe he bailed out and is a prisoner of war. The news upset Pat, for naturally she cannot help but imagine that one day I may be 'missing'.

He wasn't always so serious and mature though, as demonstrated by his account of the incident of Pat and the cakes, while he was home on leave the week before.

> On Monday we were passing through Sidcup after a delightful afternoon cycling when we decided to take home something nice for tea. 'Look out for a baker's,' said Pat. Soon we found one with just a single tray of cakes in the window. Pat went in and ordered eighteen! One bag was filled when an old woman entered and she also wanted some cakes. One by one the assistant went on filling the second bag, and as the number diminished the old woman's mouth opened wider and wider until one lonely cake was left on the tray. The woman was quite upset and said in a tearful voice, 'Have you any more of those?' Pat came out killing herself with laughter, and for the rest of the day we kept recalling the poor old woman and laughing, laughing, laughing… We were very happy that day.

*

Reading this I feel my seven decades rise up in sympathy with the 'old woman'. How dare these young people laugh at her! Why didn't they do the decent thing and offer her some of their cakes? Then I remember what it was like to be twenty and in love. And when I question Mum she assures me there were more cakes at the back of the shop.

Back in Aber, the more he thought of going to Canada the less he liked it.

Friday 17th April 1942

I curse the war with all my heart and soul. May my future children never know it.

Saturday 18th April 1942

Feeling a little more cheerful today. I still hate the thought of going overseas but it will have its compensations for me. I will at least be seeing a new strange land, new customs, new people, new places. It will be hardest for Pat – waiting…

*

The Old College, an elegant example of Victorian architecture at the south end of the bay was built in the shadow of the ruined castle as a theological college. This was where Jim had yawned with his fellow recruits through endless boring lectures, so I walk in to absorb the religious atmosphere that irritated him. The statues, the hushed silence and dark wood panelling feel ecclesiastical, so I am surprised by two young women with unnaturally coloured hair, brief denim shorts and Doc Marten boots clattering down the stone stairs. In the twenty-first century this is part of the University of Aberystwyth – still a place of learning.

St John's church, over the road, is locked but that is no great disappointment. I know my dad found no solace in religion from his description of church parades.

Sunday 19th April 1942

Why should a man be forced to attend a church? Many of us read magazines there. I got in a Stephen Leacock story quite nicely. Never known such a dull, boring, sleep inducing preacher as the one we are forced to hear. Abolish church parades! They degrade the Church and us. In spite of a glorious afternoon of sunshine on Constitution Hill I came back feeling miserable. Writing to my darling girl up there, thinking of a sad parting…

*

I discover Constitution Hill to be not a road but the cliff at the north end of the promenade. In the period ticket office at the bottom of the Victorian funicular railway, I pay my fare to a young man with an afro hairdo. The open carriage climbs up the steep gradient, the bay spread out below like a blue bodice with a necklace of Victorian buildings sparkling in the sunshine. At the top I buy a postcard of one of those early railway posters advertising the seaside resort as a 'must-see' destination, with a picture of the bay and the cliff. Licking a honeycomb ice cream, I sit on a rock and write:

Dear Mum,
I am sitting on the top of Constitution Hill in Aberystwyth, just as Dad did in 1942 when he wrote to 'his darling girl'. The weather is sunny, as it was then, and I am having fun walking in his footsteps. Tell you all about it soon. Love J.

When I descend, I walk round to the mouth of the River Ystwyth where Jim and Boon went that Sunday evening.

Boon and I hired a rowing boat and the physical exertion cheered us greatly. It is about four years since I rowed (and then badly), so I was quite bucked that I got along so well this evening.

I sit beside the river reading his diary and I, too, am bucked to read how his earnest optimism soon overcame his periods of despair.

Tokyo raided for the first time yesterday. Death, death, death. Is there no end to mankind's mass insanity? Will wars never cease? Yes, I believe they will. Maybe this will be the last great war. A change, an encouraging new spirit is abroad among people. This time they will stand no nonsense. They have endured too much to go back to the old slipshod ways of pre-war life. Collectivism is coming. It may be fascist, but I believe it will be socialist. There will be one hell of a struggle after the war, but a new free world will be established. Not by mealy-mouthed politicians, not by the oratory of magnified little men like Churchill, but by the PEOPLES of the world, by men who did the real fighting in the war, by the workers who endured the aerial bombardment, by the brainy intellectuals and technicians who are so often thwarted under capitalism. A man's character, not his wealth, is going to count. It will be a fight, and I hope I am in it. Violent or peaceful revolution, I want to be in it. For this war is but the prelude to the real war for the establishment and realization of the rights of man. If I must die, let it be in that war.

Later, I read this to my mother. 'Do you recall all this fervour, Mum?'

She shifts in her armchair, looking slightly uncomfortable, not quite sure what reply I am expecting. 'Well, yes, and I was behind him all the way of course. But he could put it into words. I couldn't. But I agreed with everything.'

I get the picture. She adored him and, to her, he could do no wrong. So of course she agreed. She didn't really think about what this new revolution, this new struggle he propounded with such vigour, would be. She just wanted the current conflict to end and to enjoy a peaceful family life with her Jim.

*

Her Jim was feeling nervously elated and not sorry to be leaving Aberystwyth. But the glorious weather of his last few days in the town had made him reassess. He writes that he liked the hills and valleys and he found nothing to complain of so far as the people were concerned. Why, he questions, was there such antipathy on the part of the English to the Welsh? Prejudice. Would it ever disappear? Prejudice against the Welsh, the Jews, the Japs, the Germans – sometimes even the French. In his view, fair-mindedness and tolerance had to be the keynotes of the new society.

Monday 20th April 1942

Goodbye Aberystwyth. I confess it is not a sad goodbye. Sometimes I have hated you with all my heart, but there are no hard feelings now. I have cursed you for being so deadly dull. I have cursed you for being at the end of the worst railway journey in this island. I have cursed you and will curse you for being the town where I first knew the terribleness of being 'browned off'. But perhaps I misjudge you. Perhaps one day I shall return with my wife and children and find a new Aberystwyth – a pretty, friendly town for happy holidaymakers. Perhaps, who knows, I may lodge here in the Queen's Hotel, maybe in one of the rooms I have occupied: 97, 87 or 67. And then, perhaps these rooms will not be austere and cold but pleasantly furnished and carpeted.

Aber, I have laughed much here in spite of you. Goodbye, I am off to pastures new. Now the real job of flying begins. Hey ho! I wonder what is in store…

*

I am here, Dad. The sun is shining on happy holidaymakers and I have stood in room 97 just before it begins a new life or meets its demise. You may have disliked the place but you tell me about your friends here.

Charles Lawrence – 'intelligent, progressive, thoughtful'. You had known him since you met him on the way to Lord's and together you had listened to a symphony on the wireless in Mrs Guthlelch's tea shop while you crammed your bellies with cakes and sandwiches. You say Charles had no use for sex; he never wanted a woman. Would a man have fitted the bill, I wonder? No. You were sure, if he survived the war, he would marry. He knew about your writing aspirations, your politics, and the full history of your pacifism. You say you disagreed on everything and yet you felt you were both on the right side of the fence. A tantalizing comment. I want to know more. Why were you such friends if you held such opposing views?

And you describe others. McGeorge, who 'warbled like a pipe organ and had ambitions to be a wing commander.' Despite his being as irritating as a hair shirt, you liked him. You would miss 'Finger' Coulson, an ex-policeman who liked 'plenty of wallop,' with his policeman's gait, his finger moustache, his broken nose and his great big grin. There was Juppy and his women; and Pinky and his women, and his inclination 'to urinate in boots when drunk.' And Smart – 'ex-communist, well-read, talkative,' and with whom you generally agreed. And Boon and Sanders and Wally Farr of the permanent staff…

What happened to these men? I feel I have a vested interest in them so I search the Internet to find out. Life was short in Bomber Command; fifty-five thousand men met their end in the sky, in the sea, or nose down in the earth, most within a few months of joining.

Smart was probably killed with his comrades on the night of 12th June 1943. Finger 'bought it' in August 1943. If Juppy's name was Arthur he met his death in May 1943, if it was Harold he lived another nine months. The most likely Pink I have found on the Forces War Records website had only a few months remaining to celebrate his conquests and pee into boots, but newlywed Les Ward, who 'disagreed with everyone about everything and was a fine fellow,' nearly made it. He was lost less than two months before VE day.

Too many Boons and Sanders at that time in the RAF Volunteer Reserve for me to identify those who shared your room, except to find they all died before the war ended. And Wally Farr, with his grand braiding and moustache, to whom no one paid any attention – was he the officer who had greeted you on arrival? He seems to have made it through to the peace.

What happened to Charles and McGeorge?

What became of Jim Gaywood?

11

Ansty

His stay at Ansty was short – only three weeks – but it shaped the rest of his life. And mine. He was not yet my father. He was nearly someone else's father, and if he had been his life may have taken a different path and I would not have existed.

A special train took them from Aberystwyth straight through to Ansty near Coventry. As the train approached Jim was dismayed.

Tuesday 21st April 1942

Well, Aber, I did at least congratulate you on your countryside. But I cannot congratulate you, Ansty! Flat, flat... unpicturesque, desolate, grim... I fear I dislike this place...

The wartime aerodrome had been converted from a peacetime civil airfield, and the living quarters had been erected in a hurry. Twelve men were housed in each corrugated iron Nissen hut which Jim describes as being like the big brothers of the domestic Anderson shelters; giant drums sliced through the middle, the flat laid on the face of the earth. Each had a coal stove to prevent them from freezing (it was one of those freakishly cold Aprils). Lighting had yet to be installed so inferior torch batteries dimmed and failed before he had read a chapter of his book. There was no NAAFI, the YMCA closed at 4pm, and the nearest pub was two and a half miles away.

Pinky, who had also arrived with the latest batch of trainees, slammed the door and slumped onto his camp bed. 'Couldn't be much worse off in the middle of the Sahara, according to Smart. "Well," I told him, "at least we'd be warmer there."'

Jim, jolted out of his dejection, looked up. 'What? Did you say Smart? Is he still here?'

'Yep. Smart, and Faircloth and Lawrence – most of C Flight. A few passed their solo and went last Friday, including McGeorge. ' Jim was incredulous, but it augured well for Mac's ambition to be a wing commander. (I know McGeorge never achieved it; his plane exploded thirteen months later.)

'Well, if it isn't old Gayboy!' The camaraderie of old friends felt like a warm safe place when Jim found them in the mess. 'Rosie Lee time, mate.' Fairclough reached for the aluminium teapot on top of the stove and poured dark stewed tea into an enamel mug and handed it to Jim. 'Milk's off, but no sugar rationing here,' he said, pushing a blue paper bag and a bent spoon towards him.

Charles Lawrence, Jim's first RAF friend, had done fourteen hours in the air and he and the others talked quite casually about flying; old hands now, reassuring the fearful newcomers.

Wednesday 22nd April 1942

Today has been spent on fatigues and form-filling – all inevitable at a new station. Tomorrow we hope to have our first trip into the air. I certainly feel better about it after the confident talk of those who have already put in a few hours.

Ooh! My head! A good night's sleep is indicated. Reveille at six again here! Oo! Reveille, ooh! Flying – ooh! ooh! ooh! My HEAD!

Thursday 23rd April 1942

Flew for the first time today. Up for twenty-five minutes altogether. Most striking thing is there is no sensation of speed. The craft appears to be static, and the ground to roll slowly below. Of course fields, hedges, towns, buildings, etc. look very tiny, but one feels quite safe. Only physical sensation was when we hit a bump and I got the same feeling as in a lift going down quickly – stomach in mouth.

Days were divided into half-lectures, half-flying. The next day he was up for eighty-five minutes, trying to gain some knowledge of the controls and attempting to fly straight and level. But his 'straight and level' was not very straight and level. Pilot Officer Buroughs was a patient instructor but he did get a little wild when Jim persisted in a slow climb. When they came down he said not to mind the binding but sometimes it was necessary.

*

'Binding.' What was binding? The word keeps appearing in the diaries, so I surf the Web until I find a site explaining RAF slang. Binding = complaining. That makes sense. Oh yes, of course, *Much Binding in the Marsh* was a comedy programme on the wireless when I was a child. I can hum the theme tune now. I think it starred Dick Bentley and Jimmy Edwards, and I remember the grown-ups laughing. My mum used bias binding when she made frocks and skirts, so I was puzzled and slightly disapproving of it being wasted and lying around in some soggy marsh.

*

Friday 24th April 1942

We looped the loop twice, and the first time I didn't quite know if we had done it or not, the effect was so much less than I had expected. The only physical effect is 'g'. One feels heavy as lead and it's quite difficult to raise one's hands. We went over the clouds. It's marvellous to see them below and stretching far away into the distance, soft as cotton wool, wispy as smoke, it was wonderful. Then we did some 'cloud hopping', that is climbing up one side of a cloud cap and down the other, and so on, time after time. Several fellows have been airsick, but the only effect on me is to leave my stomach suspended somewhere above when we go into a fairly steep dive. I certainly like flying, enjoy it immensely.

Would he be able to handle a machine solo? He had grave doubts but doesn't tell me what they were. He says he wouldn't worry too much if he failed. After all he didn't want to go overseas and Pat didn't like him flying. So that was it. Pat came first and he wanted to please her. He wanted a future. He wanted me. Nevertheless he didn't want to admit failure, so he made up his mind to do his damndest to succeed.

Sunday 26th April 1942

Up for forty-five minutes yesterday and again today, climbing, stalling; gliding yesterday and spins today. Spins are not as bad as I expected. Stalls are worse – leave one's innards in the sky when the plane dives. My straight and level and climbing were much better today, but I'm still pessimistic about getting a solo in!

Ansty may have been a desolate place but it had the advantage of being close to Coventry, from where London could be reached in two hours, so he could go home to Pat for twenty-four hours when he had a day off.

How I look forward to the happy time when we shall always be together. Pray God it may be soon. All I want is a quiet, peaceful married life with Pat and the children we shall have…

He may have said that was all he wanted when he was missing her so badly, but the socialist fire in his belly was still burning. When he pens a diary entry for Labour Day on the 1st May he is metaphorically waving his left-wing banner again. He writes that it has been a sorry year for the Labour movement. Germany is oppressing the European working class, the position of British workers is deteriorating, the Russian proletariat are shedding their blood, the Japanese are smashing their way through to India when they should be fighting oppressors at home, and India has the choice of enduring British Imperialism or Japanese invasion.

Friday 1st May 1942

Labour Day! And I expect the Communist Party of Great Britain has held a big meeting urging not 'Forward to Socialism', but 'More Production' – which means more class collaboration. And the Labour Party has probably said again, 'Victory is certain' and made no reference to socialism. There is only one truly socialist nationwide organisation left in Britain today – the Independent Labour Party who campaign for 'Socialism in Britain NOW!'

I know what it's like to feel disillusioned about the Labour Party. At least Jim had an alternative and he had hope it would succeed. He records that Fenner Brockway, the Independent Labour Party candidate, had polled twenty-five per cent of the vote in a contest against the new War Minister. That meant that one person in four voted for an ultra-left candidate! In addition, Tory seats in Rugby and Wallasey fell to Independents. It would be twenty years before Macmillan coined that memorable phrase, 'the winds of change' (albeit in a different context), but my future father thought he could feel a stirring in the air.

A socialist Britain in the West, a socialist Russia in the East, both offering a socialist peace. Will the Nazis be able to withstand the encouraged people of Germany and the Occupied Countries? I believe not. British and Russian arms, the German people's encouragement – these will mean the downfall of fascism.

What great changes there may be by next Labour Day!

May the workers of all lands be united in socialism.

My parents decided to have a baby. In the midst of an international maelstrom, not knowing if the child would be born into a fascist Britain, not knowing if its father would be alive to see it. Was it his optimism about a post-war socialist world that gave them the confidence to take this step? Or was it simply biology, the basic urge to reproduce, continue the species? Whatever the reason, I am grateful. But I had to wait my turn.

They had been discussing names for the as yet unconceived child. Mum was keen on Jennifer, but my dad was insistent that their first-born girl should have her mother's name. He makes no mention of what names they favoured for a boy. Anyway, his short, infrequent visits home produced the desired effect.

Saturday 9th May 1942

What a week it has been! I went home last Sunday night and Pat said she expected to have a baby. How happy we were! In spite of all sorts of difficulties, especially money and the fact of not having our own home, we were both proud and happy.

It made up his mind up about flying. He was miserable at the thought of Pat and the baby being left alone. At his flying test he made it pretty obvious that he expected to fail – and he was successful in that. Even so, he felt he would never have made a pilot; he just didn't fit the part. Why? He had said so often that he loved flying but his progress had been 'slow and gradual'. Perhaps he was too cerebral, not technical enough. Or was it leading and managing a crew that worried him? Whatever the reason, arrangements were made for him to remuster to a ground job: Special Duties, which meant plotting the movement of aircraft at fighter stations. Still, he doubted his decision.

Wednesday 13th May 1942

I felt rather yellow withdrawing from aircrew… And then yesterday I received a letter from Pat: 'Jim, our baby is no longer on the way, let us have another.' I could hardly believe it. We had made so sure there would be a child. I was terribly disappointed and yet half relieved. I have only just realized how much Pat wants a child.

Yesterday afternoon I applied to continue with aircrew duties. I am down for a new job which I suppose I ought not to mention yet as it is still a secret. However, it will be something like an Observer's job. So I am in aircrew and Pat desperately wants a baby. I think she shall have one. There are millions in the same predicament as myself in Russia, China, Burma and Europe. Who am I to say 'no baby in case I am killed' or 'no danger because of the baby.' My darling shall have her baby and I shall continue flying that I may not consider myself a coward. That is the best arrangement.

*

'You had a miscarriage before me, Mum, didn't you?'

'Well, yes, very early.' She looks doubtful.

'Or maybe you were just late?'

'Possibly. Who knows?'

I know how she felt, counting the days on the calendar, excitement rising as the expected date passes, then disappointment as the blood begins to flow. Whether there was a predecessor in my mother's womb or not, I would be there soon.

Like so many others, she wanted a baby for company and as a comfort if she lost her husband. Jim understood that and was satisfied with the decision he had made.

He travelled into Coventry and viewed the battered town, still watched over proudly by the tower and spire of the ruined cathedral. Rostock in Germany, York and Bath in England, had all suffered bombs that week and Jim tried to make sense of his life. He was training to kill, but hoped fervently that his killing would be justified by a new sane world emerging from the old. Could killing ever be justified? His pacifist conscience still pricked him like the brambles at the margin of a narrow path on one of those carefree Kentish rambles with his friends that now seemed part of another world. He poured his frustration onto the pages of his diary.

Thursday 14th May 1942

Oh, what a sorry state the world is in. How I loathe war! How many, many people there must be, of all nationalities, whose dream is as mine – freedom from fear and want of a pleasant home with wife and children. Surely they are simple things to ask for? We want no great riches or power, nor do we wish to harm others. All we ask is to be allowed to live peaceful lives. You 'great' men of the world who lust after power and personal greatness – I curse you. The Hitlers, Mussolinis, generals, industrialists – all who could have averted this madness, I CURSE YOU ALL!

Oh God, let there be peace in the world. Silence the cannon, make useless the bombs, divert the bullets. Let there be peace that we may reconstruct. End tyranny! END THIS WAR!!

The war had over three years of life yet and my dad had decided to fight in it. On 14th May 1942 he was posted to Brighton to await remustering.

12

Dumfries

In June 2012, puddles in the degenerate concrete reflect mature trees – hornbeam, hazel, horse chestnut and sycamore. They were not even seedlings when my father was here seventy years ago. A woman in a pink cagoule emerging from the woodland with a Labrador on a lime-green lead stands out against the surrounding grey, and pulls up her hood as she hurries towards her car. Yellow-jacketed men with theodolites record measurements on electronic pads. I have arrived just before the inexorable spread of the industrial estate gobbles up this remaining patch of runway; another piece of history. My dad's history. My history.

This is the piece of southern Scotland where Jim learnt the dark art of bombing. I retrace my steps through the car park and a few yards away the control tower sits amid assorted vintage aircraft, grounded now forever, and carefully maintained by volunteers. Two ladies of indeterminate years are chatting behind the till in the reception hut. They sell entrance tickets, postcards, keyrings with mini spitfires attached. Cheap teddy bears, manufactured in China, wear plastic flying helmets and blue goggles. I pay my senior citizen £4 entrance fee and promise to return to the coffee shop after my visit.

Rain drips from my jacket and it seems like a repeat of the June weather Jim experienced when he arrived here.

*

Thursday 4th June 1942

The glorious month of June came in rather ingloriously with a downpour of rain. After a week at Brighton we arrived here a week ago to start the air-bombers course. We expect to be here twelve weeks, and if we pass we shall get our sergeant's stripes then. I very much want to pass because Pat and I can do with the money the rank will bring, especially now that we have decided to start a family. Besides I am fed up with 'courses' and will be glad of a permanent job. Charles is one of twenty who have come here and I shall be flying with him. I am glad of that.

Despite the rain he was glad to have arrived in Scotland. Brighton had been a mixed blessing for Jim.

I hope I never go to the disposal wing at Brighton again. The station is full of petty restrictions, childishly so, and punishment is liberally doled out for the smallest offence. I came to the conclusion that the mental age of the CO could not have been more than that of a five-year-old, and naturally this childishness was reflected down to the merest corporal. At this station there is a sane attitude to discipline and life looks like being bearable.

The Sussex town had had its compensations, however. Despite the railway station being a temporarily restricted area Pat managed to get through without a permit. She stepped off the London train with a group of airmen returning from a few days' leave. Their conversation had subsided in volume and animation as they travelled through the countryside towards their base. None knew when they would see their loved ones again and, instead of sun, sand and candyfloss, Brighton now presented a reality of cold discipline and training for death.

Pat had worn her grey coat and stuffed her hair into

a matching woollen hat so that she was able to hide in the crowd as it surged past the military police checking permits at the barrier. She straightened a triumphant smile and, anxious not to provoke suspicion, strolled casually through the unlit booking hall, then paused in the spring sunshine to catch glimpses of blue sea between the grey buildings. The clock tower halfway down the hill rose out of its buttresses of sandbags and, below its four faces, giant placards announced that 'England Still Expects You to do Your Duty.' *Well, Jim's doing his all right,* thought Pat as she continued towards the seafront.

In the Star and Garter the desk in the lobby was deserted save for a small brass bell shaped like a girl in traditional Dutch costume. Pat picked it up and shook it gingerly. When there was no response she rang it harder and longer. Through the open door of the bar, walls and ceiling browned by nicotine, pre-lunch drinkers were quaffing their pints. In the main they were middle-aged and old men wearing suits with waistcoats, while some were in long brown coats with flat caps poking from their pockets. Pat saw a few women in the crowd, buxom and heavily made-up, and always hanging on to a man's arm. Although the war had caused so many barriers of etiquette to tumble, she couldn't think of walking in there, a lone woman. On the third urgent ring the wrinkled barman ambled towards her.

'S'pose you're after a room?' His cigarette clung to his bottom lip as he spoke.

'Well, yes. Just for the one night please.'

He held his fag between his forefinger and thumb as a wry smile passed across his face. She had carefully removed her left glove and laid her hand on the desk.

'Only got a small room left but it's got a double bed. The bathroom's down the corridor and I'll need payment in advance.' A flush of indignation crept up her neck at the suspicion of a leer on the old man's face. *How dare he?* she thought. I am absolutely and legally married. Avoiding eye contact, she opened her purse, counted out five shillings into his hand, and picked up the key to room 4.

Although Jim had been unable to get a 'sleep out' and had to spend the night in his billet at the requisitioned Metropole Hotel, the double bed did not remain unused.

We had a beautiful weekend and were happy as we always are together. She brought good news. Bill Mills is safe. The American Ambassador to Vichy, France has wired his mother to say that Bill is safe and well and interned at Lyons. It has made me glad. Len must have been jubilant.

My mother has mixed memories of that weekend. 'There were rolls of barbed wire all along the beach and the central sections of both piers had been dismantled in case of enemy landings, but we ignored all that; it was so lovely just to be together and strolling along the seafront. The war could have been on another planet, when suddenly Jim bundled me into a doorway, almost imprisoning me in the corner. "Jim, whatever's the matter?" I mumbled into his shoulder. I thought he had gone mad.'

'Don't move.' His snapped command was severe, professional. A second later she heard a screaming German engine in the sky and a strafe of bullets peppered the pavement where they had been walking. She had heard nothing but already his ear was attuned to danger.

They had planned to spend Whitsun together but a few days later he was sent to Scotland and it would be weeks until he saw her again, but at least that was better than spending months three thousand miles away in Canada on pilot training.

Soon after the downpour that greeted Jim's arrival in Scotland, the weather changed and it began to pour sunshine. He writes that a sunny day makes killing even more incredible.

Thursday 4th June 1942

One thinks, how can there be war on a beautiful day such as this? The birds sing, the hills in the distance look magnificently peaceful, the blue, white-flecked sky spells peace until an aeroplane appears and the air is filled with the song of war. In the distance the stutter of a machine gun on the range helps the awful chorus of the engines. On Saturday night the chorus was over Cologne. Innocent children done to death because the Nazis must be beaten. And on Sunday night another thousand-bomber raid over Essen. My German friends the Doppelbauers, of Hagen, must have spent a sleepless night.

He was embarking on an air-bombers course. Previously the observer had done the bombing but now that job was to be divided on the big four-engine bombers.

Oh to what depths have I descended! Once an out and out pacifist – now a bomber! But I suppose it is necessary. The war must be won. Somebody must do the dirty work. Who is responsible? The government that gives the orders, the workers who build the aircraft, the pilot that flies it, the observer who navigates, or the bomber who presses the button? Who dares say? All are in this war from the farmer to the airman. All must share equally the responsibility of shedding blood. Oh Lord, forgive me, for I KNOW what I do…

There is no consolation. If anyone will do their damnedest to see that only military objectives are hit, that will be ME. At least I have scruples enough left to reject all idea of letting the bombs fall any place. The blood of German workers will not be on my hands if I can possibly help it.

Service life was awful. Never before had he realised so well the benefits of home, friends, fires, armchairs, wife and family.

Sometimes, to my twenty-first-century ears, he seems impossibly high-minded and righteous, this unworldly, twenty-year-old idealist.

> In the services one just cannot study seriously. One is isolated from all that is beautiful. Life is very ugly. Sex, sex, sex… from morning 'til night there is hardly any other topic of conversation. Thank goodness I can have interesting conversations with Charles.
>
> After we had seen the film 'Mayerling' Charles said, 'You know I may be wrong about love. Those two died rather than be separated. The Duke of Windsor sacrificed a throne for a woman.' Charles, you idiot, of course you are wrong!

Political correctness, however, was unheard of in 1942 and his next entry would probably have raised no eyebrows:

> Charles and I suspect M of homosexual tendencies. He looks vaguely like Mussolini so we call him Benito Homo. When he walks in we say 'Ecce Homosexual.'

I suppose boys were, and always will be, boys but my liberal hackles rise.

> At the end of this course, providing we are successful, we shall be sergeants or pilot officers. After that a week's leave and then on to OTU. A few weeks at OTU and then on to 'ops'. It seems an incredibly short time. To think that one day next September I may be bombing a German factory, or sending a bullet into a ME-IIO! To think that one day next September I may be in the charred wreckage of a Stirling bomber somewhere in Europe! Or maybe I will have failed the course and be alive and safe for the duration by taking a ground job. And yet I want to pass. From my own point of

view I personally have everything to lose if I pass. And yet I want to. Heydrich, the Nazi terrorist of Czechoslovakia, has been shot by Czech patriots. Maybe that is the reason I want to pass.

*

Most of the buildings are gone now. The living quarters, the training sheds, the mess, the guardhouse. In the distance the last remaining hangar now serves as a store. For what? Wood? Fertilizer? Chinese imports? Certainly not aircraft. Next to the modest fire station, which now houses the visitor loos, the brick control tower sits unchanged; a three-storey bulwark against an unseen enemy.

I mount the stairs, freshly painted in wartime green and red, and watch the ghosts of my father and Charles stamp the ends of cigarettes underfoot in front of me en route to the operations room. The WAAFs, their fingers poised over the typewriter keys or plugging into radios and studying European maps, are petrified dummies. For Charles and Jim they were real, warm – essential to their safety. Perhaps Jim sneaked a look at the blackboard detailing last night's aircraft movements. In today's mock-up ten flights are listed with aircraft number, pilot and number of crew, time of take off, expected time of return, time down, and a column for remarks. DJ-564 had a useless radio but landed safely, although later than expected; DJ-548 landed on time despite heavy wind and rain; N-564 had diverted to another airfield because of engine failure and done a belly flop landing without casualties.

DJ-575 with Sgt. Woolley and four crew, which was due back at 08.00 hours, simply has 'missing – crashed' chalked in the final column. Later these transient details would have been rubbed out to make way for the record of another night of war and death.

*

Jim felt the familiar churn of conscience, the ache of indecision, and late one night after hours of teetering on the edge of troubled sleep, he gave up the struggle and took out his pen and notebook, and by dim torchlight wrote out his anxiety that the war would change nothing.

> Can it be that all will have been in vain,
> Can it be that afterwards profit and gain
> Will still retain their pride of place,
> And the soldier's bloody face
> Will be white with misery and pain.
> Can it be there will be no new world,
> Can it be that the old will decompose like corpses on the
> Eastern Front,
> Can it be that death has come to stay,
> Can it be that the play
> Has reached the last scene of the last act.
> Can it be that the earth has crashed?

On the other side of the page he writes:

> We do not ask for much.
> All we ask is a woman's touch
> And the affection of a child's lips.

The next morning he re-reads it and comments:

> Yes, I know it's not poetry. But sometimes it helps if I express
> my feelings in a few lines of pseudo poetry. I am no poet, but
> it affords me some satisfaction if I can write a few irregular
> lines that a more literary man might make into poetry.

I think it is poetic, Dad, and I press my lips to the yellowing page in a proxy kiss. When he was younger, he says, he knew what was good and what was evil; knew instinctively whether he was doing good or bad, but as he grows older the boundary becomes hazy. He is aware he is training for destruction, knowing full well that in destroying wickedness he will also destroy innocence. Is that good or bad? Who could say? He had always believed it better that the guilty should escape rather than the innocent die. What was the answer now? He knows he will go on supporting the fight against Nazism, but where does good end and evil begin?

Thursday 4th June (contd.)
Thou shalt not kill. Yes, but also, Thou shalt not let evil tramp the world, destroying good. When I was a pacifist the issue was clear. Now that I intend to fight in the war evil and good become inextricably mingled and walk hand in hand. I shall kill the innocent. I shall kill little ones that had no part in this war. I pray with all my heart that their sacrifice may not be in vain. They, as much as the anti-Nazi soldiers, die for the creation of a new world of social and economic justice. They die that my children may laugh and be carefree. Little ones of all countries who may die in this war, I salute you and feel very, very humble.

He was thinking, too, of his old friends from the Peace Pledge Union and the Independent Labour Party. Tilling, Lockyer and Rose were suffering for what they ardently believed to be right, each serving a year in prison because they objected to the war. And now Harry Phippen, the man Jim had so admired at the meetings in the Southend Crescent Scout hut, also awaited his sentence.

Friday 5th June 1942
They suffer for liberty's sake. This is a great sacrifice – imprisonment and scorn; and after the war where will they

find employment? Victimisation, revilement, the lonely cell, these they endure for conscience sake. And their counterparts in Europe – shot, tortured, enduring the horrors of the concentration camp. Who dare criticise the objector when he knows the true facts? Long live the objectors, for they keep alive the ideals and ethics that are lost in the heat of battle. May they have the strength to endure the storms and strains they undergo. May their faith be fortified and may the world recognize their heroism in the days to come. None are more anti-fascist than the pacifists. None who know them can believe the lies of the press. They are the fighters of peace. These are men and women of vision. I cannot agree with them but I salute them and give them all honour.

He received a letter from Pat:

As we expected, Phippen has been sentenced to a year. When Mum has finished with The Kentish I will send you the cutting. There is quite a good bit about it. Apparently after seven days in Brixton he complained to the magistrate of the state of the cells. He said 22 hours of the day were spent in solitary confinement, when he had to lay on a mattress ridden with bed bugs. He made a complaint to the warder and the mattress was changed but the cell was still alive with vermin. Isn't that disgusting in these so-called civilized times?

*

I am intrigued to know how my dad's days were filled, but he tells me very little; I suspect because when he took out his pen and diary he wished to focus on more palatable subjects. Yet, he must have felt a tingle of dread or excitement as he learned how and when to press the button. He would be obeying orders from on high; literally from on high. The bomb-master would be flying above the main group of planes and, when he judged the moment was right, would give the order to all the wireless operators. They would relay it to the bomb-aimers, who would press the release as soon as the target was in their sights. Obey orders. That is how war works. If individual servicemen made their own decisions it would mean mayhem and certain defeat. Did Jim feel less responsible by merely following orders? Or, now that he was an intrinsic part of a professional crew, was he able to focus on the immediate task, leaving emotion and ethics aside?

Dumfries was a training station but death still sat on its doorstep. Jim tells of two craft from the aerodrome crashing on the 5th June. One was a visiting Fleet Air Arm Swordfish. The wing fell off and the plane is said to have driven itself fourteen feet into the ground with the loss of three lives. Good fortune flew with the second – an Anson used for the Observer Training Force. It landed on the beach and the occupants escaped unhurt.

Saturday 6th June 1942

At last a day off! It is three weeks since I had one and I was beginning to feel the effects.

This morning I arose late – ten o'clock – the latest I have got up since joining the RAF, except, of course, when at home! It is pleasant to awake and think, 'No work today,' and turn over and fall asleep again.

I recognize that feeling. After researching and imagining a world so distant from mine, I read this and feel a close, human connection with my dad.

Jim describes how he and Charles enjoyed their first visit to the town of Dumfries. They sensed a friendliness about the place, so different from cold Aberystwyth and desolate Ansty.

'Blimey, it's hot!'

'Even at breakfast this morning I was perspiring,' Charles agreed as they crossed the old bridge into the town accompanied by a horse pulling a cart of vegetables, which was overtaken by a sole black Ford travelling at all of twenty miles an hour.

Sweat coursed down the runnels of Jim's lean face and he fumbled in his battledress for a handkerchief to wipe it away. 'Uniforms are definitely not the things for warm weather.' He loosened the top button under his tie and longed for an open-necked shirt and a pair of shorts.

*

Seventy years later I risk my life on the narrow pavement crossing the same historic bridge. The morning rain has abated but the heatwave my dad experienced is missing. A speeding juggernaut, with Warsaw inscribed on its side, forces me to press my back to the wall. Multi-coloured vehicles speed by; music blaring from some, well-dressed mothers with children strapped into safety seats in others. What would Jim and Charles have made of it all?

When I follow their route along the banks of the River Nith I am a solitary walker. I pause, but after the rain I do not risk sitting on the grass as they did when they…

> …spent the afternoon watching the rowing boats float quietly by, and idly listening to the cries of swimmers. We saw some urchins in a home-made boat. As the water leaked in one little kid was furiously baling it out again with an old tin can and crying, 'You'd better fetch a f— rescue party.'

He describes a boy going to intricate convolutions to cover his modesty as he changed, watched by a gaggle of giggling girls. Some of the swimmers were old men but most were children. Where were the women? I wonder. Washing the dishes after they had fabricated something approximating to a Sunday lunch from the family rations, I guess, or maybe enjoying a rare hour alone to read the *Sunday People* or *News of the World*. Despite many women working full-time now that so many men had gone to war, cooking, cleaning and kids were still considered female work. A few minutes to sit and be one's self then, was luxury indeed.

Lazing in the sunshine on the riverbank was pleasant, but Jim says he couldn't feel truly happy. He puzzled whether this was because Pat was not with him or because war was on his mind. Despite their closeness he couldn't discuss this with Charles. His friend had never been in love, never been a pacifist. How could he understand?

'C'mon, Charles, let's get going.'

They found a little tea shop run by four or five 'old' women – all over sixty! Jim describes one of them as a lovable old autocrat and recounts her conversation with a potential customer:

> A man came in and asked if there was a seat for him. 'We're fule up,' said she. He asked again. 'Get awae' wi' ye! Don't stand their blockin' te road! Oota ma wae!' The man stood aside to let her pass. 'Och! Did ye no ken wha' I said? Get ye' sel' oota here. Thair's nae rume! Awae wi' ye!' He left with an injured air.
>
> For only 1/6 each we had an excellent tea of fish, bread and butter (loads of butter), scones and buns, together with as much tea as we could drink. Such good value would never be obtained in London.

I too enjoy one of those Scottish high teas, but it costs rather more than the one shilling and sixpence my dad paid for his. Full of scones and Scotch pancakes, I follow in Jim and Charles's footsteps to the place where Robert Burns lived and died. I judge it an attractive, quiet street of red sandstone houses now it has had the 'heritage' treatment; my future father considered it rather poor, but mused that some of the finest literature has been written in the meanest of circumstances. I remember that back bedroom in the humble council house that was his childhood home. Where, as a child, I found his rocking horse, Tipperary Tim, stabled in the cupboard. Was this where he dreamed of writing a bestseller?

I agree with his description of the interior of the Burns house.

> The rooms are quite tiny – almost, I feel, as if it had been inhabited by people smaller in stature than the people of nowadays. The bed in which he died looks small, too, in keeping with the size of the room; and his study, little more than a very large closet seems incapable of inspiring song – yet in that confined space he wrote over a hundred.

Like him, I find the exhibits a little dry, but he was amused by the one letter Robbie wrote to his wife, Bonnie Jean, which began, 'My dearest love,' but, peculiarly, ended, 'I am, Madam, your humble servant, Robert Burns.' Yes, my dad was right when he commented that 'it may have been common to the times but it does sound a little formal to a wife.' But perhaps he didn't know the great Robbie also had a lover…

I am in tune also, with his opinion of the poet's work.

> He could write a pretty song but not great poetry. Or maybe one must be a Scot to appreciate it, most of his lines being in Scotch. And, too, he is essentially a NATIONAL poet, and are national poets ever really great?

Food for a literary debate there. My dad loved books, so do I. He had ambitions to write, so do I. How I regret all those discussions, debates and arguments we might have enjoyed.

On their way home they paused outside a shop window to look at a display of pictures of Scottish soldiers in the Great War. A little man approached, bent and possibly cross-eyed (anyway his eyes were very peculiar). His jaw was covered in a three-day growth of stubble and when he spoke he revealed a single tobacco-stained tooth.

> 'I was thair,' he said, pointing to a picture taken at Bethune. 'And thair.' Pointing to one of Arras, and proceeding to talk volubly in unintelligible Scotch about the pictures, moving his dirty forefinger from figure to figure, saying 'that's Haig,' and a little later, 'No, it's King George.' He had spent eight months in a German prison camp. 'These stories ye hear aboot Gairmans killing women and children in Russia, they're true ye know, we saw them in the last war. The Gairman is no' a clean fighter. They're dairty fighters. Aye dairty! When you boys go over Berlin, do na leave a house standin'.' I kept my silence but Charles, who believes in mass bombing as a means of winning the war, said, 'We'll do our best.'

I feel his inner turmoil, so I am not surprised to turn the page and read the next entry in his diary.

Tuesday 9th June 1942

I remember a leafy path in a German stadt garten. I remember Marie and I talking seriously of the coming war that came not many days later. I remember I said, 'Whatever happens, you are my friend, your family are my friends, the German people are my friends; and whatever I think of the National Socialist policy, nothing will induce me to drop bombs on this lovely land and charming people. For no cause will I kill people I like, or destroy buildings that are beautiful. You cannot bring peace by going to war. Killing will not bring you peace – only misery upon misery to all the world. I promise you I shall never drop bombs on Germany...'

Then he adds, and I can picture the look of self-disgust on his face:

Comment: 1393160 Gaywood S.J. LAC. u/t *Air Bomber.*

He describes his first flights since his transfer to Dumfries. Charles is his flying partner and it feels good to be in the air again. They had about an hour in a Battle aircraft and then an hour after lunch in an Anson. Poor Charles and three or four others suffered from air-sickness, but Jim was fine. Then he mentions that on the same day an Anson pancaked down, smashing the undercarriage. No comment on the fate of the crew, who he must have known. Maybe it was his stiff upper lip trying to subdue emotion, to look disaster in the face and not veer from the path he had set for himself.

I am on his tail again where he and Charles walked along the river to the old ruin of Lincluden College. They walked slowly:

…for the warmth and sunlight and the green, and the sounds, all made walking delightful and not to be hurried.

The path eludes me and persistent rain is once more exploring the inside of my raincoat and sending a clammy stream down my back, so I decide to take the car. The helpful woman in the Tourist Information Centre has given me a map and, after a few wrong turns, I am in a desolate post-war social housing estate. It is June, but there is no evidence of summer colour. A worn patch of communal grass is all there is to remind me that when my father was here this would have been rural pasture.

A bright red umbrella stands out against the grey, sheltering two middle-aged women waiting at a bus stop. I lower down the window and ask for directions. They point back the way I have come telling me to turn left, then take the second, or is it the third right? Anyway, past the shops and the recreation ground, then it's straight on. When I reach the shops I buy a Mars bar in the newsagent's and check. Yes, they were nearly right, just an extra right turn by the school and I am in open country by the river, and see the ruin. I am there.

It is just as he described it; founded, not as a college at all, but as a twelfth-century nunnery. But they were naughty nuns, Jim writes, who didn't know the meaning of their vow of chastity. Consequently the local lord, Archibald the Grim, closed it down and turned it into a college for aspiring clergy. Just prior to the civil war it became a private dwelling house, was badly damaged during the time of Charles the First and abandoned forever. Not much remains – just a few ruined walls and a pile of stone. Jim says:

> I wonder what those nuns would think if they could revisit
> their pleasantly situated home. What would they think of
> the aeroplanes roaring over the quietness, destroying the
> peaceful beauty. Mad, mad, mad…

I say: no heavy bombers now, but what would Jim think of the noisy line of speeding traffic on the A75 over there beyond the gentle river? Mad, mad, mad…

He was in an ethical 'no man's land' again. The war of attrition with his conscience rumbled on. Retreat was still possible – to a ground job or to regroup with his pacifist friends; or to go forward to the line and fight on. If he chose the latter course, what was he fighting for? His socialist soul was there still, like itching powder down his back.

Sunday 21st June 1942
We do much flying these days – sometimes three flights each day. Bombing, gunnery – what awful trades! What NEGATIVE work! Preventing worse evil, not doing positive

good… 'We fight for the old country,' says Revd. Elliot in the Sunday Graphic. Not on your life, Reverend! Eighty per cent of us are fighting for socialism.

Beating the Nazis is only the first stage…afterwards there will be another war – the war at home, the war for the establishment of socialism.

Eighty per cent was probably an estimate based on youthful idealism, but perhaps, in this twenty-first century of materialism and greed, we forget how many young people between the wars aspired to an unselfish, egalitarian world.

It hasn't happened, Dad. Man is an independent creature and the flame of communism, which burned so brightly in many parts of the world in the second half of the twentieth century (at the cost of millions of blighted lives and stunted talents), is all but extinguished. Once again those countries rejoice in capitalism.

A sense of humour must have been essential to Jim's sanity and I fancy I can see his mouth twitching, his eyes crinkling at the corners as he writes:

Anecdote: In bombing one must give the pilot 'corrections' in order to get the target in the sights. The bomb aimer says 'left, left,' or 'r-i-g-h-t' or 'steady'. One of the fellows on the course was with a Polish pilot. 'R-i-g-h-t,' said the bomb-aimer. Replied the Pole, 'You all right? I am all right too. Everything is fine.'

Pat was his rock, a precious thread connecting him to real life and a hoped-for future. He lived for her daily letters which were:

Full of love and hope and dreams. Much she writes of the children we shall one day have. Life is lovely when I think only of Pat. With her, ugliness is no longer ugliness, beauty brings a lump to my throat. I long to see her again…

On another foray into town he and Charles stopped outside a house to admire a jolly baby in a pram. It grinned at them and appeared to regard everything as a huge joke. Jim's thoughts turned to the baby Pat dreamed of. The child's mother came out and Charles said:

'What a fine fellow he is.'

'It's no' a boy, it's a gairl.'

'Wrong again!' said Charles as we all laughed. Later he remarked, 'I love living things. Anything that lives, I love. If I had the money I would fill my house with living things – dogs, cats, birds and all manner of creepy crawlies. But NOT babies.'

I replied, 'I was just thinking how much I'd LIKE babies.'

'What! To fill a house? What would your wife say to that!'

'Two babies can fill a house, you know,' I remarked.

There are few things Charles and I agree on. Only that socialism is necessary, and we disagree on methods about that. He is prepared to sacrifice all liberty as long as there is a socialist economy. I am more idealist, I fear…

World events did not often feature in Jim's diary. He said he wished only to write of essential, personal things, but he couldn't resist mentioning the horrible revenge the Nazis took for the murder of Heydrich, the Nazi terrorist shot by Czech patriots. The entire male population of Lidice, a Czechoslovakian village, were done to death in a reprisal.

Monday 22nd June 1942

Daily in occupied Europe the most sickening crimes are committed in the name of the German State. There can be no doubt…the Nazis must be smashed, ridiculed, reviled, and to individuals just punishment must be meted out.

Oh! What suffering there must be in Europe today; anguished souls, starved bodies, torture, death… We in Britain have not yet known suffering… In Greece hundreds die daily for sheer want of food… Famine, pestilence, oppression are like a great sore on the body of prostrate Europe… The British wonder why we suffer so many defeats. Give us a cause! Give us something positive to fight for!

Wasn't stamping out the anguish, starvation, pestilence and oppression a positive reason to fight? Or was the shining goal of socialism a greater prize?

On 23rd June, Jim received a letter to gladden his heart. His brother Len's friend, Bill Mills, had returned home after being shot down in France, and Jim's pacifist compatriot Charles Lockyer was free again. How each of them did it Jim could not imagine but, oh boy, did he feel bucked! He waited impatiently for Pat to furnish the full details of their adventures, although apparently Bill had not handed out much gen. His story came in a letter from Len, now seventeen, still working on the farm and counting the days until his birthday when he would be eligible for service.

Here is as much of the story as he (Bill) is allowed to tell. They went on a sweep and met some Jerries. Bill dived after one and then one got on his tail, and as he squirted his man the other one shot him in the engine. He crash-landed about five miles inside the coast of Northern France. He wasn't hurt so he bunked up and hid for the night.

Then, walking by night and hiding by day, he walked through to South France. For a week he lived on Horlicks tablets and bread. The people in France are really starving but he got food and money and clothes from anybody he asked. In South France he met up with a party of Frenchmen and two British prisoners of war. A guide took them to the Pyrenees Mountains by night. Then they travelled through Spain by train. From there he got to Gibraltar and then home. The trip has taken since March.

Glad you like flying. Bill told me a lot about it. You know, I feel awfully out of it. You and Bill flying and all that… I wish I could go to sea or fly or something. If I can work as hard as a man, why the hell can't I fight like a man?

I can't understand why you have so suddenly changed your attitude to the Germans or Nazis as you prefer to call them. Either you were completely potty when you were a pacifist or you are now…

(Len misunderstands. My attitude has not changed. Only my conception of the best method of combating Nazism has changed.)

In Eltham, the civilian population soldiered on in their stoical way. From Monday to Saturday, Sam took the early tram to Woolwich, laboured all day making weapons of war in the Arsenal, and arrived home expecting his dinner on the table – but not before a stop or two at the Greyhound or the Welcome Inn.

Six mornings out of seven Pat walked up the hill from her in-laws' home and turned left into Prince John Road, passing her parents' house on her way to the station to board the 8.15 to the city and her secretarial post in Leadenhall Street. As the claims for war damage dropped ceaselessly onto her desk, her knowledge of the insurance business grew. So that when the grapevine delivered news of a more senior vacancy, where she would have her own personal short-hand typist, she applied, was interviewed, and the job was hers.

'More money for our future home – the salary is sixty pounds a year!' she wrote to Jim. Her monthly rail ticket cost

£1 5s 9d – £1.30 in today's coinage. Travel was less stressful than in the worst of the Blitz, but one evening, after a long day, she was ambling down the hill from the station. A sudden burst of anti-aircraft fire cracked the still summer air, causing her to dive automatically into the nearest stretch of privet hedge for cover. *Thank God I am not wearing nylons*, she thought as she removed her gloves to rub the scratches on her bare calves, carefully avoiding the 'seams' she had painted on them that morning. After the gunfire silence filled the air, but then she heard footsteps approaching her hedge-nest and a male voice, quivering with embarrassment, enquired, 'I say, are you all right in there?'

The cessation of the tap-tap-tap of her shoes on the pavement had alarmed the commuter twenty yards ahead of her, and chivalry still being alive, if not kicking, he had retraced his steps to check on her welfare.

Still smiling, she met her mother-in-law stepping heavily off the tram from Bermondsey and regaled her with the story.

'It couldn't have been a raid, dear, there were no sirens.' The older woman dismissed the idea as they turned in to the gate, then unlocked the back door. 'Len's coming home this evening, and look, I've managed to get a knuckle of bacon for tea.' She pulled a small greaseproof parcel from her bag.

'Your hands are getting worse, Mum.' Pat took Cis's fingers in her own.

'I know, and just look at my hair.' She put the bacon on the table, removed her green felt hat, re-pinned a prized pearl-tipped hatpin to it, and touched her yellow-tinged forelock with rough fingers the colour of ripe lemons. 'We're all the same – it's the sulphur we stuff into the bombs with the cordite. The boss calls us a bunch of canaries. Oh my God, here it comes!'

A deafening noise sent them diving under the table; two heads protected, two rear ends protruding. Pat's slim, clad in a narrow blue skirt, alongside Cis's prodigious posterior buried under layers of clothing: a brown coat, a factory overall, a dress of thin blue rayon striped with green and a pastel petticoat, all piled in disarray atop a mountain of pink flannel bloomers. This was how a mirthful Len found them when he opened the back door and announced that the explosion had been the sound of a tram and a coal lorry coming to grief in the road outside.

13

In Search of a Philosophy

It seems inconceivable, almost heresy, looking back over three-quarters of a century with the benefit of hindsight, that when Jim was writing his diary, Churchill, now thought to be possibly the greatest war leader Britain has ever had, was regarded by many with suspicion, if not derision. *The Daily Herald* suggested a first class crisis was brewing and hinted at the fall of the government. Writing after the fall of Tobruk to the Axis in the North Africa Campaign, Jim says:

Thursday 23rd June 1942

In my opinion, Churchill is supported by a baseless legend. The press, films, radio, have woven a totally inaccurate picture of this oratorical incompetent. Britain has been losing the war steadily since the beginning and Churchill has done no more than any other man could have done. I have never had a good word to say for him and now my opinions (unfortunately) are turning out to be true. The people no longer have faith in this man. He stays where he is only because there appears to be no answer to – 'Who could take his place?'

Inferior tanks, guns, aircraft, generalship are all blamed for the catastrophe in the Middle East. Doubtless they were partly to blame, but why do we retreat so ignominiously and with such haste? The Russians hold on to the last – witness the siege of Sevastopol. Why? Because they have something to fight FOR! They have an enthusiasm for the war;

a terrible determination to win against all the odds. But the British are a nation of scroungers. Industry, the services, the government, are all rotten with an 'I'll look after myself' attitude. There is no feeling that we are fighting for a cause. And, as a nation, we are NOT! The nation as a whole has no lead, no indication from the government that we are fighting anything but a war of self-preservation. That is not sufficient. A cause, a great worthwhile cause, is needed before victory can ever be said to be on the way.

What an angry young man. A nation of scroungers; it sounds like a quote from the twenty-first century *Daily Mail* – surely not the chosen newspaper of a committed socialist.

Jim knew the war in the first half of 1942 had not gone well for the Allies. Singapore had fallen, the North Africa campaign was in tatters. As one of the disgruntled electorate at home, Jim cheered when John Wardlaw-Milne, a maverick Conservative MP, proposed a motion in the House of Commons:

'That this house, whilst paying tribute to the heroism and endurance of the armed forces of the Crown in circumstances of exceptional difficulty, has no confidence in the central direction of the war.'

The proposal was seconded by Aneurin Bevan, later to become known as the father of the National Health Service. Jim admired Nye, as he was known, for holding radical socialist views close to his own and vents his frustration at the defeat of the motion in his diary:

Friday 3rd July 1942
After a two-day debate on a 'no confidence' motion Churchill yesterday obtained 475 votes against 25 in the Commons. Once again that incompetent fool has made a wily, cunning

speech that has the effect of saying that after all, we are still in a good position to win.

The press today hails Nye's speech as one of the finest expositions against the government for a long time. As Bevan said, the services are riddled with class prejudice.

Churchill, in spite of his victory in the Commons, now stands lower than ever in the eyes of the people. Surely we are not going to tolerate him much longer? Surely if Alexandria falls we shall give him no more opportunities for losing more battles?

We need a cause, a people's war, a people's government.

Ten days later Jim managed to get home to celebrate Pat's twenty-first birthday. They stole upstairs to examine their wedding gifts and everything they had since accumulated as the beginnings of their future home. Mum tells me how they hugged each other as they looked forward to a future when they would drink tea from the bone china cups decorated with a wide pink band edged with gold. They laughed as they pictured Pat up to her elbows in suds, making use of the box of Reckitt's blue-bags and the thick ribbed glass of the washboard, wedding presents from her practical granny.

Jim felt civilised, normal, human again. Going home accentuated the craziness of service life. When he returned to Scotland he was lonely for Pat and shuddered to think what life would be without her.

She is as necessary to my soul as food is to my body. What fools that insist love is only physical. It is more than that. It is more than a union of bodies, it is the union of hearts and minds and souls. Love is also comradeship.

The thought of time off was always uppermost in my dad's mind and he decided that for his next leave Pat would join him in Scotland. They would have a proper honeymoon in

Helensburgh. For a few days they would turn their backs on a troubled world and find peace and happiness together.

On 5th August, Jim records that he has been busy – and successful – with exams. He was one of six recommended to be instructors and he wondered how he would take to the role. It was tempting in many ways, and he speculated that he and Pat could get a flat so that he could 'sleep out'. And yet he felt a little ashamed – so many were dying. But, he asked himself, why did he think so? Instructors were as necessary as bullets. They were doing an essential job. 'No,' Jim decided, 'I will stay in aircrew.'

Maybe these thoughts led him to Russia again, where things were very bad.

Tuesday 4th August 1942

The Germans are smashing their way through, getting nearer and nearer to the Caucasus. Is it possible that the USSR may even sue for peace? Russian streets run with blood, many children die, her industries are captured. How long can a nation stand it? Even valiant Russia?

Where is the world going? Is mankind really marching to extinction? Will man destroy himself?

I ask myself the same question daily, Dad. It is not only the suffering that man continues to inflict on his fellow man, or the conflicts that occur endlessly in this world, that make me ask that question. It is also that, through man's greed for power, he is destroying the very planet that gives him life. My hope is that his common sense will recognize it and his ingenuity will find a way to turn back from the abyss.

Hope is a persistent human emotion. Even when buried under apparently insurmountable odds, it continually reignites with the slightest puff of oxygen. Sometimes, Jim felt an inexplicable optimism burning within him, a feeling that out of the bloody struggle would arise, phoenix-like, a new world. Maybe, after all, the war would be the birth pangs of a loftier civilisation.

He remembers his Scoutmaster, Leslie Duerr, saying, 'Man is hard to teach and must go through a terrible experience before he will exert himself and wholeheartedly attempt to make his relations peaceful. Man learns through torment and suffering.'

Jim comments that man suffered plenty in the last Great War but learnt little.

Wednesday 5th August 1942

Death stalks the earth – mechanized death, death on wheels, death with wings, floating death. The world is a charnel house. Corpses litter the fields and decay in the sunshine. The innocent and the guilty – all are paying the price. I glance at a newspaper on the floor. Two words stand out – FOR WHAT?

The boys went to a dance at the Airmen's Club in Dumfries. Jim stood at the bar with Charles, watching as ballroom dances alternated with Scottish reels. The waltzes he found nauseating. The couples slithered around the floor, clinging to each other, looking vulgar and sexy. But the reels! Couples whirled with arms flying, shouting, yelling, screaming with enjoyment. Round and round they spun, changing partners almost every second. It seemed the music would go on forever; it seemed the dancers would go on forever, their joyful laughter piercing the air. A beery-looking man in a battledress from south of the border was laughing and, every few seconds, he shook his head saying, 'Bloody mad, bloody mad.' Perhaps it was mad but Jim was loving it.

What a pity the English folk dance is dead. If the primitive is jolly, then for God's sake let us be primitive. Not even this terrible war can kill the dance. It is fundamental to man. He will dance though the earth is cracking.

In 1942 the earth was cracking, but it had not quite fallen apart.

*

Following my father around Dumfries has been exciting, satisfying. I am disappointed then, to find that the King's Arms Hotel, where they held an end of course celebration, has been replaced by a brutal 1960s block of shabby shops, bereft of customers, and with peeling window stickers announcing their imminent closure.

The site was lively and fun in 1942, and I am happy for Jim as I read his account of the party. After a meal there was the usual singing, storytelling, etc. All the speakers patted each other on the back and the drink flowed freely, engendering much merriment.

Tuesday 11th August 1942

As is usual at RAF functions of this nature, most of the stories and songs were indecent. People do not laugh at them for their indecency, but rather for their ingenuity.

Coming home on the bus we sang continually, roaring lustily until our throats were sore.

Before they'd set out there had been a discussion in the mess about the situation in India. The papers had been reporting on the long-simmering dissent that led to Gandhi's call for passive resistance to the British. Now he and Nehru had been arrested and imprisoned and riots were erupting in Indian cities. Jim was scandalised that the Congress party had been declared illegal. Back at base after their riotous evening the boys continued the argument.

One a.m. found me in the billet fervently advocating the Congress cause. Half a dozen of us were at it hammer and tongs. Charles is wholeheartedly anti-Congress on the present issue, and I found myself literally coming to grips with him!

Monaghan sided with me even though he was drunk. Parker, who rarely comments on anything, said we should concentrate on winning this war before we think about bloody India. On the whole I enjoyed the evening and was quite sober. Well, not quite, but at least my head was clear. I felt merry and talkative, that's all. I have never been drunk. I suppose I ought to try it one day. Just for the experience...

Despite the alcohol his sense of injustice made for a restless night so that before dawn he wrote by torchlight:

Congress doesn't want the British so the British must arrest the Congress leaders without further ado.

Ah! Dear Britain! Free the Czechs, the Poles, the French, the Danes. The Norwegians, the Dutch, the Belgians, free them from foreign rule! But, dear Britain, don't free the Indians. That would never do. 'We have mills in Bombay, doing very nicely thank you! Calcutta is a growing centre of industry! Free India? Oh my goodness, no! Don't you see we must protect her from that bloodthirsty monster, Gandhi? And Nehru? The man is a socialist! A socialist as a responsible Indian cabinet minister? Unheard of! Preposterous! Madness!'

Jim the internationalist was not to be confined by events in Europe; his concern was justice for all.

The next page of writing makes me prickle. Jim's view of women in society horrifies me.

He was in the Airmen's Club drinking tea at the same table as some WAAFs and other airmen.

Saturday 15th August 1942

The WAAFs were telling stories – not just smutty, but dirty stories. I mention this because I regard the enlistment of women into the services as one of the worst evils of this war. In civvy life the various types would seldom meet. The girl with the dirty mouth would tell her stories to other girls with dirty mouths. But in the services they are all lumped together with the result that the normal, decent girl finds herself imitating her shameless sister. There is nothing more horrible than to hear a woman relating a 'joke' about sex and making pointed remarks in her conversation. It is all the more distressing when they talk in mixed company.

It is all too apparent that service conditions lead to a moral laxity that is very alarming. Too often one hears that such and such a WAAF has been with so and so, and so and so, and so and so.

How terrible it is that a girl from a decent home with a normal moral outlook should be conscripted into a life where such immorality is taken for granted! She will learn a large vocabulary of the most distasteful oaths in no time. Men still prefer to cherish ideals about women, modesty among them. But service women have the attitude of amateur prostitutes – and few men like it.

He tries to redeem himself when he says he fears he generalizes too much. He is not condemning all women in the services, but a tendency of some towards immorality that is going to be a terrible thing in the life of the nation. In the next paragraph he describes the attitude of those women as asking to be treated as whores.

Oh no! Can this really be my father writing? The hero I have always been so proud of? A small asterisk at the end of the sentence corresponds with a similar one at the bottom of the page and my rage abates slightly when he comments, *This was nasty and unjustified.* He says he is no prude; prides himself on having a broad outlook on relations between man and woman.

Hmm… Women are human beings, Dad, not dolls or

sex objects! And I thought you were against prejudice. In 2014, gender discrimination is at the forefront of political correctness but women still fight for full equality with men. Reading your diary, however, reminds me of how far we have come.

I keep telling myself that you lived in a different era, a different world. I believe you would have changed your view, Dad. You may have found the excesses of the sexual revolution hard to take. You certainly would have disapproved of our first female prime minister, but not on grounds of gender. But surely you would have rejoiced in seeing your daughter, granddaughter and great-granddaughters embrace the opportunities and responsibilities a more equitable world has offered them.

On 17th August, Jim bade farewell to colleagues leaving for Operational Training Units all over the country.

> What can one say when friends and comrades leave? Many of them I shall never see again. Nay, most of them. Perhaps I have looked my last on Charles. Death is very near them now. In a few weeks they will be facing it twice a week. To see them go and not be with them – it hurts. Friends for a few weeks, and then gone, to be seen no more. 'Ships that pass in the night.' But I shall always remember them. Sachs, Leadbetter, James, Wargent, Palmer, Chisholm, Lennon, McCabe, Evans, Fuller, Pottier, Midgley, Monaghan, Williamson, Richards, Lawrence – I shall remember them all. My comrades. A fine bunch. They go to face death. May God have mercy on them.

Together with King and Dando, he was frustrated at the delay in his own posting. After qualifying as air-bombers it was discovered that all three had below average night vision and should never have taken the course. They were now to be deployed as instructors. After enjoying the advantage of seven days' leave and adjusting to the fact that they would not be flying, they were recalled by telegram and told an instructor's life was not, after all, for them. They would be posted to Brighton to await a navigator's course. The coincidence of all three having defective 'owl eyes' seemed too much and they pleaded for another vision test.

With no time to organize a 'honeymoon' in Helensburgh, the date of the leave had been fortuitous – it meant Jim could be at home to celebrate his twenty-first birthday. Pat produced an iced cake with twenty-one candles and presented him with a soft leather writing case. His mum promised him a watch as soon as she could get to Woolwich and his brother Len gave him a book token for twenty-one shillings and sixpence, and a photograph album. Overwhelmed, Jim says he feels he did not express his gratitude adequately.

While at home he made a film, tentatively entitled *The Nine O' Clock News*. Was he still using the borrowed camera, I wonder? It was the first film he had attempted by artificial light and he was eager to see the result. Did he ever see it? He doesn't tell me and when I ask Mum she says she remembers the filming, but not the outcome.

Waiting impatiently for his next posting, he reflected on coming of age.

Monday 31st August 1942

I am legally a man! Of course I feel just the same, but it is gratifying to know that I am responsible to no one but the law, and now I have the doubtful privilege of the vote. Privilege? I mean RIGHT!

Looking back over his minority years he felt that, save for his marriage, they had been a dismal failure. He had made no career for himself; contributed little to the happiness of mankind. Since leaving school, he says, he had begun the task of educating himself. In those five years he had learnt much, and now had sufficient knowledge to form his own opinions and judgments. But he had lost what he had believed to be a lasting, unshakable philosophy for life: the philosophy of pacifism. It had informed his outlook and given him an inner peace and tranquillity. Now all that had gone. He had rejected pacifism and found nothing to take its place. He was lost.

> I have no religion, for my religion was peace and love. I hold firm only to the principle of socialism, but my socialism has lost much by my rejection of pacifism. In the last five years I have followed false creeds, travelled wrong roads and now I am at the beginning of the journey again. I know the creeds, the roads to avoid. And yet…sometimes I cannot suppress the feeling that maybe pacifism IS the right road. Only sometimes. It does not last for long…

The one thing Jim congratulated himself on was his marriage, in which he had found something to make up for his lack of a philosophy. It could only temporarily fill the gap, however, as no man could live without a purpose in life.

Then my father talks to me. He dreads becoming a crabby, narrow-minded man in his middle-age.

> In case I do, and in case my children should ever read this, I say to them: if I ever disapprove of your love affair and oppose your marriage, and if you are truly in love, utterly certain of it; if you feel you love as your parents love, then ignore my foolishness, even if it hurts me. Break with me completely if I am so stupid as to stand in your way. Only this, my dears; be certain of your love, completely certain.

I was certain, Dad – and you would have approved.

14

Russians, Poles and the Big Dipper

Jim sensed his twenty-first birthday had coincided with a crucial point in history. Never before had humanity been so degraded. He cites an article in the *Daily Sketch* on the 29th August about a Russian woman who wore the Order of Lenin and had been wounded four times. She looked more like a student than a sniper who had terrorised the Nazi ranks. Asked how she felt on killing a man for the first time she replied, 'How can a human being feel when killing a poisonous snake?'

I wonder if it was the toll of Miss Pavlichenko's victims that depressed him or because even his esteemed Russia was barbarising the fairer sex?

I am writing as Russia is commemorating the seventieth anniversary of the relief of Leningrad. When my father was writing the people of Britain knew nothing of their Russian allies' suffering. The news blackout in the West was total. Jim would have been ignorant of the horrors being inflicted on the city that had been the cradle of the Russian revolution. Leningrad was besieged for nearly two and a half years. Hitler intended to starve the population into submission and it was said in Germany that he was so confident of success that he had already printed the invitations to the victory celebrations. By the end of the siege more than a million and a half people had died – nearly four thousand perishing on one bitter Christmas Day alone. Beds, chairs, tables, books were burned in cold grates all over the city, the heat from the short-lived flames charring numbed frost-bitten fingers held too close to the fire. When all the cats, dogs and rats had been eaten, leather shoes and belts were boiled to produce a thin, foul-tasting gruel. Stale bread was wrenched from the grasp of the dying in the streets, and rumours abounded about the bodies themselves being eaten.

Had he been aware of the horrors, Jim would have applauded the courage of those who risked their lives attempting to smuggle in meagre supplies; the drivers who sank with their lorries when they were too desperate to wait for the ice on Lake Ladoga to thicken enough to support them.

Disease, starvation, and those who perished attempting to flee the city accounted for unimaginable misery, but Jim would have been proud that the city never gave in; the siege was only lifted after the Germans retreated in the face of the advancing Red Army.

Although he knew nothing of the suffering in Leningrad, the Russian socialist system remained iconic for my father. In his diary he relates with disbelief what his Polish colleagues in the RAF had to say when describing Soviet life.

'When they are seven the children are taken from their parents, who never see them again,' said one man.

Another nodded his head and added, 'There is no home life in USSR; all meals are taken in community feeding centres and workers are likely to be moved from one town to another and cannot take their belongings with them.'

More animated voices joined in. 'The whole of the northern USSR is one vast prison. In Siberia, men work under appalling conditions.'

'And if they prove difficult they're sent to special camps where they are forced to work stark naked in temperatures below zero. Forty-eight million Poles have been transported to Siberia.'

'There are about two million Russians who live well and,

except for the Red Army, the rest of the population is underfed, ill-treated and illiterate.'

Jim refutes such exaggerated tales and dismisses them as:

A natural outcome of a hard-pressed nation at war. The Essential Works Order in Britain has meant a move away from home for many an Englishman. And what about the British Restaurants we have in towns all over Britain serving cheap food? They are little more than community feeding centres.

As for the allegations of Siberian work camps he says:

I must enquire further – but it smells too much of Polish government anti-communist propaganda to be taken seriously. And as for an underfed, ill-treated, illiterate people, the Russians are showing an amazing enthusiasm for the defence of a system allegedly responsible for such conditions. Forty-eight million Poles transported to Siberia? – Well! I feel sure the whole population of Poland was not near that figure.

He was right, the angry Poles were exaggerating; the total population in 1939 was thirty-five million, but history has shown that not all their tales were fiction.

Jim asked about the opening of a second front and the Poles replied, 'You must wait until the Germans have weakened Russia. If you help Russia now she may win, and Europe will become Bolshevik.'

According to my father's diary their war experience explained their misguided thinking.

Some of them fought the Red Army when it marched into Poland, were caught and spent two years in Russian prison camps. When Russia entered the war against Germany they were released and worked in Russia before coming to England. That is their authority for making such statements, but one cannot help but suspect them.

He was shocked that his Polish colleagues, in spite of the humiliation, degradation and suffering imposed on them by the Nazis, seemed to regard the USSR, not Germany, as the main enemy. Their nationalism appalled him too.

Saturday 11th September 1942

Talking to three Poles I asked where they came from. One drew a rough sketch of Poland and marked a spot in the south-west corner near the German frontier. Another said he came from Warsaw, enlarged the map to one of Eastern Europe and proceeded to show me the 'Greater Poland' that will exist after the war! This area included the Polish State of 1939, Lithuania, Latvia, Estonia, Eastern Prussia, Czechoslovakia and a large slice of Western Russia. 'That,' he said, 'is Poland as she will be after the war.' The aspirations of the Sikorski government are well known, but it is disappointing to find an ordinary rank and file airman so aggressively nationalist. One can only hope that these views are not general among the Poles – but I fear otherwise. Altogether I get a picture of a Poland violently nationalist, violently anti-communist.

A pity…the Poles I meet are extremely nice fellows and I like them a lot.

I wince as I read Jim's comments. No wonder poor Poland, squeezed between Germany on the west and Russia on the east, felt the need to assert itself as a sovereign state. The country was writhing under the German jackboot and enduring the extermination of not only its Jewish population, but all its ethnic minorities, its artists, its dissenters, its freethinkers, even those who displayed simple human kindness.

My first son married Malgosia, a girl from Warsaw. I wish my dad had been able to hear her stories.

Like Jim, her grandfather, Jan Budzynski, did not live to see his only child. Warsaw was in Hitler's grip when he obtained a travel warrant to visit his sick father in the country. A fellow traveller later told Jan's pregnant wife what happened on the journey.

'He fell into conversation with a middle-aged lady standing with us in the corridor of the train. A guard pushed through the crowd and demanded his pass. After careful examination it was declared to be in order. The German thrust it back into his hand and turned to the woman. As she fumbled in her bag his eyes fell on her gold watch. "Where is your star?" he snapped. "You are a Jew."

'She stuttered, "N-n-no. I am n-not a Jew, my father was from, was from... Here, see, here are my p-p-papers."

'The official studied the documents which proved she was right. Not wanting to lose face, he said, "You will have your papers and I will have your watch," and he grabbed her wrist. It was then that Jan made his big mistake. He protested and pulled at the guard's sleeve. The German didn't even look at him; he didn't shout. He just signalled to another uniformed man who nodded his head and came to join him. The train was travelling at some speed when they opened the door, took your husband by the arms and threw him out. Then they shut the door and continued along the corridor as if nothing had occurred. I am so sorry, madam, I could do nothing; I knew what my fate would be.'

There were two funerals for Jan. The body parts were found months apart.

*

In Warsaw with Alice, my Anglo-Polish granddaughter, we added to the hundreds of candles illuminating the memorial to the Polish Underground Home Army who rose up against the Nazi oppressors in 1944. On that visit Alice was only nine years old but she knew how the German guns had mown the patriots down and, as I watched her solemn face in the candlelight, I grieved for all those children who died when Himmler ordered that all the inhabitants of Warsaw be killed and the city bombed into oblivion. The Russian army, watching from the opposite bank of the Vistula river, obeyed orders from the high command and offered no assistance to the beleaguered Poles. They stood by and allowed their common enemy to demolish the city and slaughter its people.

'Warsaw was rebuilt,' Malgosia told me as we toured the city, 'but look what the bloody Russians did. They made it ugly, brutal.' My daughter-in-law grew up under communist rule and, like many other young people in the 1980s, could not wait to leave her home country.

'But just wait until we get to the old town, Granny!' Alice was excited. 'The people who came back to the city rebuilt it just as it used to be.' My granddaughter is proud of Warsaw, proud to be half-Polish. She is proud that after fifty years of her mother's country being the prisoner of its neighbours – crushed by Germany, then ground down by Russia – Poland is now free.

I wonder if any of Jim's Polish colleagues lived to see it.

The ideal of communism appeared to Jim to promise a peaceful, equitable society. But it failed. It failed because mankind is not peaceful or equitable.

*

Dumfries was blessed with a good bookshop and Jim was pleased with what his book token bought: *The Complete Verse and Prose of William Blake*, Rousseau's *Social Contract* and *De Quincy's Confessions of an Opium Eater*; all books he had long wanted to own.

The war was about to enter its third year and Jim recalled in his diary the Sunday when his mum was chatting to Mrs Blendell over the backyard fence. In September 1939, Chamberlain had just broadcast to the nation that the country was at war with Germany. Then the sirens began their awful wailing.

Thursday 3rd September 1942

It was three years ago today that I ran out to Mum. 'Listen. Sirens. Air-raid,' I said. She was not in the least alarmed. Unconcernedly she replied, 'It's only a practice'.

Only a practice... Even after the declaration it was difficult to realize that the war we had dreaded so much was now upon us. It just couldn't have happened. It was only a practice...

How often since that Sunday morning have we heard the sirens play the overture to bombs and fire. It's not 'only a practice' now. We have had a bellyful of war. My mother, so unconcerned that first day, has sometimes been near to hysteria.

On the next page he writes about carefree days out to Margate when he was a child; the exhilaration he felt when the car on the big dipper climbed higher and higher, then the terror when it plunged at speed, as if to bury itself and him into the ground. Over the past few years, he says, his life has been like riding a big dipper. There has been the high of holding firmly to his belief in pacifism, the low of rejecting it; the high of learning to fly, the low of a constantly troubling conscience. He reached the height of happiness when he married Pat, and it is not her fault that now he is plunging again. He dreads to think what the future holds; he can envisage nothing but fresh horrors.

The war showed no sign of an end. However, morale was holding up pretty well and if food supplies were moderately sufficient, and if the military situation improved, he thought the British people might be able to take another two or three years of conflict. But what then? Anxious about his friends in the Ruhr valley, he tried to imagine how Germany was coping. The papers were full of propaganda. According to the British government the situation of the enemy was so dire they would capitulate at any moment. Jim knew this to be political bravado.

I think I can hear my future father sighing as he writes about mankind continuing its headlong drive to destruction. This time the metaphor is not a big dipper but a train.

Friday 4th September 1942

The passengers on the train are arguing, disputing, fighting, as the train, with ever gathering speed, rushes towards the abyss. Nobody thinks of stopping and reversing the engine, they are all too busy fighting their neighbours. No. I am wrong. A few want to stop the train but they are locked in the guard's van. I imagine I can see H.G. Wells furiously banging on the window, but no one pays any attention to him. I sometimes feel I too am in the guard's van. Yes, I am there, but silent, weak; making little effort, rousing only to pull faces at the Nazi on the running board…

A couple of days later Jim climbed onto his sexist high horse again and wrote to Sir Kingsley Wood, his MP, and Ernest Bevin, the Minister of Labour, urging them to oppose the conscription of childless wives of serving men:

I would deeply resent my wife being placed willy-nilly into such a life… The atmosphere between the sexes among service personnel is not the sort into which I would wish my wife to be forced… The conscription of single women was bad enough; the conscription of married women will be monstrous.

His despair at where the world was heading wasn't the only reason his spirits were low. He was plagued by writer's block.

> Tuesday 15th September 1942
>
> I cannot write nowadays. It is nearly a year since I came into the RAF and during that time I have written only a short play called '18B'. I have never pretended I could write well, but secretly believed that with practice I could learn to. In civil life, if I felt like writing, I just sat down and wrote… But now – now I cannot write. The effort is too great, ideas for subjects will not come. Is it because the passionate desire to write – what almost amounted to a need – has diminished? Or is it because this life, being so completely alien to me, deadens and frustrates all creative desires? It worries me…

It was the same with reading. He used to read 'difficult' books with pleasure but now he found them hard work and he seemed less capable of assimilating what they had to say.

He shakes himself out of despondency the following week and writes:

> Monday 21st September 1942
>
> Laziness! That has been my trouble! I CAN put pencil to paper and write something approaching a short story; I CAN read a good book and enjoy it. In the last three days I have written a story called 'Flyers are only Human' and read Thomas de Quincy's 'Confessions of an Opium Eater'. Laziness was my trouble. The story I consider a very bad one, but at least I have convinced myself that I still have the will to attempt writing. The truth is I have been making service life an excuse for my own intellectual idleness. From now on I intend to write at regular intervals and any excuse for not doing so can only be

pressure of work. So there, Jim Gaywood! Don't get in a spin about it again. Service life is not conducive to writing but it is no excuse.

'The talk in the mess got round to brothels. Brothels are talked about a great deal among servicemen. It relieves the boredom', Jim writes. He recounts the story told to him by the only man he had met who had been inside one; at least the only one who admitted it. Bill Kierson, a workmate from the Albion Sugar Company, had been working in Montreal and was returning home with friends from a football match. After a good deal of drinking they stopped at a brothel in the town. Dim, rosy light fell on the girls as they sat around, wearing nothing but stockings. There was only one place for the girls to stow their earnings so the men hatched a scheme they thought a huge joke. One man was deputed to stand by the light switch and, at a given signal, the light went off and each man grabbed a wad of notes from the nearest girl's stocking. Away they went, out of the house and down the street followed by the cries of the madam of the establishment. No doubt my sexist father enjoyed telling that story, but I don't enjoy reading it.

Jim and his colleagues, King and Dando, had now waited three weeks for a simple night-vision test, and all that seemed to be holding it up was reams of red tape. The thought of a weekend pass at the end of September cheered him considerably. Pat and he would have an early celebration of their first wedding anniversary. It turned out that they had something much more thrilling to celebrate.

He arrived home in Eltham about seven o'clock on Saturday morning. Pat heard him open the door, ran downstairs and flung herself into his arms, saying, 'We are so glad to see you – both of us!'

'You mean…?'

She nodded and Jim lifted her high in the air and danced her round the kitchen.

'So a child is really on the way this time?'

'Yes, yes…' Her grin was wide, her eyes sparkled.

Jim could hardly believe the news. 'When…?'

'Around the 20th of May.'

He set her down again and she took a breath; tried to be sensible, grown up. 'I've already booked a bed at the British Hospital for Mothers and Babies in Woolwich.'

When he returned to Scotland, Jim confided in his diary that he couldn't find the words to express his feelings. He was proud, happy, overjoyed. He was to be a father. My father.

> Monday 28th September 1942
>
> Pat and I the parents of a child – our very own child – part of us – born of our love. Words cannot describe it. We are the happiest, proudest couple in the world. Never have I been so glad, never so sweetly content. This is glorious! How gladly I accept this responsibility!

Ah, that word – responsibility. It brought him back down to earth. He'd made up his mind that even if there should be a baby he would remain in aircrew. But now a child was definitely on the way it was difficult to be so sure. Supposing Pat and the child were left alone? How would they take care of themselves? Should he take this opportunity to remuster to ground staff? There were, after all, hundreds of single men without responsibilities only too keen to fly.

> Oh, my God…what shall I do? I cannot make up my mind. The war must be won. My child must not suffer. What course should I take? I know what Pat wants. She is hoping I will stop flying. I certainly have no desire to go on 'operations', but

something indefinable holds me back. What right have I to be 'safe'? But then it is not for myself. It is the child that must be considered. Oh dear…what shall I do? What shall I do?

He was still tussling with the problem a week later on 4th October – a year since the wedding. They had spent so little of their marriage together but it had been a beautiful time. Every leave had been a honeymoon. Now all he could think of was Pat and the child. Hundreds of miles separated them, but on their anniversary, knowing she was thinking the same, he felt very close to her.

O humanity! Come to your senses. Cease this bloody fighting! Let families live in peace and contentment; let October 4th 1943 see me reunited with my dear wife and the child that will then have been born. This is a forlorn hope, but I pray that at least I shall still be alive then, that I may spend my second wedding anniversary with my beloved Pat and our child.

The next day he received a telegram:

'Nobby Clark. Prisoner. Safe and well. Fondest love. Pat.'

The emotional big dipper soared towards the sky once more. His dearest friend, the boy he grew up with, the one who could not wait to get a gun in his hand when they surveyed the carnage of the Blitz together, was living, not dead. In a Japanese prison camp, to be sure, but alive! Alive! Alive!

Dear old Nobby will come back again and we will have a drink in the 'Who'd-a-thought-it?' and once again we'll air our views as we used to do. My dear friend has been resurrected from the dead. No cross for him! Relief and joy for his safety!

The euphoria was short-lived. Self-disgust took hold and he quotes a poem he had torn from a page of *Punch* in 1940.

> Walking alone at break of day
> I saw the man I planned to be –
> He beckoned me in a friendly way,
> Then disappeared mysteriously.

> Walking alone in the evening light
> I saw the man I used to be –
> I hailed him with a friend's delight,
> But he cut me most discourteously.

Friday 9th October
We are in a train hurtling along towards a bridge that isn't there.

He was back on the metaphorical train with H.G. Wells heading for the abyss or hurtling to the ground on the big dipper.

15

The Run Up

In the middle of October, Jim was back in Brighton – *blasted Brighton* – with Dando and King, making further efforts to unravel red tape.

Tuesday 13th October 1942

Much money has been spent on training the three of us and if we go on a navigator's course it will all have been wasted. One simple night-vision test might mean the saving of hundreds of pounds – but red tape makes the simple complicated. No wonder we are losing the war! Three trained men fighting the authorities for the right to help win the war! The position is absurd. Navigator or air-bomber I have made up my mind. I shall stay in aircrew.

A few days later they were back at the Aircrew Reception Centre at Lord's where, for Jim, it had all begun a little over a year ago. This was the venue for the long-awaited night-vision test which, as they expected, all three passed. Jim took advantage of a few hours in the capital to spend a couple of them with Pat. He left his colleagues to join the Saturday afternoon amblers in Regent's Park while he retraced the route he had taken so often the previous year, to Charing Cross Station.

He didn't have to wake her in the night this time; she was waiting under the clock in the station. It is said that if one stands there long enough, the whole world will pass by. Pat and Jim were the whole world to each other; for them there was no one else on the crowded concourse.

'Jim suggested tea and cakes in Lyons Corner House,' Mum tells me, 'but I was feeling a bit queasy so we decided on a stroll through St James' Park instead. Jim kept insisting we sit on a bench so I could rest. He seemed to think a pregnant woman was made of Dresden china.'

I can't help but see the irony. Eighteen months later allied bombing smashed not only the china but the city of Dresden itself.

All too soon it was time for Jim to head to Victoria station for the Brighton train. The frequency of their partings made them no easier and now Jim was conscious that he was saying goodbye not to one, but to the two people he loved most in the world.

> Blast the war! Life is just beginning for me. I never wanted to live so much as I do now. If there is a God, a good God (how one doubts it these days), I pray that I may be spared death until my three score years and ten are past. I am too young to die. Pat, my darling, you are my life, my happiness. I don't want to leave you now. Oh Death! I fear and hate you.

It was more than a month until Jim resumed his diary. Now he was Sergeant Gaywood and after six days of leave at home with Pat he arrived at Operation Training Unit, Honeybourne, on 10th November. The course, near Bristol, was expected to last until March when he would proceed to a conversion unit ('four-engine jobs there'), and thence to a squadron of Bomber Command to commence operations.

Bitterly cold weather, unheated Nissen huts and minimal rations resulted in Jim contracting a cold which became a persistent cough. The Medical Officer was concerned and sent him for a chest X-ray. When Jim went for the result the MO asked his colleague to listen to Jim's chest and the two men spent about a quarter of an hour discussing the case out of Jim's hearing. He was alarmed.

Sunday 22nd November 1942

Obviously the MO is thinking of TB, and so am I. Dad had it at the time I was born, as a result of gas in the last war, and also his brother died a few years ago from the dread disease. I do not altogether trust service medics. No, I think that on my next leave I'll go to the TB centre at home (where I've been before) and see what they think of it. With the child coming I must take no risks, and if this thing is liable to affect me (as it is) I must catch it before it has a chance of taking hold of me.

After three weeks of ground school he went on leave for ten glorious days and returned, feeling much better.

Sunday 13th December 1942

My cough having gone a few days before leave, I decided not to go to the TB place. I feel quite sure it was a false alarm, although the MO is still keeping a weight check on me weekly.

I share his relief. I am glad he didn't have the disease. If he had, however, he would not have flown to Germany and I would have known my father.

With TB dismissed, he could concentrate on an exciting prospect ahead. Pat's parents were moving up the social ladder into home ownership so Pat and Jim decided to try to take over the tenancy of the house they were leaving. When they told Sam and Cis of their plan, Jim's mum could not share their excitement. 'But

I thought Pat would stay here until you came back to civvy street.' She had enjoyed the companionship of the younger woman when Sam was out working, gardening, gambling or at the pub. Now she would be lonely without her daughter-in-law.

'I know you're disappointed, Mum, but really it will be better for Pat to have her own home now that the baby is coming. You can see that, can't you? And after all, she'll be just round the corner.' His only fear was that Pat would get lonely and brood over the danger he was in, but she said she would never feel completely married until she had a home of her own to take care of.

His kit bag of flying clothes had been tossed into trucks, thrown over his shoulder and dumped unceremoniously on the bunk in his new quarters. When he unlaced the cord at its neck and began to unpack there was evidence that mice had found a home in the dark warmth. Jim swore as he surveyed chewed socks, nibbled underwear. When he pulled out his sheepskin-lined leather trousers a tiny rodent ran out, and paused, swaying like a drunkard. Jim briefly considered killing it but then, as their eyes met, he turned away and the creature found enough strength in its legs to dart into a dark corner where, no doubt, it found an escape route. Another mouse crawled out of the bag, dazed and helpless. 'Look,' said Jim to D, one of his hut-mates, 'another of the little blighters.' D's instant reaction was to stamp on it. It lay petrified on its back. Minutes later Jim thought he saw its body shudder. 'It's still alive!' He was incredulous.

'Nah,' his companion sneered, but then the creature's tiny legs twitched, stretched, and tentatively clawed at the air. D stood staring at it as if hypnotised, then his great rubber boot slammed down on the mouse's head. Blood spurted and Jim's stomach turned over.

Saturday 19th December 1942

I thought of Gulliver. I thought: there is no good God. Everything is out of harmony. Animals kill each other, we kill animals, we kill each other. Everything is out of tune. We are all members of a discordant military band.

His personal life was on a high; he was in love with his beautiful wife and about to embark on the adventure of fatherhood, but his pessimism about the future of the world persisted. His contention that there was a new spirit among the British people remained unaltered, but he feared it would not be strong enough to stay the hand of fascism. Not the fascism of Hitler's Nazis, but that of totalitarianism. A mild form of fascism, Jim acknowledges, but who knew to what dark depths it might descend if hunger and unemployment were to stalk the streets after the war ended? As the pacifists had foretold years before, one-party dominance was firmly entrenched in every corner of the globe – more firmly than before the war.

Even the so-called democratic nations, under the impact of war, have succumbed to that dread 'ism.'

I wonder what Jim would have thought had he known that the dread 'ism' in the post-war world would be communism, his vision of a perfect social order.

*

Like any couple anticipating their own fireside, Pat and Jim began to look around for furnishings. New furniture was of poor quality and the prices horrified my parents-to-be.

'I looked in the For Sale columns of the *Kentish Independent*,' Mum remembers, 'and I bought the dining suite – sideboard, table and four chairs – from a lady in Sidcup at a ridiculously cheap price. Sorry, but I can't remember exactly how much.'

I smile. 'Well, it was an awfully long time ago!'

'Oh, and there was that cheap furniture shop opposite Hitch's garage. I bought a Utility fireside chair from there. It had wooden arms and very little springing.'

'Mm, I remember Utility furniture. Wasn't it pretty basic stuff – poor quality, but all you could get in the war, I suppose?'

'Well, I expect the nobs who shopped in Harrods got better, but that was all that was available to us. It was okay, though. I got an occasional table – dark wood, with a lower shelf, and a square Utility carpet for the bay window room. The stair covering was hardwearing but certainly not carpet – you may remember it.'

Oh yes, I remember it all right. It was the coconut matting that scratched my feet when I ran down the stairs to open the door to my fantasy dad.

'And then, a bit later, I got a settee and two armchairs. Not sure if they were second-hand or Utility.'

I puzzle to recall them. 'What colour were they, Mum?'

She throws her head back and guffaws. 'Brown, dear. Everything was brown!'

A few days after our conversation an email from Mum appears in my inbox:

Memories

I remember when Jim was home on leave, we were on a bus in Eltham High Street when I overheard someone say there were saucepans for sale in Woolworths. Much to Jim's surprise, I insisted we got off the bus and queued up for some shiny new pans. I don't remember being successful.

On another occasion we heard that the fish shop up near the Welcome Inn at Shooter's Hill was frying that night (a rare occurrence). So we jumped on a tram and joined the queue. I had to leave Jim to do the buying because I was pregnant and the smell of fish and chips made me ill.

More memories dear, as they come to mind.

Cheerio for now.

Love Mum x

*

Sunday 20th December 1942

Politicians are mouthing phrases about the 'New World' – vague, foolish, empty phrases that deceive few people – that will come after the war. But they lay no foundations for this New Order. Churchill and co. insist on 'winning the war first'. Fools! Of what use will victory be unless preparations for the peace have been made?

I and so many others are sacrificing much. Many of us will die, as many have died already. We are 'heroes'. But when I close my eyes, or gaze into the embers of the fire, I can see my son, a young man, doing battle in the skies, fighting as I fight, for false promises and 'new worlds' that will be new only in that there will be a newer, more efficient way of killing people. His reward, if he survives, will be the same as ours – The Kingdom of Hell Upon Earth.

By God! If I live I must fight for a real New Order. I must fight with a fervour, an enthusiasm that I cannot muster in this present war.

H.G. Wells was on the radio tonight, urging yet again World Federation. Of course he is right, right, right! Yet will it solve man's ultimate problems? Man needs, desperately needs, a new spiritual conception of life, but who will lead him to that newness of spirit? The churches are dead and refusing to be buried. The corpses stink to high heaven.

Despite his personal happiness, Jim had once more sunk into despair. He says he has no faith in anything now; feels everything had gone when he lost his belief in the way of peace. He had believed that he could help mankind; that he was among the few who were not lost. But now, he says, he too is unable to find a way forward. He is fit only to murder and kill, maim and torment. Reality, life, the struggle for existence, have made of him a person both mad and evil.

I am not unique. We are all mad and evil these days.

Sometimes he wished he could run away from it all, but there was nowhere to go. There was no way of escape except through death, and he didn't want to die. But had he not found happiness with Pat, he wouldn't care much about holding on to life.

I guess we deserve all our sufferings. I guess we are just not good enough for this sweet earth. I guess we don't deserve to see the glorious majesty of the setting sun, the symmetry of hills, the rhythm of rivers, the strength of the ocean. I guess we deserve nothing of God.

My heart goes out to this passionate young man. When we are young many of us want to change the world; many of us try, but unlike him, we are not looking death in the face and most of us have feet of clay. We do what we can and make the best of what life throws at us. Our reforming zeal is lost in everyday living.

A few weeks later, however, he is elated that he and Pat have been granted the tenancy of her parents' house.

At last – a home of our own! I feel proud and happy that we have managed it. When the baby comes life will be very thrilling.

But once again he was thinking of chucking it all in. Flying had been giving him bad headaches and a feeling of dizziness. If it continued, he decided, he would get out of aircrew and with no sense of shame. He refused to throw his life away like a cigarette end and he was not going to take the lives of men, women and children for a cause that was not worth tuppence.

Tuesday 16th February 1943

It is tragically amusing that I once imagined I would be able to hit military targets! Good God! What on earth made me think you could pick out a factory at night aided only by flares and be sure you had a good chance of hitting it? I must have had some queer notions.

Surely I cannot go through with this terrible business. Surely my conscience would ever be haunted by the sight of broken bodies, homeless families, weeping mothers. Civilians, workers of my own class – no I cannot murder them. The 'New World' is not worth it. Nothing is worth it. I must get out…

He was not alone in his dejection. Of the seven men sharing his hut four were in the process of getting out. All the members of Bomber Command were volunteers and free to resign at any time. According to Jim, it was not foolish cowardice that impelled his comrades, but disillusionment with the rotten social system and cynicism about what was promised for the future. D was all for revolution when the current conflict ended. He said, 'The end of the war will not be the time to hand in your guns – it will be the time to use them.' D was also the man who smashed the harmless mouse to a bloody pulp. I am not sure I would trust him in a revolution. But the discontent of these men helps me to understand why Clement Attlee, the Labour politician, led his party to a landslide victory over Churchill, the great war leader, in the 1945 election.

It may not have been as radical as you wished, Dad, but a new world was on its way.

Jim didn't get out, he didn't even try. However, his respect for the government didn't increase. Another four weeks of indecision resulted in this diary entry:

Sunday 28th March 1943

It is no use. There can be no 'getting out'. There is only one way to get out of this stupidity – finish the war quickly. Only by one side winning can this be done. Peace by compromise is impossible…and anyway in my heart of hearts I know that fascism must be crushed.

British men are enduring agony and death in every corner of the world, but in this tight little island plans for re-feathering the capitalist nest are being discussed, perhaps even implemented. Men are DYING for freedom, for the idea that their children will have a better life than they did. They are being shot, shelled, bombed, bayoneted. Some die slowly with their entrails grilling in the desert sun, some die quickly – so quickly that their bodies are in a million pieces; some are crippled, their eyes gouged, maybe, or their genitals ground to a sticky mess under the heel of a heavy boot. Some die of thirst, some of hunger. Some are cremated in blazing aircraft. In Europe there is famine, suffering and persecution. And the businessmen sit on their arses and plan the maintenance of the system that caused this war. Is it any wonder that I want to stick bayonets in their bottoms?

Operational Training finished at the beginning of March and Jim went home for twelve days of 'the happiest leave yet'. He tried his hand at home decorating and acknowledged he was not very expert, but it made the house feel their own.

Yorkshire was his next posting and the prospect of operations on four-engine bombers. I am pleased to find him more positive as he writes on his first night there: 'No getting out. Finish the war. Finish capitalism. Ops soon. Lovely leave. Heigh ho! To BED!'

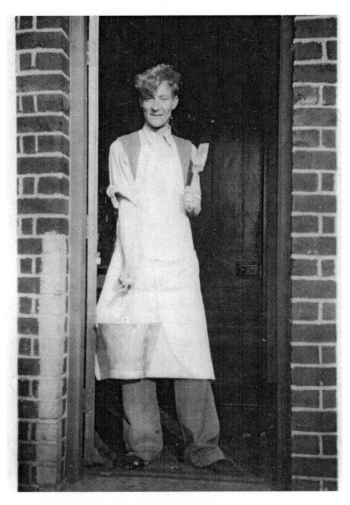

Jim the decorator

On the second anniversary of their marriage ('in the lovers' sense') Jim phoned Pat.

'Five weeks today, darling, only five weeks!' she said as soon as she heard his voice.

'Is that what the doctor said?' He grinned into the black mouthpiece of the telephone.

'Yes, and she predicts I will have an easy time with no difficulties. Oh, Jim, will I see you before then or must I be patient for five whole weeks before you come home to US?'

'I don't see much chance of leave, darling. But the moment he is born you must get the nurse to phone and I'll fly home. Well, not actually fly; don't think they'd let me have a plane, but I'll be on the next train. Five weeks! I am so happy, so proud. I've never been so proud before. Now take very good care of yourself, my love. Five weeks and then...joy!'

Thursday 8th April 1943

I am at Ricall and the flying field looks like a junk heap! Kites prang here often. Bert Fraser is in hospital suffering from burns after a miraculous escape from his aircraft. So is Reg Brand. I met Selman today. He has come to find another crew – his kite hit a tree, killing three and putting two in hospital. Whittle has 'gone for a Burton' over Berlin. Daily one hears, 'I say, old so-and-so has bought it!' We joke about it in a grim sort of way. One dare not think too much. Eat, drink and be merry! And lately, I have been drinking and getting very merry. Merry, not helplessly drunk, but one must go out sometimes and find a sense of security – even a false sense of security.

Sunday 2nd May 1943

Yesterday I arrived here at the operational training squadron near York. So I have reached the stage for which I have trained these many months. I am here to begin my career of destruction. In a few days I will be on ops. My feelings are mixed. There is fear – yes, we all fear the untried and unknown. There is a little thrill of anticipation – I am going to know war. I am going into action. I am going to be shot at, chased by fighters, rocked by flak. I am going to kill. I am going to know the real thing.

> A tour of operations consists of about thirty trips. Once thirty seemed such a little number, but now... Oh well, I guess I'll get hardened after the first five or nine – or is it softened to a jelly? Like the London Blitzes – you either get used to them or your nerves get the better of you.

The reality of war was very close now; the man who was to head Jim's crew was going on his first operational flight that night. 'See you in the morning, Taff,' Jim writes, with what sounds like forced optimism. In the morning he learnt that Taff had to turn back before reaching the enemy coast. His pilot had a cold and couldn't hear properly so felt it best to abandon the mission.

Another mate, Bert Winn, described the Pilsen raid he had been on with several others from the station. He had never witnessed anything in his life to compare with the bombing of the target. 'We were afraid of being hit by other people's bombs. It must have been hell down there. When we dropped the incendiaries it looked as if molten metal was being poured down. A man who says he is not afraid of operations is a liar!'

Fifty-five aircraft failed to return from Pilsen that night. Jim's thoughts were in turmoil.

Some of the crew he would be flying with he knew already; others were complete strangers and he describes them in his diary.

Taffy Rees, the pilot, a short lad of nineteen, was originally from Swansea but now lived in Ebbw Vale. From the age of eight to fourteen he had been a child singer and had won the Eisteddfod three times in succession and toured Canada singing in concert halls. He was a good, confident pilot, easy to get on with and Jim liked him very much.

Fred Rose was the navigator. At twenty-four he was older than the rest. In civvy life he was a machine tool setter, married and had just learned he was to be a father. At times rude and complaining, my dad liked him all the same. When drunk he was screamingly funny, taking 'a dim view' of everything and everyone. Born in Paddington, he lived in Middlesex but spoke like a Yorkshireman – a trait the rest of the crew never tired of teasing him about.

The wireless operator was a twenty-year-old native of Leeds, Denis Birkhead. Fond of beer, fond of riding women, a humanist of the crazier variety, Jim found him quite likable.

At six foot four inches tall, London cockney Bill Oliver had earned himself the unsurprising nickname of Lofty, sometimes varied to Shorty. Aged about twenty-one, he was in love with a girl in the Wrens, fond of a glass of beer and a diverting woman. Lofty was the flight engineer.

There was another Taff – Evan David from Cardiff. A quiet twenty-one-year-old, he was addicted neither to drink or women. Jim got on well with him but found him something of a mystery man who never spoke of his home life or civilian job.

The rear gunner, their tail-end Charlie, was Frank Farnell. He was from Birkenhead and had worked on the Great Western Railway. At twenty-two he was a boozer and womanizer. Although Jim says he was impossible to dislike, he found his unfaithfulness to his wife *('who we gather is a charming girl')* sickening.

> He always gets any woman he wants. Women are queer creatures with queer tastes!

The crew was completed by the air-bomber, Jim Gaywood.

> Yes, a mixed bunch but we get along together very well. An aircrew must do that; it is half way to seeing the end of ops.
>
> Seven young men of Great Britain, prepared to kill, to die if need be. Oh, Britain, will you give them a new world that will be worthy of it all? If they die will you take care of the widows, the children? Oh, Britain, how doubtful I am.

Tuesday 11th May 1943

Today is Len's birthday – and I have forgotten to send him my greetings. Queer to think he is a man. I still think of him as much younger than myself. At eighteen I thought I knew a lot – yet I suspect that Len knows more than I did.

Then the thing Jim had feared happened. There was a split in the crew. Denis and Frank had been out drinking and made a hell of a noise when they returned. Fred Rose told them to shut up and it looked as though a fight would develop, but Evan managed to separate them. Denis made a lot of detrimental remarks about Fred and the crew in general. According to him, Fred couldn't navigate, was a spoilsport and was thoroughly unlikable. The upshot was that Fred said, 'I'll not fly with this crew again!' Attempts to get either of them to see reason failed. Denis would not apologise to Fred. Fred would not fly with Denis.

This is a very bad thing. It is essential that all members of an aircrew should be on good terms and trust each other on the job. If it had to come, this should have occurred long ago, not so close to operations.

The top brass were all present and correct on 12th May for a visit from Air Chief Marshal Sir Arthur Harris. Bomber Harris, the Commander in Chief, was doing his rounds to raise morale and encourage the troops. Jim is mysterious about the talk he gave the men:

Much of it I may not record for he spoke 'confidentially'. I wish I could do so, for what he said was an eye-opener. I suppose the details will be known soon enough.

Only four days later the Dam Busters launched their famous raid. Was it bouncing bombs that were 'an eye-opener'?

Wednesday 19th May

My beloved went into the Maternity Hospital yesterday and baby is due any day. I wonder if it has happened yet? Or must we wait a few days longer? My nerves are a bit on edge and I feel agitated. I pray that Pat will be spared unnecessary pain. Oh, but today I love her a thousand times more!

Frank went on the Dortmund raid a few nights ago. They were attacked by fighters and the aircraft was hit in several places. A cannon shell exploded inside the kite and stunned Frank for several minutes. It is a marvel they got back at all.

The next time we fly will be as a crew on our first operation.

I pray I may see baby before then...

16

Sunday 23rd May 1943

Why did he write no more diary entries after the 19th? Did he and his crew fly on an op? Probably not; there had been a respite from the 'Ruhr Ops' for over a week and it seems unlikely they would have been destined elsewhere. If they had flown on a mission, they all returned intact.

The British Hospital for Mothers and Babies had been evacuated to a safer location in Kent. Pat wrote to Jim every day, willing her baby to arrive so that he would be granted compassionate leave.

Moatlands. Thursday 20th May 1943

My Darling Husband,

Jim, I miss you very, very much – even more than I do at home. No letters yet – I did expect one today.

Oh, Jim, please take care of yourself. Please. I couldn't bear it if anything happened to you.

They say I was talking about you in my sleep last night. When I woke they asked me what your name was and when I replied 'Jim' they were relieved! They thought they'd caught me talking of someone else. If only they knew us! Jim, my own, I do love you… I do hope there is a letter tomorrow.

I've just seen the doctor and she is 'very, very satisfied' with me but she doesn't think he'll be here before Saturday. I wanted to go to the village but she says I mustn't do much walking –

not even in the grounds – because of the veins in my leg.

Don't forget you can phone me before I go to bed – although I suppose it won't be much good telling you that – by the time you receive this letter I shall probably be...

If all goes well I should be 'castor oiled' tomorrow morning and then the fun should start.

Two more girls were born last night. That's four since I've been here. However, speculation about my having a boy runs very high. I hope they're right, although you know I would feel no different towards a girl. She would be ours and that would be all that would matter.

Darlingheart, remember the footpath marked on the map? Well don't follow it all the way into the grounds of Moatlands. When you come to cross the lane, turn left, then it is the first turning on the right – you can't miss it.

Beloved, I am tired; I am going to have a sleep. Goodnight, God bless you and keep you safe for your adoring wife,

Pat xxxxxxxxxxxxxxxxxxxx

It feels intrusive to read, let alone print, these intimate lines. But I rejoice that my parents lived in a time of romantic love letters and I am envious of their readiness to commit their devotion to paper.

Three days later, as he picked up his pen, Jim felt a pang of anxiety for his parents. His mum's nerves had been ragged ever since November when a shard of a firebomb had crashed through the roof of number 17 and caused a fire in the back bedroom. During his short leave, Mum tells me, they had come to take their wedding presents to their new home and stayed for Sunday dinner. While his dad was at the pub and the women cooked and gossiped, Jim retreated to his childhood bedroom to thumb through old notebooks. He took his fountain pen from his pocket and began to write. After increasingly impatient calls that dinner was getting cold, he closed his book and ran downstairs, full of apologies.

The scrag-end of beef was full of gristle. It was all the butcher had left but they filled up on plenty of home-grown veg. Jim and Pat cleared the table and the bowls of half-eaten rice pudding. 'You have a sit down, Mum. We'll wash up.'

Sam was looking up the racing tips in the *News of the World* and it wasn't long before the young couple in the kitchen heard the regular breathing of Cis snoozing.

Pat poured away the washing-up water and shook her head. 'Why is there always a teaspoon left in the bottom of the – Oh my God, what was that?'

An almighty bang made their ears ring. Jim and his dad were halfway up the stairs before the sound had faded. A corner of the bedroom was ablaze. Sam yelled, 'Get some fucking blankets.' Cis, startled out of her nap, heaved herself upstairs, ripped the covers off the beds to smother the flames. Pat filled pails of water in the kitchen and passed them up to Jim to douse the smouldering pyre.

Mum tells me the fire and water between them destroyed most of their wedding gifts as well as Jim's books and pen. 'No harm to any of us, thank goodness, but those beautiful embroidered … Oh well, never mind, they were only pillow cases.' She wipes the memory away.

Now, as he sat down to write in Yorkshire, Jim remembered the nervous, expectant look on Pat's face when he unwrapped her Christmas gift of a new fountain pen. And her relieved expression when he danced her round the living room and covered her face and neck with kisses. Before he removed the black cap with its gold clip he fingered the shiny bulbous barrel and remembered laying his palm on her smooth round belly hoping for that frisson of excitement when he felt the movement of a determined child within. He frowned at the thought that, even at this very minute, Pat may be suffering the pain of bringing their baby into the world.

Melbourne Nr. York. Sunday 23rd May 1943

My own darling,

I have had no news yet, but perhaps tomorrow I will, for if doctor said 'not before Saturday' maybe baby has come today. I hope so, my love, for I am longing to see you both very soon. I am thinking of you continually.

Oh! But I am glad I met you, married you; overjoyed at the prospect of your bearing me a son or daughter.

Thank you for all the great happiness you have brought me, for all the delight we have known together, for all the happiness and delight we shall know together in the future.

My dear, darling wife, you are the light in this dungeon, the world. You bring beauty to ugliness, divinity to beauty. When I am with you I see a new world and in it I find a supreme joy.

I wait confidently but anxiously for the happy news that at last Baby has come. What a happy family we shall be! This war will end, and I shall come home to you, my dears, and stay with you for always. Always I shall love you – always, my darling.

Goodnight, beloved.

Your adoring husband, Jim xxxxxxxxxxxxxxxxxxxxx

Not a word about what he had been doing; not a word about her careful directions to the nursing home. *Goodnight, beloved,* tells me it was written in the evening of a tumultuous day which was to be followed by a tumultuous night. That night, eight hundred and twenty-six aircraft took part in the biggest raid of the Battle of the Ruhr. Jim's Halifax II was one of them.

How had he spent the day? Now that I have researched

the routine of a Bomber Command Station, now that I am beginning to understand my quiet, thoughtful father, this is how it might have been.

Since the morning 'prayer meeting' when they were told they would be flying on ops that night, conversation had been sparse. No one discussed what the night may bring. Jim was in no mood for the half-hearted dirty jokes rattling round the mess and felt the need of a breath of fresh air. It had been a good decision to bring his bike back with him after his last leave. It had always been his passport to freedom. He saluted to the guard in the gatehouse as he cycled into the flat landscape of the Vale of York. His chest expanded as he breathed in the country air and the wind ruffled his hair. Thoughts of bombing and carnage were blown away. As he pedalled faster and faster, his spirits lifted further into the atmosphere of the quiet Sunday afternoon. All he heard was birdsong in the hedgerows and, when he reached the village, the sound of a piano floating through an open window. An old man in shirtsleeves was hoeing a vegetable patch and tipped his cap to Jim as he cycled past. Beyond the rotting lock gates on the disused canal, a couple of boys were optimistically dangling homemade fishing rods into water clogged with silt. Jim found a secluded clearing and propped his bike against an elder tree laden with clusters of flowers like little sunshades decorated with white flowers for an Edwardian lady. He flopped down onto the grass and listened to the comforting sound of cattle chewing the cud on the other side of the straggly hedge. Squinting at the sun in the cloudless blue sky, he tried to decide whether he felt guilty, frightened or excited. Within a few hours he would be up there, roaring through the night, bent on destruction. The warmth of the sun was soporific, and he drifted in and out of the edges of sleep, half-thinking, half-dreaming, of his life back home – his real life.

He sat up, fully awake. This was his real life. This was

the here and now. He pushed back the cuff of his grey-blue battledress to check the time. Yes, this was reality. He stood and climbed back onto his bike. When he rounded the bend in the perimeter road of the airfield there was organised activity on the aprons in front of the hangars. Dozens of figures crawled over the bombers, preparing them for action. Jim was reminded of the sketch in his *Encyclopaedia Britannica* of shoals of tiny cleaner fish grooming a gigantic whale. He turned his wheels, parked his bike in the shed with the others, and retreated to the mess. Like the rest of D flight, the crew of DT-789 sat around smoking, snoozing and reading the Sunday papers.

'Cor blimey,' exclaimed Bill Oliver, 'they've gone and tested that jet plane everyone's been talking about.'

'And did it stay up? I reckon nothing could go at those speeds without coming to a sticky end,' replied Evan David, the upper gunner.

'Well, you're wrong. It says here it's the "plane of the future".'

Taffy had been playing with the wireless and, at last, got a crackly voice reading a news bulletin. 'Bloody hell, Jerry's bombed Bournemouth. Must be getting desperate if all they can aim for is kids building sandcastles.'

Others were composing their letters.

Jim tried to ignore the preparations going on beyond the windows criss-crossed with tape. He'd had enough practice runs to know what the maintenance crews were doing: checking the undercarriage, testing the engines and controls, pumping fuel into the tanks, loading the ammunition and 'bombing up'. Some of his mates were out there watching, but Jim had no wish to see the tractor pulling a trailer loaded with the enormous tanks of explosives – their fuses already in place – and the cranes loading them into the bomb bay. The squads were expert and well practiced but that didn't stop Jim praying that they would align them very carefully with the lugs in the hatches. If they got it even slightly wrong he wouldn't be able to release his bombs.

Release his bombs! Oh dear God, is this what it had come to? His promise to his German friends rang in his ears. He would never do anything to harm the German people or their beautiful country. He had meant it. He had continued to mean it. But then he had volunteered, and now here he was, a bomb-aimer, setting off to destroy the factories of Ruhr. Jim began to regret his dinner of cottage pie and cabbage as his stomach churned and threatened to return it to the floor. How could he be sure no stray bomb would explode on a house, a church, a hospital – on Ernst and Maria? Was this really him, Jim Gaywood, the erstwhile committed pacifist, who had sworn never to harm civilians? *No*, he answered himself. This was not the same Jim. This was a highly trained Jim. A Jim who was determined to bomb, as accurately as possible, only the industrial target he was aiming for: the factories that were producing the tanks, guns, fighter planes and bombers with which to destroy the civilized world.

The WAAF known as the Map Queen had prepared the 'gen' for Fred Rose, the navigator. Evan David asked where they were bound but she just tapped her little snub nose saying, 'Wait and see!' But Evan had watched the ground crew fuelling the aircraft and a quick calculation of flying distance per gallon gave him a fair idea of where they were bound.

When the crew had been fitted for their parachutes it was a bit like being measured for a new suit, inside leg and all. Frank Farnell, the rear gunner, had encouraged the WAAF fitting his to move her hand a bit. 'Up a little, gorgeous, and then under.'

'Like this, you mean?' When she had trussed his chute tighter and a little tighter still until his voice went up an octave, the rest of the crew had urged her, through their laughter, not to slacken it off.

'Don't forget, boys, if your chute doesn't open you can always bring it back,' she said. After a couple of seconds their laughter faltered as the point of her joke sank in.

Writing his letter, Jim smiled at the memory; then smiled again at the thought of his baby. He never doubted that Pat would sail through the delivery and produce a beautiful, healthy boy. His brow furrowed, however, at the thought of her bringing up the child without him. He must survive. He would survive.

Bill Oliver, the flight engineer, cuffed him on the shoulder, 'C'mon, mate, leave the scribbling, it's supper time.'

'Finished yours, Bill?'

'Ain't writing one, mate. I'm coming back.'

'Me too, just as long as we can dodge Jerry. Remember, I'll have a child to come back for. But just in case...' Jim pressed the page of blue-black writing to a well-used piece of pink blotting paper leaving the imprint of twenty-one kisses. He slid the two neatly folded sheets into a small blue envelope, licked the flap and the back of the King's head and pressed down with a trembling finger.

The irresistible smell of supper lured him to the canteen where he joined the crews tucking into sizzling bacon, eggs, beans, fried bread and mugs of steaming tea: the traditional fry-up for all men about to go on ops.

The plane was fuelled, the guns belted up, the bombs loaded, the engine checked and rechecked by the time the boys were called for their briefing. Jim filed in, found a rickety wooden chair, sat down and noticed the windows were shuttered. An RAF policeman locked the door behind them and remained on guard. The station intelligence officer stood in front of them – serious, businesslike. Taffy Rees called 'here' on behalf of his crew when the roll call was taken.

'Right, men, this is your route for tonight.' A screen was drawn back to reveal a large-scale map of Europe with the target pinpointed.

'It's bloody Sprat again, I knew it would be,' muttered Taffy. Jim, a freshman, was not up to speed on codenames. He cocked his head and raised his brow into a question mark.

DORT... Taffy wrote the letters with a finger on his palm. *Ah, Dortmund.* Jim nodded.

'The route is marked by the wide red tape,' continued the officer. 'Lancasters from No.1 group will make up the first wave. You will be in the second and will muster with the other craft from No.4 group, here.' He pointed to open country close to an area of blue. *Mm,* thought Jim, *that's Rutland Water.* 'Then head out over the North Sea and cross the Dutch coast here, at Egmond.' He tapped the map with his pointer. 'As you fly east you will take this dogleg line to avoid known flak positions. You will find plenty of searchlight cones here, and here. Pathfinders will drop flares to highlight the target. If everything goes to plan, the defences at this point, here, will be disabled. If not, you will take avoiding action. Take a good look at the photos of the target, particularly you bomb-aimers.

'In order to minimize collision risk you will fly at maximum height and take as little evasive action as possible.'

A heavy cloud of silence hung about the men in the room, all thoughts of home, babies and fry-ups wiped from minds focused entirely on the night ahead.

'On your return, after you have achieved your objective, you will follow this route – here.' There was an audible sigh of relief as the intelligence officer dragged his cane westward across the North Sea, over East Anglia and back to Yorkshire. 'The Met men have indicated a clear night.' But one could never be quite certain – some wag had stuck a notice on the door of the Met Office that afternoon renaming it Depression Villa.

The flying control officer took over then to give the details of which runway to use and the order of take-off. Jim's plane would be third up.

'We will now synchronise watches at' – he stared at his wrist for a full three seconds and a roomful of eyes waited for the command—'nineteen-forty-eight hours exactly.' Jim adjusted the hands on his twenty-first birthday present in unison with his colleagues.

'Any questions?' The officer's eyes swept the room. 'No? Then I wish you good luck for a successful operation.' The screen was drawn across the map and the door secured behind them as they filed out and crossed the tarmac to the locker room where they were handed their bags.

Small change, an old bus ticket, his notebook of unfinished poems; all these Jim was happy to toss into the canvas bag he would collect on his return, though he couldn't really see what use they would be to the enemy if they remained in his pockets. But he delayed dropping in the letter Pat had written for as long as he dared. This last connection. These small pages she had held, covered on both sides with her pencil. He placed the envelope carefully in the bag, not to crease it, and vowed he would come back to claim it again.

'Collect your escape kits over there.' The instruction jolted Jim back into the moment and he stared at the Perspex pack with a wry smile. This was what was supposed to save his life if he was shot down or forced to bail out: glucose sweets, foreign currency, a small compass and water purifying tablets. Tucked in his inside pocket was the silk handkerchief, all eighteen square inches of it, printed with a map of the whole of Europe.

The room was busy but silent; apprehension surrounded the men like the invisible weight of air before lightning and thunder. Focused on the task ahead, they decided what to wear under their flying suits. Jim wore his heavy roll-neck sweater; he might as well be comfortable and he doubted the alternative, his service dress jacket, would impress if he found himself in a POW camp. He pulled on fine silk socks, his fingers enjoying the smoothness as they slid across the fibres. Then he tugged thick woollen ones over the top. Leather trousers and Irvin jacket with their sheepskin linings were bulky and weighed him to the ground like chainmail. But he knew he would be grateful for them when the temperature was sub-zero and he was lying face down in the bomb-aimer's compartment, aligning his sights on the target. Lastly, he donned a Mae West in case he ditched in the sea. Before lacing his boots and picking up his flying helmet, his lips brushed the letter he had written and he handed it to one of the map clerks with the fervent wish that Pat should never read it.

Then he braced thin shoulders, dwarfed by kit, and strode out to board DT-789.

17

The Flight

It is 2012, and my mother and I are spending a few days on the Suffolk coast. Blue sky and spring sunshine are tempting but the keen wind forces us to hunch our shoulders and retrace our steps after only a brief stroll along the beach. We decide on a drive through lanes edged with emerging primroses and picnic in the warmth of the car while we watch a hen harrier quartering over the marshes.

Winding our way through the Waveney Valley we come across a barred gate and a notice proclaiming that we have arrived at the Norfolk and Suffolk Aviation Museum. We think it's closed, discover it's not, and agree to see what it has to offer. A band of busy retirees welcomes us and we are directed to a display of Bomber Command memorabilia. My father never flew from here so we don't expect to unearth any treasures. Mum sees a silk handkerchief printed with a map of Europe and points excitedly. 'Your dad had one of those, just like that. I wonder if I still have it. Oh no, I suppose he would have had it in his pocket.' I search her face for sadness, the vestige of a tear, but recognition and excitement are all I see. Is it all too long ago or does she, like me, keep her flask of emotions firmly corked, only allowing it to leak onto her private pillow?

We explain our interest to the eager volunteers and the word goes around. 'It's Bill they'll want. Where's Bill?'

'Probably in the workshop.'

'Or in the office.'

'Ask George.'

George appears. 'Bill's not here today I'm afraid,' he explains when he hears about our quest, 'had to take Beryl to Lowestoft to have her feet done so he changed his day to Friday.'

'Well, you'll certainly need to talk to Bill,' says the lady in the green cardigan who has made our mission her own, 'he's got all the books.'

George agrees. 'Oh yes, books wall to wall in his house; Beryl says if one more war book comes in the back door she's out the front. Come back on Friday.'

We can't come back on Friday so I leave my name, a few details and my mobile number. George promises to pass it on to Bill, the fount of all Bomber Command information. No sooner are we back at base than my phone rings and a booming voice fills my ear.

'Mrs Denny? Can't help you I'm afraid. No record of a Denny lost in May '43.' A click and he is gone.

When I call him back and explain it is not Denny but Gaywood he is seeking, he hoots and shouts, 'It's OK, Beryl, I got the wrong name so I'm off again.' I hear the receiver crash onto a table.

Beryl's distant voice tells him to get down off that ladder, his dinner's ready; but I can hear him muttering, '1943, May…' The sound of footsteps taps across a hard floor and the phone is picked up. A female voice enquires my name.

'Janet,' I reply.

'Tell 'im to have his dinner first, will you, Janet? Just shout.'

So I yell into my phone and imagine the sound issuing from an old Bakelite handset. 'Bill, I've waited since 1943; I can wait until you've had your dinner.'

'Okay, Janet,' he replies, 'I'll work on it after I've done the washing up and then I'll post it to you.'

I am dictating my address as he says, 'Got to go now,

sausages are sizzling. Cheerio.' I can almost smell the bangers and hope he got the details noted before he hung up. The scene is so vivid I feel I've known this pair for years.

A few days later a recycled brown envelope drops through my letter box. A white adhesive label on the front is covered in a firm hand addressing it to Mrs Denny/Gaywood. I slit it open and take out four pages of yellowing lined foolscap, covered on both sides with unpunctuated words all in capitals.

Bill has researched all available information about No. 2 squadron, the crew of DT-789 and the details of its last flight.

The letter ends:

RIGHT MUST GET ON MRS DENNYGAYWOOD DINNER TO PREPARE FOR MY PARTNER MANY BOOKS TO CLEAR AWAY BEFORE SHE ARRIVES
        FROM ME BILL OAP

*

The western sky was deep umber turning to indigo when seven young airmen jumped off the tractor that had transported them across the airfield. They gathered around the nose of the plane for a last cigarette. The night was to be a big one, they knew that. The whisper in the mess was there could be up to a thousand bombers heading for the Ruhr. Twenty-one were flying from their squadron alone. Taffy Rees felt his responsibility keenly. This was not his first op. Every newly qualified skipper did two runs as a second pilot before commanding a crew of his own. Taffy had flown on the Dortmund raid on 4th May.

'Piece of cake, lads,' he told his boys with a doubtful grin when he returned. 'No, seriously, with luck, care, and bags of pukka gen, I'm sure we'll get through okay.' His second op had been on the Bochum raid which he reported as being, 'pretty hot, but then it was Friday the 13th!' There had been no flying for over a week since then because of the poor weather, so tonight was his first time leading a crew.

'All right, Denis? Okay, Fred?' Taffy reached his arms round the backs of his wireless officer and navigator.

Denis shrugged free and turned away, stamped his boot on the butt of his fag and glowered silently.

'Any reason I shouldn't be?' Fred's lip curled as his eyes bored into Denis's back. The rest of the crew had worked hard to knit up the differences between the two men who still refused to make eye contact. At every opportunity they muttered obscenities about each other under their breath. Their colleagues continued to keep the conversation light, careful not to deepen the rift.

'How was your fry-up, Bill?' asked Evan David.

'Bacon was burnt, mate.'

'Yeah, mine too. Hope the WAAFs remembered to put the coffee on board.'

'Essence of dandelion, you mean,' Frank butted in. He had a taste for coffee but not its wartime substitute.

I guess my dad would have remained silent, perhaps thinking about Mum and my imminent arrival.

Their planned take-off was scheduled for 22.34 hours. A camouflaged Albion ambulance drew up alongside the aircraft. Jim acknowledged the raised hand of the driver, feeling simultaneously alarmed and reassured by his presence. This was a routine standby, but the grapevine was alive with tales of disastrous take-offs, when it had been necessary (or useless) to have medics on hand. The ambulance would be there again when they landed. The ground crew, vital to the flyers' safety, checked once more the hydraulics serving the flaps and the gun turrets, then fitted the camera loaded with film and an automatic flash. It would record the scene on the ground thirty seconds after Jim released his bombs. The plane was then handed to the aircrew.

Ever the ladies' man, Frank was exchanging kisses, blown

from a distance, with the laughing WAAFs who had cycled out to witness the take-off. The captain called him to order for the checks. Each crew member had his own responsibility.

'Pitot head cover off?'

'Yes, Skip.'

'Chocks in position?'

'Yes, Skip.'

'Fire extinguishers?'

'Okay, Skip.'

'Controls and tabs serviceable?'

'Yes, Skip.'

Taffy signed Form 700, agreeing all was in order. 'Okay, men, let's get going.' He adopted a light-hearted but efficient tone, attempting to imbue his crew (and himself) with confidence.

'Right, Skipper,' came their replies, almost in unison. They climbed the short ladder to board, and slung their parachute packs onto a line of hooks. All except for Frank Farnell, who turned to the right, ran his fingers along a few of the ten thousand bullets on the conveyor belt feeding the tail guns, and heaved himself and his chute pack into the rear turret, locking the door behind him. Proud of his physique, he'd been irritated by ribald jokes about Michelin Man when he had donned his bulky heated suit. But the rear turret lacked the primitive heating in the main body of the aircraft, so it would be essential when they climbed high into the freezing sky.

It was as if there was an anaesthetic in the air, stopping the men in their tracks, glazing their eyes for a second before they shook themselves back into the moment. As they continued with their duties one or two had to discipline themselves. Aircrew were trained to think only of the job in hand, but keeping minds on a narrow technical path and preventing thoughts straying towards homes and loved ones was a skill some had yet to master.

Fred Rose settled into his navigator's seat, checked the

compass and studied the map. Bill established the engines were operating smoothly and recorded the oil pressures and temperatures in the log book. Next, he compared the petrol consumption with the engine running at various RPMs and ensured the fuel system feed to each tank was in order. Taffy Rees assured himself the instruments were working as they should. Evan made sure all the hatches were secure. Jim concentrated on preventing his hands from trembling as he adjusted the sights and noted the bomb release was in place. Taffy pressed the starter button and, when the engine fired, snapped it to 'slow running'. Directed by the torchlight, each engine was started individually and DT-789 taxied out onto its allotted runway.

The crew ensured the tail wheel was straight, tested the flaps (again), checked the gyro compass was on the correct magnetic heading and waited for the WAAF in the control tower to give permission for take-off. Radio silence was observed but Jim's heartbeat sounded to him like an industrial hammer as the ground controller signalled with his Aldis lamp. Taffy stood hard on the brakes and pushed the control column away from him, thrust the throttles forward, then released the brakes. Bill didn't wait to be asked – he knew his Skipper needed help keeping the throttles open. Together their knuckles whitened as their hands pressed on the column. Halfway down the runway, as they gathered speed, Jim attempted to swallow his apprehension; the back of his throat rasped against his uvula and he felt a momentary desire for an acid drop. Pat liked those, he remembered.

The aircraft left the ground like an ungainly grey goose lifted on the currents of air beneath its wings. The web of tension in the plane relaxed a little, but there was more to be done. When the undercarriage had been raised, Fred, the navigator, gave his pilot the course to steer. Frank, in his transparent eyrie at the rear, grasped the handles (so reminiscent of the handlebars of his Raleigh bike) and swung his guns from side to side, as if in a war game. But Frank knew this was no game as he loaded and cocked them and reported back to his captain. Some gunners would ask permission to test their guns over the sea, but there was no way Frank was going to risk wasting precious bullets or attracting the attention of the enemy, even in a friendly sky. Isolated from the rest of the craft, he felt disconnected from any sort of reality he'd ever known. His world consisted of a starry sky over a darkened earth – and his memories.

DT-789 met up with scores of other planes at the appointed position and flew in practised formation, leaving the coast somewhere to the north of Great Yarmouth. That night there was no moon to reflect on the calm black water below. Jim found comfort in the sound of dozens of friendly engines around them as they crossed the North Sea.

'Sandwich, Jim?' Denis delved into a greaseproof parcel, 'ah, cheese, lovely.' Jim showed his palm to his colleague; food was the last thing on his mind.

A few tense jokes passed round the cabin and after a visit to the Elsan, Bill exclaimed, 'That thing stinks – must have been on some shitty flights.'

The laughter died when Fred, the navigator, interrupted. 'Stand by, boys, back to your posts.' The watery coast of Holland was showing on the radar. Jim positioned himself face down on the hard grey bomb-aimer's couch, stretched his hands forward over the armrests and peered down through the transparent nose of the plane. A shudder of fear – or was it anticipation? – ran through him. That was enemy territory down there. He glanced at his watch. Midnight had passed. They had flown into the next day, May 24th 1943. Did he think of Pat? Did he wonder if I had been born? Or was he one hundred per cent focused on what he was about to do?

Dozens of searchlights combed the sky above the Dutch town of Egmond but the beams, wandering around apparently aimlessly, were little more than a warning. The whole formation of bombers avoided them and flew on.

'Thirty miles to target, Skipper.' Fred Rose raised his voice above the roar of the engine.

It was not long before Taffy took a deep breath and announced, 'Here we go, men.' Seven pairs of shoulders tightened. Seven pairs of eyes focused on the columns of white light ahead, piercing the dark sky and swinging to and fro, searching for prey. Jim was transfixed as he watched them catch a Lancaster and hold it in a giant cone of spotlights. He thought what a fabulous subject this would be for a film. Surely someone would record it? The bomber ducked and dived, a fly avoiding the spider's web, but the beams moved with it until, at last, it was able to squeeze through a darkened gap and evade the flak exploding around it.

DT-789 wove around and escaped the monstrous search-light traps, but it was held for a couple of minutes in a smaller cone. 'Must have school kids manning the ack-ack guns tonight – they're missing us by a mile,' Frank's voice piped up from the tail as they flew unscathed back into the dark.

Seconds passed.

'Bloody hell – look at that!' Jim gasped. There was no need for the yellow flares the Mosquitos had dropped to mark the route; the fires were visible from miles away; scarlet and gold flowers bursting out of the black earth, new blooms unfolding by the minute. No stars were visible, although the sky around them was full of incandescent bursts of fire.

The aircraft juddered.

'Fucking Mary, we've been hit,' Bill's words trembled over the intercom.

What felt like a long silence was finally broken by Evan's voice, from the mid-upper-turret. 'It's okay, boys, the tail's taken it, but no major damage done.' A second later, his voice again – urgently. 'Fighter. Turn to starboard.' Taffy practically turned the plane on its wingtip but the fighter banked in unison and came in firing. Simultaneously, Frank and Evan aimed their guns at the enemy. A flame shot from the top of the German fighter and it limped away wounded.

'Sooner we get rid of this bomb-load the better.'

'Agreed, Skipper.' Jim's words were heartfelt. Then he realised what he had said. The moment was upon him. He was about to take the step he had vowed he would never take. He was about to do his bit to destroy Germany. He was about to bomb the German people: innocent babies, old people who wanted no part of this war, German pacifists, insurgents who were fighting Hitler on the ground. He might incinerate Jews hiding in garrets. He tried not to think of Ernst and Maria. He drew in a long, slow breath of air in an unconscious effort to gain control of his emotions. He tightened his lips and clenched his trembling hands. *Do your job, Jim,* he told himself, *you mustn't let the crew down.*

The red target indicators dropped by the pathfinders were a waste of time. Spotting them below was like searching for the light of a match in a crackling bonfire. Jim could see a few green markers round the perimeter of the flames, and between the plumes of smoke he could just make out the shape of burning buildings below. The bomb-master's muffled voice could be heard in his headphones, but goodness knows if he was giving the order to press the button.

'Left, left…right, steady.' Jim guided Taffy to the centre of the area marked by green flares. Lining up the target in the sights was a challenge – the aircraft was bounced and jolted by surrounding explosions. When he judged the orange cross to be as perfectly aligned as possible in the maelstrom, Jim carefully reached for the bomb release and pressed the button. Hundreds of tons of high explosives and incendiaries rained down to add to the conflagration below. He'd done it. He had blood on his hands now. Jim swallowed hard to subdue the acid burning his throat.

'Straight and level, now, Skip.' His words were almost a whisper.

A sitting target among the mayhem, they hung in the air for the longest thirty seconds of their lives, until the automatic camera flashed.

'Okay, let's get the hell out of...' A deafening explosion drowned Taffy's words and tossed the plane in the air like a ping-pong ball. Denis shot from his wireless operator's seat, smashing his face into the hooks holding the chutes. Jim slid from his couch and was flung against the metal spars in the wall of the aircraft. Willing himself not to pass out he felt his right knee burning like the fires beneath them. When he tried to regain his position he found he had only one functioning leg and a trickle of blood was interfering with his eyesight. Shards of metal dropped from a hole in the side of the fuselage. It had been dealt a glancing blow from a bomb dropped by the Stirling flying above them. After a few seconds of safe silence Frank's disembodied voice came over the intercom from the rear turret.

'Mm, close shave there, thought they were meant to be on our side.'

Taffy turned the Halifax away from the gates of hell, dodging flak and searchlight cones like a wounded game bird avoiding the guns of aristocrats, until the skies became darker and quieter.

Jim tried to bring down mental shutters on what he had just done and turn his thoughts to Pat. She was probably in labour now, he thought. Or maybe the pain was over and his baby was there – in the world – waiting to be held in his arms; waiting for a happy family life with two loving parents. The pain in his knee subsided a little and he stretched the tensed muscles in his back. He had achieved his target and now tried to think only of the long-term consequences. Maybe this war really could be won and a new world created for his family, his child.

Evan had the advantage of a 360° view from his bubble on the roof. 'Nearly there, boys, Dutch coast in sight, then it's over the pond and by four o'clock we'll be in the mess drinking a nice cup of Typhoo.' The plane and its occupants all seemed to exhale in relief; Denis inclined his head to Fred, who almost managed a smile in return.

Whump! The impact heralded a sustained burst of flak from the ground just as they crossed the coast.

'Fighter coming in from port, Skipper.' Bursts of fire from the attacker were returned by both gunners and Jim felt as if they were careering round a dodgem track. The sound of the bullet-belt feeding the guns was like chattering teeth. A figure dropped from the disabled Messerschmitt. As the parachute opened Jim smiled and nodded his head, then gagged when he saw the body consumed by flames.

'Don't worry, Skip, we got him,' came a triumphant report from the mid-turret as the German fighter fell away in a ball of fire.

'Bang on, Evan.'

'Just doing my job, Skipper.' Jim could hear the pride in Evan's voice.

'And you, Frank.' The captain was proud of his crew. No reply came from the tail gunner. 'Frank? Frank, come in, Frank.'

'Want me to check, Skip?'

'If you would, Sergeant.' Taffy's tone was formal, concealing his concern.

Jim had done his main job of the night so he crawled to the back of the plane, wincing as he dragged his leg. 'Frank, Frank…' Silence. 'C'mon, Frank, stop playing possum and give us a shout.' Jim hammered his fist on the locked door of the turret but was met with – nothing.

'What can you see, Evan?' Taffy asked.

Evan, half-standing, peered from the mid-turret to the rear of the plane. 'Tail end's blown apart, Skipper. No sign of Frank.' They flew on in silence.

Back in position, it was Jim who caught sight of the lone ME-110 approaching as they gained the comparative peace of the skies over the North Sea. The tracer was floating towards him like a string of coloured balloons. He braced himself at the forward gun to fire his first shot in anger, directly at the pilot. *Oh God,* he thought, *I can see his face.* But the fighter managed to duck underneath the Halifax and aim his fire from there.

'Night-fighter attacking,' Denis reported to base at 02.27 hours.

'Corkscrew, corkscrew!' Bill's voice squeaked.

Taffy pushed the control column this way and that, turning his unwieldy charge in an attempt to lose the attacker.

'Gain height, Skip.' Jim's stomach leapt to his throat. Taffy's teeth clenched. His mouth was made of sandpaper. Could he lose the enemy while retaining control of the aircraft?

DT-789 pulled away.

18

The Aftermath

Pat had no letter after 20th May. *Well,* she thought, *Jim's busy, isn't he?* But if he was on ops she knew he would write the minute he returned, and ops were only for a few hours...

*

We sit drinking coffee in my mother's comfortable retirement home in Sussex. Sunshine lights up the rose garden beyond the windows and glitters on the lake. Beyond, sheep munch contentedly in the field beside the country church. All is right with the world – at least with this little corner of it. I am about to take her back to a very different time.

'Tell me about when I was born, Mum.'

'Oh, it was a long while ago and you know what my memory's like these days. What do you want to know?'

'Everything. Everything you can remember.'

She sits up straight and launches into her story. 'Well, I had to report to the British Hospital for Mothers and Babies in Woolwich on May the 18th; you were due on the 20th. I was taken by car to Moatlands near Paddock Wood in Kent. It was a large house. The hospital had requisitioned it as its country home – to avoid the bombs I suppose. I hear it is a golf club now.' Every detail is as clear to her now as it was seventy years ago. 'The weather was lovely – warm and sunny – so I took a walk in the grounds and sat down on a grassy bank. I must have dozed off – don't know for how long, but I was woken by some nurses who thought I had gone into labour and needed help, and I was forbidden to go into the grounds alone again.'

'Sleeping in the sun is an odd sign of labour, Mum.'

'I suppose it is,' she smiles, 'but at that stage I didn't know any better.' She hesitates and any evidence of humour is wiped from her face – her thoughts have fallen back in time. 'Anyway, about midnight on the Sunday the pains started.'

'That was the 23rd?' Just as Jim was flying towards the target.

'Yes, but you were a reluctant little thing. The contractions stopped completely after a couple of hours or so.' Just as Jim's plane exploded.

'They let me have a night's sleep – not that I slept much – and then they broke my waters, but you still took your time. You weren't born until 2.45 on the afternoon of the 25th. As soon as you arrived I insisted the Sister should ring the RAF to stop Jim flying. Whether she did, or whether she knew what had happened, I don't know.' My mum's gaze fixes on the horizon beyond the lake.

After a minute I nudge her back into the present. 'And then?'

'Oh, yes, sorry, dear. Then I was moved from the labour room to one of the eight beds in St Gabriel's ward. Mine was right by the window and your friend Lesley's mum was opposite me. You were whisked off to the nursery with all the other babies. I only saw you at feeding time when the nurses brought all the babies to their mothers. You were always the last one because they said you were so quiet they got the noisy ones out first.' She smiles, proud of me.

'Days passed and I was really worried; the daily letters from your father hadn't come.'

'Did you think they might just be delayed?'

'Oh no, the post was much more reliable then. In my heart I think I knew, but I concentrated on not thinking the worst and imagining Jim's delight when he saw you. Then, when you were a few days old, I looked up to see my mother walking into the ward. In those days only husbands were allowed to visit so I knew she must be bringing bad news. I remember looking at her and saying, "It's the sea, isn't it?" It must have been my sixth sense – somehow I felt he was in the water.' A long silence, until she fills it. 'New mums stayed in hospital for a fortnight then, so it must have been the 8th of June when I came home.'

'Did you go to stay with Granny or Nanny? Or did someone stay with you?'

'Oh no, I went straight to 19 Prince John Road. I remember my drama group friend, Etta, coming to visit, but no one stayed. I had you in the little basket cot beside my bed.'

I am angry – angry with all four of my grandparents, my aunts, my uncles, my mother's friends, the neighbours. She was twenty-one, with a new baby and a missing husband who may well have been dead. And they left her alone.

Back at home I turn to the brown leather writing case I'd discovered beside the dustbin with the diaries. When I first opened it my hopes that it would contain a treasure trove of my parents' correspondence had been dashed. Yes, there were the final letters they had written, but no others.

Knowing they corresponded daily, on my next visit I ask Mum what had happened to them all. She shrugs her shoulders, avoiding my eye. 'I suppose they must have been destroyed.' I detect discomfort in her voice. Then she protests, 'But I kept them for years in that blue box on the bottom shelf of the linen cupboard.' Do I remember it? Perhaps.

When she remarried she was beginning a new life, starting again. Why carry all the evidence of the distant past into a new future? She disposed of the diaries and I am fortunate to have found them. I regret that I didn't lift the lid of the dustbin – the letters would surely have been inside. But they were private, written for each other and have nothing to do with me. I have no right to them. Maybe it was right for them to be consumed by fire as, perhaps, Jim had been.

What I did find in the writing case was a sheaf of official letters on small thin sheets of ivory paper.

The first notice from the casualty branch of the Air Ministry was addressed to:

S.G. Gaywood Esq. 17, Eltham Hill, London, S.E.9.

'Why?' I phone Mum to ask. 'You were his next of kin. Whatever were they doing writing to Grandad first?'

'Because your dad, bless him, had asked that if anything happened, his parents should be the first to know – so they could break it to me gently. Of course I knew anyway – I'd had no letters.'

I suppose that was thoughtful of him, but if I had been in Mum's shoes I would have felt belittled.

The RAF Benevolent Fund was swift with their letter of sympathy, financial assistance and practical advice about benefits. If she found herself in need of temporary assistance now or in the future she should contact the Fund. The Air Ministry paid my mother £3 per week (the family allowance rate) for four months. This payment was extended for two more months but then reduced to the 'pension' rate of £1 18s 6d when it was judged that he was not merely 'missing in action' but 'missing, presumed dead'. I can't think why this meant a reduction in benefit, but it was then that Mum took advantage of the Benevolent Fund's offer of help and they awarded her thirty shillings per week for three months.

'Was that enough, Mum? Could you manage, or did your parents help you out?'

'Of course I managed.' She is indignant. 'There were lots worse off than me you know, and I was not going to go running to Mum and Dad for help. I was an independent woman.'

She still is. She is strong and brave. My mother doesn't often cry; she grits her teeth and gets on with what she has to do. Tears for her beloved Jim must have flowed, but I haven't asked. I have questioned her enough and I won't invade her emotional privacy further.

While I slept the first weeks of my life in my pram in the garden of 19 Prince John Road, Mum was busy writing letters. They are not in the writing case but the replies are there. As I read them I feel the strength of her determination. If she couldn't have Jim himself, she demanded to have his possessions returned to her.

On 12th June, a note from the Air Commodore commanding Jim's Yorkshire base said he was seeking permission to release his bicycle. Two weeks later she received an inventory of his effects. I study the list and notice it includes three notebooks and a leather writing case containing personal letters. I reach out to touch them and the years fall away. His bicycle was retained pending disposal instructions. Pat was not satisfied; his bike had to come home. In addition to that, only one pair of pyjamas was listed. He had definitely had two and she wanted them back. Her complaint resulted in a letter dated 1st July from Squadron Leader John Allenby who regretted that 'after a most careful search and exhaustive enquiries, no trace of them could be found.' I suspect my dad had been wearing them under his flying suit.

'Did you get his bike back, Mum?' I ask when she comes to stay with me.

'Certainly did,' she replies with a slight nod of the head, a tight-lipped smile and a victorious twinkle in her eye.

On 18th December 1943, after seven months of tentative hope, Mum received the worst Christmas present she has ever had – a letter from the War Organisation of the British Red Cross Society and Order of St John of Jerusalem:

Dear Mrs Gaywood,

We feel you should know of some very grave news which has reached us about a member of the crew in which your husband, Sergeant S.J. Gaywood, 1393160, was serving when he was posted missing.

A telegram from the International Red Cross Committee at Geneva states that the body of Sergeant Rees was recovered on the shore near Bingon, East Friesland, Germany. We fear that this report must indicate that the disaster to the aircraft most probably occurred over the sea.

We are continuing to make enquiries on your behalf and need hardly say that should any news come through about your husband, it will be at once communicated to you.

Please accept our very sincere sympathy in this prolonged period of anxiety and suspense.

Yours sincerely,

Lady Margaret Ampthill

We read it together. 'So that was it, Mum. I suppose you had to accept that he wasn't coming back,' I say.

'Oh no.' She sits straight and throws me a look of shocked surprise (how could I think that?). 'I never accepted it, I never gave up hope. Right through the war – and after it was over – men were still filtering back. Some had been prisoners, some had lost their memories but somehow found their way home.' Like the man I saw in the *Daily Herald*. The one with the chewed-up hair; the one who had walked all the way home from a prison camp; the one who made my five-year-old self dream that my dad might return.

In the writing case I find an undated newspaper cutting about two inches by four. On one side is a report that 'Hot Ice', Brighton's first ice-skating revue for eight years, opened at the sports stadium to an audience of three thousand. Peace must have arrived; the population of Brighton were enjoying life again. I turn over the cutting and read:

THE MISSING

Relatives ask for news
Relatives seek news of these missing men:

A score or more servicemen's names and the addresses of those seeking them are listed, including: *Sgt S.J. Gaywood, RAF Dortmund raid, May 1943 (Mrs P. Gaywood, 19 Prince John Road, Eltham).* My mother didn't give up.

'There was that time at London Bridge station, long after the war, when I thought I saw him down the end of the platform. I tore past all the rush-hour crowds and nearly knocked an old woman's bag of shopping flying, I was so sure it was him.

'As I got to the man he turned and held his arms out to break my run. "Whoa!" he said. "What's the hurry, luv?"

'"None of your business," I spat at him. Poor fellow,' she presses her fingers to her lips to suppress a laugh, 'it wasn't his fault his eyes were the wrong colour.'

I offer her a cup of tea but she doesn't hear me; she is back in another life.

'I was polishing the dining table once, in the bay-windowed room at Prince John Road, when I looked up and saw a man in Air Force uniform walking down the road from the station. You were crying in your pram in the garden. Normally I would have rushed out to you, but I couldn't move a muscle; just stood there with the duster in my hand until he got close enough for me to see.' She gives a little resigned laugh. 'It was the brother of the woman at number 2. What was her name now?' Mum creases her brow. 'No, it's no good, I can't remember. Isn't that dreadful? Can't remember a thing these days. Old age must be setting in!'

In 1951, Woolwich Borough Council came to the conclusion that a three-bedroom semi-detached house was more than a young woman and her child needed and Nanny and Grandad were now the sole occupiers of a house with four bedrooms.

Mum had decided that Haimo Road School, which had been good enough for her and Jim, was not good enough for me. The RAF Benevolent Fund had offered to pay the fees at a small independent school near to one of the estates which were gobbling up farmland on the edge of suburbia in the post-war building frenzy. Two brand new adjoining flats provided a solution. I could walk home from school and stay with Nanny until Mum returned from her job in London.

I phone Mum. 'How did you feel, Mum, leaving Prince John Road with all its memories?'

'I'll think about that, dear, and email you.' She thinks for a day or two and then this appears in my inbox:

Memories

Leaving 19 Prince John Road after nine years as Pat Gaywood and the previous fifteen years as Pat Sheridan was a big, but practical step to take. Actually the emotional side of such a move didn't hit me immediately. One didn't get time off work for moving house so it was all a bit of a rush.

We took Sandy the cat and I remember when we got there I shut him in the larder so he didn't wander and get lost – which after a time he did and sadly we were without him.

Love Mum x

I can't believe the only regret was for the loss of Sandy.

Had the fog already begun to surround Nanny? Was it then that the trillions of tiny lights, the cells which made up her brain, started to degenerate and die? It was a slow process – years. Grandad cared for her as long as he could, working nights so he could be with her all day. But it couldn't last and they took her away. Every Sunday for months – or was it years? – Mum and I took the 161 bus to Shooter's Hill and walked down the hill to the Brook Hospital, a maze of long single-storied huts which had been built for wounded soldiers returning from the Great War. We tramped through the open walkways, roofed with corrugated iron, where the wind whistled round our ears in an attempt to whisk off woolly scarves and bobble hats. I was torn between hurrying to achieve the warmth of the long, cheerless geriatric ward and dawdling for fear of what I knew I would find there.

Demented cries reached us before we opened the door. Old women, like ghosts with straggly hair, stared at us as we walked past the endless rows of beds. Some reached out in the hope that we were their family come to visit them, then dropped their arms and their heads when our pace did not slow beside them. The smell of disinfectant did little to mask that of decay and excrement, so my hankie was always at my face and Mum wondered if it was some kind of allergy that affected me when I entered. In a way, it was.

One thin crone with wild hair and hideously ulcerated legs frightened me by constantly climbing from her bed to shuffle across the scrubbed wooden floor. I shrank away when she stroked my hair and shouted to the world that I was her Sylvia come back from the dead. Mixed emotions of relief and sadness beset me as the nurses led her, protesting, back to bed and imprisoned her with metal cot sides. I tried to keep my eyes from another old hag who held an incomprehensible conversation with her thick brown stockings as she rolled them down thin white legs bound with blue venous ropes which, to my child's eyes, seemed to have bunches of grapes attached. She cackled as she waved her stockings in the air before aiming misshapen toes at them and finally, after many failed attempts, inserting her feet and rolling the twisted garments up her legs again. Not even one moment of triumph did she allow herself before rolling them down once more. The whole process would repeat and repeat for the entire thirty minutes of visiting time. I shivered and turned away from the witch-like creature but, as if watching a Boris Karloff film, I could not prevent my gaze returning again and again to the horror.

Nanny did not cry out, wander, or indulge in strange rituals. She merely lay in her bed, like a beached whale, staring at the ceiling, waiting for the ebbing tide to carry her away. But even as the fog was growing thick enough to consume her consciousness entirely, the few remaining beams of light shone onto her bright, blond, blue-eyed boy. On one visit the only words she uttered were, 'Did Jim get his tram all right?' Mum assured her he had and she sank back, satisfied, onto her pillow.

Shortly after that, the last light was extinguished.

At thirteen I was considered too young to attend her funeral so I took the pocket money Grandad gave me to Broadmead's in Eltham High Street and bought my first record, 'Rock Around the Clock' by Bill Haley & His Comets with 'See You Later, Alligator' on the B-side. The world was just beginning to rock and roll.

Perhaps the lights went out for Grandad too. Family folklore has it that his hair went white overnight when Jim was lost. After Nanny died he had a spell as a school lollipop man and moved to a bedsit round the corner where I did not visit him often enough.

One day I decided to be a dutiful granddaughter and help him tidy up. Sorting through the old newspapers under the low table with the leg which had been broken and badly set, I came across a small, well-thumbed magazine. *Health and Efficiency* was its innocent-sounding title, but when I opened it I found naked women on most pages. By today's standards they were decorous enough, but in the straight-laced fifties, shocking. I was not shocked but felt a rush of love for Grandad, sad that this was where he found comfort in the twilight of a comfortless life.

After enduring the gas, the blood and the mud of Flanders, he had taken a wife who came complete with child, father and brother. Then, sick with tuberculosis and with three children to support, jobs came and went and so did his earnings – on food, rent, beer, horses and dogs. His boys would do great things, he knew that. But then Hitler took Jim, and Len opted for the rural life and married a woman Sam did not understand. A day trip to Margate, where he rolled up his trousers for a paddle and made a sunhat out of newspaper, was the nearest he ever got to a holiday. When the wiring in Cis's brain failed he continued to clean trams and buses until he could draw his small old-age pension.

He needed the glamour girls on the pages of *Health and Efficiency*.

Those hypocritical, thin white tubes of tobacco and pints of beer continued to comfort and destroy him. He proudly coughed his way through my wedding, but the gas and nicotine-induced cancer did not allow him to meet his first, bright, blond, blue-eyed great-grandson eighteen months later.

19

Yorkshire 2013

Here in Betty's Tea Room in York, I am tempted to get up and dance. The fingers of the white-haired gent at the piano move rapidly, note-perfect, through tunes my dad may have danced to. I can't decide whether to join in 'The Lambeth Walk' or to 'Tiptoe Through the Tulips' 'By the Light of the Silvery Moon', so I behave myself like the decorous tea-drinkers around me. Waitresses, clad in black dresses and snowy frilled aprons, glide between marble-topped tables dispensing tea, cakes and old-fashioned civility to their customers. It is worth the queue in the cold. It is worth the top-end prices. Beyond the art deco stained-glass frieze above the windows, ice-blue Christmas garlands already twinkle, despite November clinging to its last few days.

In the forties Betty's was famous, not only for its glamorous decor reminiscent of the *Queen Mary* liner, not just for its tea and cakes, but for its bar. As war approached, the founder, Frederick Belmont, was triumphant when he obtained one of the few liquor licences available in the city. The Dive, as Betty's basement bar was known, became the unofficial off-station headquarters of the Bomber Boys posted around York. Countless men gathered there to drown the horrors of past ops or the fear of those to come; to meet up with colleagues from other squadrons; to exchange gossip and news. All too often the news was bad – 'Old Johnson went for a Burton on the Essen raid', 'Charlie Chawton bought it at Bochum...'

A lone lady in a faux-fur hat is sitting at the next table.

She smiles and, in true English fashion, comments on the bitter weather. Glad to have someone to chat to, I explain the reason for my visit and she recalls family tales of airmen in York all those years ago.

'My Dad kept the newsagent's in Elvington and he loved to chat to all the Canadian airmen stationed on the nearby airfield. Dad had a sister in Winnipeg, you see, and he thought one of them might know her.' She hoots with laughter and bids me goodbye and good luck. Picking up her bill she makes for the cashier's desk. Then she hesitates, purse in hand, and turns.

'You know about the mirror, of course?'

'What mirror?'

'Why, Betty's mirror, downstairs. Ask the waitress, your father's name might be on it. Must rush. Bye.'

Rose, the lady in the navy suit who oversees the smooth running of the café, explains. The mirror hung behind the bar downstairs and hundreds of airmen scratched their names onto it, some say with the barmaid's diamond ring, before they went on missions. Yes, of course I can go down and see it; she will see if she can find a typed list of the names.

The mirror now hangs in an elegant corridor – Betty's no longer has a bar. Rectangular, in a gilt frame, it makes me think of the mirror in that famous Manet painting of *The Bar at the Folies-Bergère*. If the barmaid in York really did lend her ring to scratch the glass she was a jollier character than her French counterpart in the picture.

Gaywood, Gaywood, Gaywood... My eyes are reflected back at me as I search the glittering glass for my dad. The scratched names are so close in places they run into each other or into doodles of parachutes or planes. I find a few dated 1943, but no sign of Jim or any of his crew. The signatories on the mirror are just a few of those who faced the possibility of imminent death in the skies.

Rose touches my elbow. 'I've copied the list for you. It

includes all the names we could read. Some we just couldn't decipher.' She laughs. 'The beer must have got to them.'

I scan the alphabetical list and pause at the Gs. No, my dad didn't put his name on the mirror. Perhaps he never came to Betty's. Perhaps he was too well brought up to deface a beautiful mirror. But others were not, and I am glad. I look up and catch myself smiling as I imagine the relaxed comradeship, the mischief of young men far from home but close to death. I say a silent thank you to Betty's for preserving this informal memorial to many who never wrote their name again.

My son Matthew has taken the train from Cambridge and phones from York station.

'I'll be outside the Minster in five minutes, Mum.'

Lady Luck is on our side when we enter, one minute in advance of a tourist ban. Only those attending a service are admitted after 17.00.

We are here to see the Astrological Clock – a monument to the airmen who took off from Yorkshire, Northumberland and Durham in the Second World War and who did not return. My father's name was not on Betty's mirror but I know I will find it here. Matthew visited a few years ago and discovered his grandfather. The Duke of Edinburgh was here when the memorial was dedicated in 1955 and the full cost was raised by subscriptions received in response to a joint appeal by the British Legion and the Royal Air Forces Association. Quite unlike any other clock I have ever seen, it is an intricately decorated and carved giant cube, the height of a double-decker bus. Designed and built at the Royal Greenwich Observatory it depicts Greenwich Mean Time, solar time and sidereal or star time which is four minutes adrift of solar time. The guide book tells me that aircrews navigated by the stars and worked on star time and in this way Dr Atkinson felt his design forged a slender link with the men it commemorated.

The astral dial on the east face charts the stars the airmen would have seen as they flew. On the west zodiacal face the edge of a large convex disc represents the horizon as seen by the navigator flying over York on the flight south. There is even a plan of York showing the Minster and the walls of the city. An inscription reads:

> They went through the air and space
> And the shining stars marked their shining deeds.

The book we have come to see, *The Roll of Honour*, is the essential heart of the memorial. It lies in a locked illuminated glass case at the front of the clock and contains the names of some 18,000 men from all parts of the Commonwealth and those of continental allies who fell while serving in the area. The page on display today records the names and ranks of men whose names were Smith and Sullivan, Short and Sikorovski – a man who never made it back to his native Poland. We search for an official who may be able to turn the page to G, but in this vast silent space we see only a young priest comforting a weeping woman in a red coat, while a young girl in a school blazer sits beside them twisting a wet handkerchief round her finger. At last a rotund, cassock-clad figure approaches. His badge announces him to be a verger and he offers a cheery greeting.

'Hello there, can I help you?'

'Yes please.'

'Of course I can,' he replies when I make my request. 'Just wait a tick while I get the key from my colleague – I think he's still here, should be here 'til half past, but he has to catch a bus.' As he crosses the nave towards a small brown door, the organ bursts into life and the golden voices of boys, as if carried on angel wings, unfurl high into the air at the opening of evensong. Matthew goes to look at the nearby memorial to women who gave their lives in the first Great War. I slip into a pew and am relieved to see the woman in red is smiling now and holding the girl's hand as they make their way out into the cold. The few worshippers kneel, and I wonder if I should do the same, but then the verger reappears brandishing a brass key, and beckons me to the clock.

'Now, dear, what name was it?'

'Gaywood. S.J.'

Matthew has appeared at my side and we watch the verger reverently turn the thick vellum pages, sighing, 'All these brave young men – gone into the stars. Makes you think, doesn't it? Ah here we are, Gaywood.' He takes a few steps back, leaving us alone to scan the list of names in neat italic script.

Here he is, my third lost man – my father:

Sergeant – Gaywood, Samuel J. – R.A.F.V.R. 10 Squadron.

'Isn't it beautiful, Mum? Would you like a photo?' I nod silently and he focuses his iPhone on my dad's, his grandad's, name.

The next day, after a full English breakfast in a comfortable B&B, we drive out into the flatlands of the Vale of York for a private tour of the only restored Halifax Bomber in Britain.

The Yorkshire Air Museum seems all but deserted, save for the voice of Vera Lynn floating over the windswept airfield, assuring us that 'There'll Always Be An England'.

Historic aircraft, large and small, stand apparently ready for take-off. Single-storey buildings are painted in camouflage grey. Erected hurriedly in the anxiety of war they are now lovingly tended in their old age.

'Where is the Halifax?' Matthew asks a grey-haired man in a boiler suit.

'In that hangar over there.' He points to the far corner of the airfield. 'Have you booked?' We show him the paperwork and he scratches his head. 'Didn't know we had any tours today. Hope Phil knows.'

The hangar is cold and echoey but the plane is unmistakable, dwarfing its companions. Phil, an amiable Yorkshireman in working overalls, meets us beside the dark metal giant. He has worked on the restoration of this plane for many years and freely admits it is like a child to him. He knows every nut and bolt, every detail of its history and generously shares his knowledge with us. We are transported back seventy years. We study the instruments, the oxygen supply, the belts loaded with bullets and the primitive computer. We laugh at stories of the frequent use of the Elsan chemical toilet on 'hot' flights, and imagine a pigeon cooing in its basket, ready to be released with a message for home if the crew had to ditch in the drink. Phil tells us the story of how the fuselage and its interior have been pieced together from sections of Halifaxes begged, borrowed and donated from locations throughout Europe. We hear how he and his team have carefully restored them into this lumbering beauty. We shudder at the vulnerability of the tail gunner in his lonely turret, and marvel at how the crews survived the sub-zero temperatures in the unpressurised, single-skinned cabin.

When I lie prone on the air-bomber's hard couch and look down through the Perspex nose, I line up the target in the centre of two crossed orange lines and push the bomb release button. My target is a stain of oil on the concrete floor. I can only imagine how Jim felt looking down at a blazing inferno and releasing his bomb-load to add to the destruction.

'Lunchtime, Phil,' echoes a disembodied voice across the hangar. We bid our guide a grateful farewell and move to the exhibition of photographs and memorabilia donated by those who survived Bomber Command, or by the relatives of those who did not. So much to see, so many stories to read; we vow to return.

Cold to our bones, a familiar smell entices us through the swing doors of a building marked NAAFI. Lasagne would not have been on the menu in 1943, but the place looks much the same as it does in the period photos that surround us as we tuck into our lunch. An old upright piano stands open, ready to be played when the bar in the corner opens in the evening. Our only companions are a group of men at the next table. No longer in the bloom of their youth, they chat animatedly about engines and wing flaps and their days in the RAF. They are the volunteers who come here to offer their time, their talents, their enthusiasm – and to enjoy the camaraderie.

'Where to now, Mum?' Matthew asks as we make for the car.

'Well, I think he went to Pocklington first and then finally to RAF Melbourne. That's where he took off from on his final flight.'

Phil has told us that the airfield at Pocklington now serves a gliding club. When we arrive we see a modern pre-fabricated building and a restored runway. There is no other evidence of World War Two. I can find no connection here with my father.

We follow the map on Matthew's phone which shows us that Melbourne is four and a half miles to the south-west. I point out the canal where Jim might have cycled on his last day and then we enter the village. Where is the airfield? The place seems deserted. No piano music floating from a window; no gardening local to tip his hat to us. We stop to enquire in the pub and find it closed. The November sun is sinking, lending a warm glow to the western sky which belies the outside temperature. The car's dashboard shows three degrees. I sigh. 'Perhaps we have to admit defeat.' Then I remember reading somewhere that the old RAF site is now used for motor racing. When we drive, for the third time, along a deserted road out of the village we notice a grubby yellow sign at the entrance to an overgrown track, saying:

YORK RACEWAY
(NO RACING TODAY, NO TRESPASSERS)

'Want to try it?' Matthew asks, looking doubtful.

'You decide, you're the driver,' I reply. My inner voice shouts: *Please, please say yes!*

He turns off the road and we bump along grooves carved by giant wheels. Brambles squeak along the side of the hired car and lofty trees block out the sky so that we wonder how deep into this forest we can venture. At last the track opens out to a vast concrete apron in front of a yellow painted guardhouse and a striped red and white pole barrier in its upright position. The whole place is deserted. Our eyes meet and, like schoolchildren on an illegal adventure, we grin in tacit agreement. Matthew depresses the accelerator and we glide through the entrance.

'This is it. We've found it, Matthew. Look over there – World War Two buildings.' A group of Nissen huts clings to the ground in the desolate distance. We drive on and to our left we see a banner announcing future racing dates. It is attached to a low grey building beside a wide metalled road which snakes away out of sight.

'Look, they're using a runway as a racing track,' says Matthew.

'The Internet says there were three runways at Melbourne,' I reply, 'so let's not trespass on that one.'

A hundred yards further on, another strip of concrete unrolls in front of us, weeds forcing up through the cracks. We pick up speed as our wheels travel along the runway.

'Mum, the prevailing wind is westerly, so assuming they took off into the wind, this is the last view your dad would have had of England.' He puts his foot down. 'Ready for take-off?'

My shout of triumph has difficulty getting past the lump in my throat so I screw my face into a tight grin as Matthew reaches for my hand.

Epilogue

I am the child you missed by just one day, Dad, when that young German flew his fighter out of the night sky and blew your plane apart. I have wondered if he could have been one of your German friends; whether he survived to see his family again. I think I know you well enough now to believe you would be glad if he did.

You swore you would never kill. You wrestled with your conscience time and time again, but you made your decision, and on your very first bombing raid you were lost. Mahatma Gandhi, a hero of yours, said, 'An eye for an eye leaves the whole world blind.' Some zealots might say you were punished for abandoning pacifism. No. Your death was nothing to do with retribution. History has shown you fought in a war that, if not always just, was at least necessary. If you had stayed at home my life would have been different; I would have had a father, but would you have been a hero? I think you would. If you and others who doubted the morality of conflict had taken a different road, who knows how it might have affected the outcome of the war? Perhaps Hitler would have triumphed and ground Britain under his heel. Europe would have been a dark place and many more would have lost their lives. I wish you had not lost yours, but I thank you, Dad, for taking that risk.

In 2013, I am trawling through websites for information about your last flight. I type the number, DT-789, into a search engine and suddenly time is suspended. My eyes lock on to an image of a pleasant, smiling young Luftwaffe pilot chatting to his crew; another woman's son, perhaps another woman's husband, maybe another child's father. This was him. The caption below the photo details his service record showing that this was the man who killed you. Your plane was the eleventh kill of his career, the second on that night alone. In recognition of his achievements he was awarded the Knight's Cross of the Iron Cross, the highest honour available to the Luftwaffe. After notching up another year of life and a further twenty kills, he did not return to his family. He died after his plane was attacked by two young Englishmen flying a Mosquito. They themselves were killed a couple of months later.

The German crew who shot down DT-789

I howl into the silence of my comfortable study at the loss of all these brave young men.

'I have found an amazing picture on the Internet, Mum,' I say when I visit your beloved Pat the following day. I show her what I have found.

'Well, isn't that strange. Cousin Anne in America emailed me a photo yesterday – something to do with Jim and the war, she says, but I can't seem to open the attachment.' A few clicks later the image I hold in my hand appears on the screen. Your niece and your daughter found the same photo on the same day.

Mum takes the picture from me and I watch her reaction. She breathes out slowly and her shoulders slump. 'He was only doing his job, just like Jim.' She studies the face for a long moment more before handing the page back to me and closing the lid of her laptop. She enquires how my garden is doing to bring her back into the present, distancing her from the pain of the past.

Later that day I take a call from my son. 'Mum, guess what I've found on the Net about your dad.' Yes, he found it too; the same picture on the same day. If I believed in ghosts...

For seventy years your bones have been scoured by cold northern waters. Your grandson, Matthew, at seventeen, crossed that sea on a school trip to Norway. He told me he had stood on deck in the moonlight, looked into the cold, black water and thought, *My grandfather is down there.*

How you loved my mother and how you loved me, your unseen child. As you died she laboured. And there I was – death and life in thirty-six hours.

I am Patricia, named for my mother, as you wished. But I have always been known by my second name, Janet. My first son, his life only a little longer than yours, bore your name, James, but was always known as Andrew. Your beloved Pat, strong and resilient at twenty-one, remains thus at ninety-three.

I was all she had, but she was never possessive; she let me lead my own life and made no demands. For that I have always been grateful. I had a long, happy marriage, just as you anticipated for you and Pat. Then I, like her, felt the pain of widowhood. I have been a nurse, a midwife, a health visitor and a businesswoman. You will be glad to know I have never been a clerk! I have voted Labour for most of my life but now the planet is so endangered I give my support to the Green party which seeks, against the odds, to save it.

Dad, I think I have found you. At least, I think I have discovered the young man who died. But where would life have taken you? Would you have achieved your writing ambitions? Would you have been a Trade Union activist? A politician? No, not the latter – you were too honest for that. I like to think of you as a left-wing journalist and imagine a small picture of you, a man with altruistic fire in his eyes, beside your latest article in *The Guardian*. Perhaps, though, that fire would have been diminished to an ember had you lived to see the rise, corruption and ultimate fall of the communism you admired; to witness, and benefit from, the post-war innovation of the National Health Service; to see your children (I would surely have had siblings) take advantage of the good, free education on offer. But then you would have watched, with unease, the metamorphosis of the Labour Party as it edged further and further to the right to become New Labour – a different party for a different world. Witnessing the rise and rise of King Capitalism as it widens the chasm between rich and poor, I believe you would have applauded the young people who camp in the financial hearts of cities in peaceful protest.

The Woolwich Free Ferry still transports some workers across the Thames. Now, though, most of them commute on the Docklands Light Railway (with driverless trains) from their smart apartments on the old Arsenal site where your father worked for a pittance assembling weapons of war. Gone are the blue boiler suits and flat caps, the tweed jackets and trilby hats, the headscarves, the overalls and the steel-tipped boots. Now the men wear sharp suits and colourful ties (or no ties at all). The long, glossy hair of confident, educated young women swings above the collars of their short-skirted business suits as they strut on stiletto heels. Few commuters converse with one another; most are speaking into, or studying, small black tablets which keep them informed, communicated and entertained. Many have little wired plugs in their ears delivering private music to which they hum or jig their shoulders. You would believe them to be mentally disturbed. They are destined not for smoking factories or noisy docks, but for offices in glass and steel towers which thrust ever higher into the clouds; those same clouds you flew over to build this brave new world.

But it is not nirvana for them all. Some study reports of war, injustice and the climate change which threatens to be our Armageddon, and they scratch their heads uneasily.

Young men and women throughout the world still fight and die: for their country, to stamp out evil, to satisfy power-hungry leaders, for misguided religious beliefs, for comradeship or merely to earn a crust.

The indolent, the selfish and the evil will always be with us – we are human, after all. But there will always be those like you, who love unconditionally, search their consciences for the right course of action and then fight in their chosen way for justice, peace and freedom.

This is how the world turns.

THE END

Jim 1941

Pat 1941

Acknowledgements

My thanks are due to so many. To Stephanie Norgate and all the tutors on the MA course at the University of Chichester, to Blake Morrison, Helena Drysdale, Mark McCrum, James Long and all the other writers who have taught and encouraged me at Ways With Words.

I would like to thank my writing workshop colleagues, especially Kim Hope, Yvonne Phillips and Jane Venn; their input has been invaluable. Thanks to all the friends and family who believed I could write this book and the team at SilverWood Books who have ironed out glitches and been unfailingly helpful.

Ania and Gwynned at the Ceredigion Archives, the staff at Flixton, Dumfries and Yorkshire Air Museums all have my gratitude for their helpful enthusiasm. In particular I would like to thank Phil Kemp, who brought my father's last flight to life with his unstinting information about the Halifax bomber. I am grateful to the Aircrew Remembrance Society for the use of the picture on page 258.

Last, but by no means least, a big thank you to my mother and uncle for trawling their memories and allowing me to write this book.

Glossary of WWII Terms and Slang

ARP	air-raid precautions
Aldis lamp	green signalling light
ack-ack	anti-aircraft fire
Anson	British aircraft
bang on	term of approval
Battle	British aircraft (Fairey Battle – an early bomber)
bought it	killed
CO	Commanding Officer
conchie (CO)	Conscientious Objector
corkscrew	avoidance manoeuvre
gen	intelligence
gone for a Burton	killed
Halifax	British bomber
Heinkel	German bomber
Hurricane	British fighter plane
Irvin jacket	leather jacket, sheepskin lined
Lancaster	British bomber
Mae West	life jacket
Messerschmitt (ME-110)	German fighter plane
Mosquito	British fighter plane

NAAFI	Navy, Army and Air Force Institute
NCO	Non-commissioned Officer
pathfinder	planes dropping target indicators
pitot	wind speed indicator
prayer meeting	briefing meeting
play possum	lie low, hide
pukka gen	accurate intelligence
Rosie Lee	tea
Spitfire	British fighter plane
Stirling	British bomber
TI	Target Indicator
WAAF	Women's Auxiliary Air Force
Winco	Wing Commander

Bibliography

Of the many books, reference centres and websites I have read or visited while writing this book, I have found the following especially helpful:

Beardmore, G. *Civilians at War: Journals 1938-1949*, (John Murray, 1984)

Berlin, S. *I Am Lazarus*, (Galley Press, 1961)

Birkerts, S. *The Art of Time in Memoir*, (Graywolf, 2008)

Blake, L. *Red Alert – South East London 1939-45*, (Lewis Blake, 1982)

Cooper, A. *Air Battle of the Ruhr*, (Airlife Publishing, 1992)

Dunmore, H. *The Greatcoat*, (Random House, 2012)

Frayn, M. *Spies*, (Faber & Faber, 2002)

Minns, R. *Bombers and Mash*, (Virago, 1999)

Moreton, C. *My Dad Was a Hero*, (Penguin, 2004)

Morrison, B. *And When Did You Last See Your Father?* (Granta, 1993)

Morrison, B. *Things My Mother Never Told Me*, (Vintage, 2002)

Partridge, F. *A Pacifist's War*, (Orion, 1996)

Waller, M. *London 1945: Life in the Debris of War*, (John Murray, 2004)

Waters, S. *The Night Watch*, (Little Brown, 2011)

References

Peace Pledge Union – Conscientious Objectors
Greenwich Heritage Centre
National Archives – Military Training Bill – Bomb Damage in London
The Eltham and *Kentish Times*
The Kentish Mercury
Yorkshire Air Museum
Ceredigian Archives
The Norfolk and Suffolk Aviation Museum
Dumfries and Galloway Aviation Museum

Websites

Eyewitness to History
    www.eyewitnesstohistory.com
WW2 People's War
    www.bbc.co.uk/history/ww2peopleswar
BBC History
    www.bbc.co.uk/history/worldwars/wwtwo
Forces War Records
    www.forces-war-records.co.uk
Peace Pledge Union
    www. ppu.org.uk
Spartacus History
    www.spartacus.schoolnet.co.uk
Revolutionary League
    www.wikipedia.org/wiki/revolutionaryleague(UK1938)
Peace News
    www.wikipedia.org/wiki/Peace_News
Airfields of Britain Conservation Trust
    www.abct.org.uk/airfields/melbourne
A Vision of Britain Through Time
    www.visionofbritain.org.uk/unit/10217660
Creative Nonfiction
    www.creativenonfiction.org/what-is-creative-nonfiction
Aircrew Remembrance Society
    www.aircrewremembrancesociety.co.uk

Lightning Source UK Ltd.
Milton Keynes UK
UKOW04f2115051215

264185UK00005B/354/P